SOME OF THE SCHOLARS IN THIS BOOK

Praise For WHO LEADS?

"This is a masterpiece! Succinct yet filled with information, reasoned yet inspiring, easy to read yet scholarly. Quotes many key scholars in a great mix of older and newer sources, and I learned something new in every chapter."

Ellen Duffield, Coordinator, Paul E. Magnus Centre for Leadership Studies, Briercrest Seminary, Canada

"Jane L. Crane does an excellent job presenting my research into ancient Bibles on whether women are to stay silent in church (I Cor. 14:34-35)."

Philip Payne, PhD, Cambridge-educated New Testament expert

"This book gives the reader a concise look at the work of world-renowned scholars, illuminating God's intentions for leadership through His Word. It is simple to read and understand but also has meticulous notes for deeper study."

Andrea East, University of the Nations, Community Development and Justice Center

"Disagreement around the relationship of women and men within the teaching and leadership ministries of the church, and in marriage, continues to disfigure and divide God's people. The Lausanne Movement's *Cape Town Commitment* (IIF.3) calls upon "those on different sides of the argument to study Scripture carefully together, with due regard for the context and culture of the original authors and contemporary readers." This impressive short book by Jane Crane, a Lausanne colleague who has researched, taught and written on this topic for years, provides such a careful study. But it does so in a superbly concise way, combining an approximately three-hour read of the main text with detailed endnotes to support her condensed but clear biblical interpretation with thoroughly documented and up-to-date research from dozens of well-respected evangelical scholars."

Christopher Wright, Global Ambassador, Langham Partnership. Chief architect of the Lausanne Movement's Cape Town Commitment

"You can read this book in two ways: you can follow the well-researched summaries in the front half of the book, or you can also dig in and read through all the quotations and arguments cited in detail in the latter half of the book. What a wonderful way to help both lay readers and theological scholars gain from this condensed insight!"

Elke Werner, Germany, former Board Member of the International Lausanne Movement

"When I hold this book in my hand, I cannot believe how much it says in so few pages, and so clearly. It brings a cloud of witnesses of leading scholars and is well organized and highly annotated. A concise tool for study by pastors, congregations, leaders, and many others who want an up-to-date understanding of this topic."

Mimi Haddad, PhD, President, Christians for Biblical Equality

"Fascinating! Reads at times like an Indiana Jones movie. And so clear, concise, and easy to follow."

Andrew Alden, Gen-Y Entrepreneur

WHO LEADS?

WHO LEADS?

A Concise Look at Top Bible Scholars
on the Male/Female Question

Jane L. Crane
Foreword by Rev. Dr. James D. Smith III

WIPF & STOCK • Eugene, Oregon

WHO LEADS?

A Concise Look at Top Bible Scholars on the Male/Female Question

Copyright © 2024 Jane L. Crane. All rights reserved. Except for brief quotations in critical publications or reviews, no part of this book may be reproduced in any manner without prior written permission from the publisher. Write: Permissions, Wipf and Stock Publishers, 199 W. 8th Ave., Suite 3, Eugene, OR 97401.

Wipf & Stock
An Imprint of Wipf and Stock Publishers
199 W. 8th Ave., Suite 3
Eugene, OR 97401

www.wipfandstock.com

PAPERBACK ISBN: 979-8-3852-2327-5
HARDCOVER ISBN: 979-8-3852-2328-2
EBOOK ISBN: 979-8-3852-2329-9

Except where noted otherwise, Scripture quotes are taken from the HOLY BIBLE, NEW INTERNATIONAL VERSION. Copyright © 1973, 1978, 1984 International Bible Society. Used by permission of Zondervan Bible Publishers.

Scripture from the Holman Christian Standard Bible® is used by Permission of HCSB ©1999,2000,2002,2003,2009,2013 Holman Bible Publishers. Holman Christian Standard Bible®, Holman CSB®, and HCSB® are federally registered trademarks of Holman Bible Publishers.

With honor to God for the guidance and joy I felt daily during the three years of writing this book.

Contents

Foreword by Rev Dr James D. Smith III	xiii
About this book	xvii
1 What does the Bible really say?	1
2 Male and female	5
3 Old Testament and "Days of Mingling"	9
4 Jesus and women	15
5 Early church and women	23
6 Women silent in church?	31
7 Man as "head" of woman?	39
8 Submission?	47
9 Teaching and authority over man?	55
10 Church leadership?	63
11 What the Bible does not say	71
12 What remains	77
Notes	87
Works cited	167
Art and photographs	179
About the author	181

Foreword

When first invited to offer a brief foreword to this insightful volume, the bold title and perennial life question stood out: "Who leads?" My only faithful response was clear: "God." So, engaging the subtitle—"A Concise Look at Top Bible Scholars on the Male/Female Question"—I hoped for a compact, well-researched exploration of God's Word. I am deeply grateful this unique presentation offers exactly that. Its years of painstaking research are artfully condensed and readable at one sitting with detailed references inviting further study as desired.

Jane Crane's volume calls us back to the Genesis of human relationships—engaging key issues illumined by a host of first-rate Bible scholars and informed by decades of discussion. The first half examines biblical topics, texts, translations, historical factors, and hermeneutics vital to the Body of Christ. The second half invites further research through bibliography and detailed notes. In my various roles—as husband/father/grandfather, pastor/professor, and friend/neighbor—I've already been blessed by this presentation!

As pastor and professor of church history for over 35 years, I especially appreciate the historical inclusions in this book. The Scriptures direct us to value history. As we are called to worship only the Lord—not nostalgia or novelty—we're meant to discover treasures new and old (Matt. 13:52), emulate faithful ones across time (Ps. 101:6), and examine all things, holding onto what is good (I Thess. 5:21).

I first became aware of church history through Dr. Issa Khalil at San Diego State University—and the dynamics of tradition and Scripture translation. In my studies at Bethel Seminary, Dr. Millard Erickson reflected on how these aspects shape theology and stated (as cited in this book) that women have been highly influential throughout Christian history—because of what God has done. In doctoral studies in church history at Harvard University, through Drs. Margaret Miles, Eleanor McLaughlin, Clarissa Atkinson, and David Herlihy, I also engaged specifically in research on women in church history. I found the insights so enriching that I have taught seminary courses on this topic for over 20 years.

Studying the lives and contributions of gifted women in the church, we note scholars like Ruth Tucker and Barbara MacHaffie (see Works Cited at the end of this book)—and earlier, Edith Deen. Her classic *Great Women of Faith* (1959) was written because those who loved her *All the Women of the Bible* (1955) were eager to see how the Lord inspired his daughters in the Faith across all generations. Her work drew my attention to Julia Kavanagh's 1852 Women of Christianity—for which I wrote the Foreword introducing a new 2006 edition.

After decades of pastoring and teaching, my focus on the male/female question remains "What was God's original intent?" Genesis 1:26-27 offers a two-fold answer: as humanity we are created male and female in God's image for loving relationships and called to dominion together over the created order. Even after Adam and Eve chose paths of cursed, fallen disobedience, the divine *chesed* inspired Old Testament figures like Abraham and Sarah, Moses, Deborah, David, and Esther to Kingdom faithfulness. Then, through Jesus' unique life and sacrifice, perfect redemption came! The curse was lifted—freeing men and women of faith to fully partake of the Holy Spirit, proclaiming the "good news" to all. This "greatest story ever told" changed my life!

Given the fresh insights and illumination provided in this book—and reflecting the divine character of the Father, Son and Holy

Spirit—let us all "be imitators of God as beloved children." And, in lives of fruitful service together, may our loving, Spirit-led responses to one another grow "out of reverence for Christ . . . " (Eph. 5:1, 21).

                Rev Dr James D. Smith III

            ThD, Harvard University
            Faculty – Bethel Seminary, Pacific
                Theological Seminary, Richmont
                Graduate University
            Associate Pastor – La Jolla
                (California) Christian Fellowship

About this book

I needed a book, a simple book. One that pastors and others could read in a relatively short time to learn what top Bible scholars say today on male and female leadership. I had heard some teaching I knew to be very unbalanced and it upset me. But I could not find such a book. Then God began to move on my heart. . . .

I had taught this material on five continents. I had read thousands of pages on the topic. I had studied this because God had called me to organize Christian events. With all glory to God, I had been a key catalyst in bringing Billy Graham to San Diego in 2003 for one of his last crusades and opened in prayer for him at our stadium. I had organized two of the country's largest National Day of Prayer events and a March for Jesus on San Diego's waterfront Harbor Drive with tens of thousands of people. I had served in leadership with the international Lausanne Movement (started by Billy Graham) and had my writing on this topic published by them.[1]

So I began to write. . . . And read what turned out to be thousands more pages of the most recent scholarly work. I thanked God I had been trained for two years in doctoral-level research through the Oxford Centre for Mission Studies in Oxford, England, so I knew how to study scholars. And I thanked God I was gifted with the ability to present complex information in a clear, simple way.

I decided to present the research of top scholars, most of whom teach at the seminary level.[2] I chose to focus primarily on facts rather than opinions and leave conclusions to the reader. I also worked to give references to multiple scholars wherever possible for each point made. These references are found in the back half of this book with detailed explanations for those who want that. But the front half of the book gives an overview for the average reader that can be read in a few hours.[3] I also wanted to include cultural background that brings the text alive.[4] I worked intensively for three years to do this.

I can honestly say that I studied with the fear of the Lord.... Were my past conclusions about the relevant Bible passages biased? Did God want to show me something different? It felt risky and vulnerable, but right. I believe each of us needs to do this. Like good scientists, we need to be open to new information as it emerges to check our assumptions. And we need to know personally what God is saying to make informed decisions for our own lives.

Billy Graham called for Christian leaders to work together for the Gospel in humility, friendship, prayer, study, partnership, and hope.[5] May we all follow his worthy lead and study this information with humility and prayer. And may we all know richly what God's plan is for leadership in the home, church, and beyond, following God with trust and joy.

> Jane L. Crane
> San Diego, California USA

1

What does the Bible really say?

How the Bible came together is quite a story! Who wrote it, the materials used, a famous librarian who ran in the night from a fire with an ancient Bible under his arm. A Russian czar, British kings, Napoleon, an intrepid researcher who traveled far and wide to find ancient manuscripts. Shepherds in caves in the desert, persecution, exile, the Vatican. Scribes who hand wrote copies of ancient texts. The unavoidable errors of omission and addition.[1] The papyrus sheets first used as paper for the New Testament that did not last more than a decade. No original manuscripts but ancient copies maintained as treasures. Dramatic discoveries of fragments. At least one scholar reportedly working to his dying breath on an important translation.[2]

Translation of the Bible is itself quite a story. The first known translation of the Old Testament happened about 300 years before Jesus' birth. Many of the Jews had lost their knowledge of Hebrew during generations of captivity. So the Old Testament was translated into Greek, the widespread language then.[3] Seventy Jewish scholars were reportedly brought to Alexandria, Egypt, to prepare a translation for King Ptolemy's famous great library there. Then thousands of copies were made and sent to Jews across the land. This translation, called the "Septuagint" from the word for seventy, is the version Jesus himself quotes.[4]

Today, copies of the Septuagint remain and are still used by scholars, but we have no original Old or New Testaments. Translators must compare the oldest manuscripts available, and teams of scholars are still needed. In addition, the languages of the Old and New Testaments can be especially challenging to translate. The ancient Hebrew of the Old Testament (with some Aramaic) has no vowels, and spaces are often omitted between words to save space.[5] It can also require twice as many words in English and other languages to convey its meaning.[6]

In the 900s (and before), a group of Jewish scholars near the Sea of Galilee worked together to standardize a Hebrew version of the Old Testament.[7] This work is still referenced for translation of the Old Testament into other languages. The scholars, however, decided to add some vowels to help with understanding and this opened up the possibility of changes in meaning.[8] An eminent Old Testament scholar believes the addition of these vowels may have impacted the translation of an important statement about women in Genesis.[9] (The next chapter explains.)

In the 1940s, scholars the world over were thrilled when Bedouin shepherds discovered old scrolls in caves that contained parts of the Old Testament. These "Dead Sea Scrolls" were probably hidden to protect them from marauding enemies of the Jews. Much older than the Galilee translation, they are an invaluable resource.[10]

The ancient Greek of the New Testament is also challenging. It is very different from today's Greek and has no modern punctuation, verse numbers, or paragraphs to guide the reader or translator.

A single Greek word can have multiple meanings and may require a phrase or sentence to translate it into another language. Greek verbs and rare words are especially difficult to translate.[11] Scholars point out that the Greek of the New Testament can also be "free," taking on new meanings in the context of the Gospel.[12] And both Greek and Hebrew speakers indulge in plays on words (a favorite of Paul) that can be impossible to translate fully into other languages.[13]

Bruce Metzger, longtime professor at Princeton Theological Seminary and chair of the translation committee for the New Revised Standard Version of the Bible, says no translation of the Scriptures is perfect, "as anyone who has tried to make one will readily agree."[14] Duplicating another language in translation is considered virtually impossible, and there is always room for improvement.[15] The New International Version agrees that the work of translation is never finished. "This applies to all great literature and uniquely so to the Bible."[16]

So we continue to have new translations, aided by dramatic discoveries of ancient documents and ongoing research by scholars illuminating the texts.[17] And part of this work is to correct bias, conscious or unconscious, in translation choices. Scholars tell us that such bias has occurred even since the earliest known translation, the Septuagint.[18]

If bias occurs in the verses related to male and female leadership, this can have significant impact. Some instances of such cases have been addressed and changed in current translations, but others have not.

So what does the Bible really say about male-female leadership? This is still being debated, and the following chapters explore top scholars' work on this topic. One translator said he needed to spend as much time on his knees praying for God's guidance as doing the actual craft of translation. May we follow his lead as we study.

WHO LEADS?

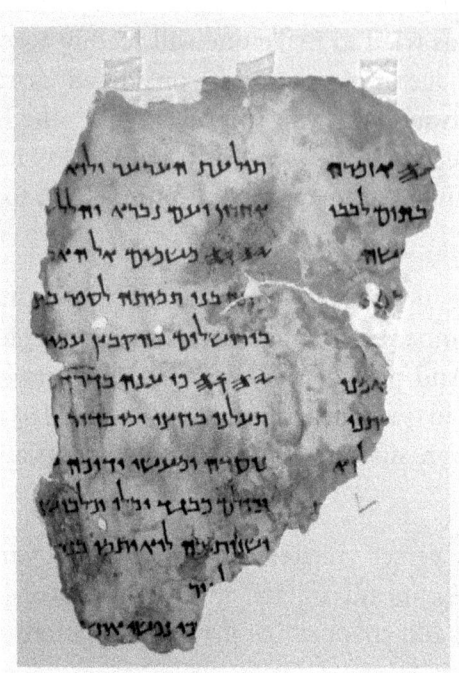

DEAD SEA SCROLL (DIGITIZED)

Ancient Hebrew has no vowels.

2

Male and female . . .

In the beginning, God created male and female in his image, blessed them, and told them to rule over the earth.[1] Scholars tell us that the word for that first human, 'adam, means "made from the earth" and carries here the meaning of "humanity." Adam as a personal name does not appear until later in Genesis.[2] From the side of that being, (said to be more accurate than the "rib"), God forms woman.[3]

The woman is described with a two-word Hebrew phrase sometimes translated as a "helper," a "helper suitable," or a "helpmeet."[4] "Helpmeet" came from the King James Version of the Bible in the 17th century, when "meet" meant "fit to" or "corresponding." Through time it morphed into the English "helpmate."[5] When the King James Version was written, though, Hebrew had not been in use much for centuries, and the understanding of its vocabulary was inadequate, including apparently the word sometimes translated "helper."[6]

Distinguished Old Testament scholar and seminary president Walter Kaiser says that in the ancient Hebrew the first word of the phrase, sometimes translated as "help," should be "strength" or "power."[7] In fact, this word is used more than a dozen times in the Old Testament to describe the kind of help God himself gives.[8] It is not one of the four Hebrew words that describes a subordinate help. Kaiser says a more accurate translation of the original two-word phrase for the creation of woman would be "a power or strength corresponding to the man."⁹

WALTER KAISER

Rather than "a helper suitable," a more accurate translation is "a strength corresponding."

Before the woman was formed, God gave instructions to the human being about the tree of the knowledge of good and evil. From what the woman says, the man, not God, told her about it after she was formed. But she is deceived by the serpent into eating from that tree. The man, who the Bible says is there with her, eats of it too.¹⁰ When God confronts them, the woman tells God the serpent deceived her. The man then blames God for creating the woman who gave him the fruit.

After God curses the serpent and prophesies of one who will come through the woman to crush the serpent's head, God speaks of the future of both the man and woman. Some translations in English say God will increase the woman's pain in childbirth. Walter Kaiser, however, points out that God is not the source of evil, and vowels added to the original Hebrew by a later group of scholars could have affected this translation.¹¹ Kaiser considers a more accurate translation to be, "A snare [*from the enemy*] has increased your sorrow and sighing."[12] To the man, God says he will toil for food on ground that is now cursed.

Scholars address whether the sin of the man or woman was greater than the other. What was the impact of being deceived versus willful obedience? The woman blaming the enemy but the man blaming God? The man hearing the prohibition directly from God but the woman hearing it from the man? The woman tasting of the fruit first and giving some to the man? The man not speaking up about what God had said to him? Some verses seem to point to greater responsibility by the man, for whatever reason (it is not stated), but unquestionably both sinned.[13]

When God says the woman will "turn" away toward the man, scholars have said this may mean turning away from her sole dependence on God in the Garden.[14] Some translations say instead that the woman will "desire" the man. But reportedly the meaning of "turning toward" the man was used almost universally in the twelve known ancient translations and by the early church fathers.[15] This includes the version of the Old Testament that would have been used by Jesus and the Apostles.[16] The phrase "desire the man" apparently first emerged in 1528 when a Dominican monk used the teachings of the rabbis in the Talmud about ten curses on Eve, including that she would lust for her husband, instead of the ancient translations.[17]

After sin enters in, God says the man will rule over the woman, in the first statement of male dominance. Scholars have pointed out, however, that the Hebrew verb here for "rule" is in a future tense indicating what will happen, not in a command form.[18] Roger Nicole, an eminent Bible scholar who has been called a giant in his field (and was president of a prestigious society of scholars), wrote that God's words were "a divine description of what would occur, not a mandate which obedient servants of God should attempt to carry out."[19]

WHO LEADS?

ROGER NICOLE

The Hebrew grammar indicates that man ruling over woman was a description of what would occur in the future, not a command.

After the fall from grace, the man calls the woman "Eve" (*havvah*), meaning mother of all the living. This reflects God's words that her offspring will crush the head of the enemy.[20] God does not want man to eat of the tree of life and live forever in a sinful state. So God banishes man from the Garden to work the ground from which he had come. Adam and Eve leave the Garden, Adam lays with Eve, and she becomes pregnant. Then Eve, unabandoned by God, says God helps her to bring forth a son.[21]

3

Old Testament and "Days of Mingling" . . .

Numerous godly and courageous women appear in the Old Testament. . . . Miriam, a leader and a prophet in Israel. Deborah, called the judge and leader of Israel. Queen Esther, appealing to the king at risk of her own life to save the Jews. Abigail, a wise and courageous woman providing for David and his men when her husband will not, preventing a slaughter. The daughters of Zelophehad, boldly asking for their own inheritance of land when they have no brothers, and God telling Moses to give it to them.[1] Huldah, giving the king a prophetic word that triggers a great revival (when the prophet Jeremiah was alive but she was the one brought to the king). The wife of the great prophet Isaiah, also called a prophet.[2] The prophet Joel proclaiming that sons and daughters will prophesy and God will pour out his spirit on both men and women.[3]

Yet the Old Testament also sometimes paints a picture of male dominance, polygamy, and privilege. Women are mistreated, sometimes in horrible ways. A concubine is sent out to a group of marauding men rather than giving them the man they wanted. A wife is required to drink bitter water if a husband suspects her of unfaithfulness, possibly harming her health. But the same does not apply to the husband.

DEBORAH'S SONG OF TRIUMPH

The Old Testament calls Deborah the judge and leader in Israel.

Moses establishes a law regarding divorce due to the hardness of the people's hearts, as Jesus said, but not as God's ideal. The Jews have a tendency to protect and confine their women and children during times of captivity, such as in Babylon, to preserve important traditions,[4] but this apparently continues in some measure after captivity too.

Then we have what is called in Jewish history the "Days of Mingling," a pivotal time. These 400 years happen between the Old and New Testaments, when the Jews live as a minority, a ruled people in the Roman Empire.[5] Palestine is surrounded by Greek cities in which many Jews mingle freely with the heathen population. The days before Christ are called desperate, with the Jew "a beleaguered figure in his own land."[6] There is great pressure to conform to Greco-Roman ways, and Greek is the commonly spoken language throughout the Greco-Roman world, including by the Jews.[7] The Old Testament is even translated from Hebrew into Greek in Egypt about 250 BC as a major event.[8] Greek spirit and forms of thought have a significant influence on the Jews.

Greek thought, including much anti-women bias, is generally revered by the Romans in this period and quite pervasive.[9] Aristotle writes that the female is a "monstrosity," a "deformed male."[10] He says man is by nature superior to the female and should rule over her.[11] His conclusions are very influential, and women as a group in the Greco-Roman culture are considered inferior to men.[12] This includes physically, intellectually, and spiritually, therefore, women should be subordinated to men. In the vast majority of cases, they are, both socially and legally. Baby daughters are often not welcomed, and infant exposure to the elements, especially for daughters, is practiced (though this would be more frowned upon by the Jews). Women are blamed for man's ills, as in the Greek myth of Pandora, who opened the box to evil. It is considered a cruel fate to be a woman.

WHO LEADS?

Jewish writing reflects Greek thought. Woman blamed for evil like Greek Pandora.

© RMN-Grand Palais/Art Resource NY

For the first time, scholars say, some Jewish writings follow suit.[13] They blame women for sin's entering humanity and say that woman is cursed with multiple curses (though Genesis never says the woman, or the man, is cursed, only the ground and serpent). Jewish women do not normally engage in many of the religious privileges that Jewish men do.[14] In a common daily prayer of the time, Jewish men thank God that he did not make them women.[15]

The Old Testament itself shows high regard for women's religious rights, including being present for the public reading of Scripture.[16] But close to the time of Christ, in 19 BC, Herod the Great builds a temple for the Jews with a separation of men and women. Women are restricted to the Women's Court, and only Jewish men can enter the next inner courts.[17]

Jewish women receive respect in certain ways, but activities for most Jewish women are usually quite limited.[18] Some rabbis write that it is disgraceful for Jewish women to study the Torah in-depth as men did (although there are documented exceptions).[19] Women at this time do not generally speak in the synagogues.[20] A Jewish woman is not supposed to speak in public to a man other than her husband.[21] In the culture at large, women's testimony is generally not considered reliable,[22] and women's worth is usually seen as childbearing, especially of males. Woman is considered man's possession.[23]

This varies somewhat by region and class, and Roman women generally fare better, especially by the first century.[24] Some Jewish women are also able to take initiative for their lives and activities, with even one a queen of Judea for nine years who is appointed by her husband on his deathbed and praised for her own accomplishments.[25] But first-century Judaism overall takes place in a wider Eastern culture where there is male dominance, women participate little in public life, and beliefs of women's inferiority as a group are common.[26]

When Jesus is born into this, as we will see next, he treats women differently.

4

Jesus and women . . .

Into the "Days of Mingling," Jesus is born. Kenneth Bailey, called the premier cultural interpreter of Jesus' life, said the "radical nature of the changes in attitudes toward women that Jesus introduced are beyond description."[1] In fact, it has been said that nearly every action by Jesus regarding women that is recorded in the Bible is considered revolutionary for his time.

KENNETH BAILEY

Jesus introduces changes in attitudes toward women that are "beyond description."

Even Jesus' birth is countercultural for its honoring of women. His earthly DNA comes just from a woman, when the culture exalts the man's role in procreation. An angel gives his name to Mary first, when the father has the power of life and death over a child, including its name.[2] Mary believes the angel's words, in contrast to Zechariah, a priest, who does not.[3] Two women, Elizabeth and Anna, prophesy of Jesus' lordship when he is still a baby.[4] All of this occurs when women are considered by the culture at large to be inferior spiritually to men.

Jesus tells parables about both men and women in a time when women are generally not a topic for discussion in literature, except negatively.[5] He even uses a female image for himself, saying he is like a hen wanting to gather her chicks.[6] He cites positive examples of women in his teachings and parables.[7]

Jesus teaches spiritual truths to women, including Jewish women, when normally they do not study the Torah.[8] This includes Mary, at a time when "sitting at the feet" of someone is a known phrase meaning to be a student.[9] Scholars tell us that most Jewish women in Palestine would have been surprised that Mary was sitting and learning, generally a male activity, rather than helping Martha with hospitality, the traditional Jewish women's role.[10] Two people have revelations themselves of Jesus as the Messiah, one of whom is a woman, Martha.[11]

When Jewish men are discouraged from even speaking to women in public, Jesus publicly affirms a woman for her faith.[12] He heals a woman with an issue of blood who touches him, when contact with her is supposed to render a man "unclean," and he makes no such reference.[13] He even heals a woman on the Sabbath, violating religious regulations and angering the rabbis.[14] Even though women are considered inferior spiritually, Jesus affirms multiple women, often in the presence of others, for their faith and actions.[15] He calls a woman a "daughter of Abraham" as he heals her, when that was unheard of, and only "sons of Abraham" are mentioned.[16]

Jesus allows women to follow him, with the same Greek word for follow (*akoloutheo*) that is used repeatedly elsewhere in the sense of being a disciple of Jesus.[17] Women travel as part of his ministry, leaving their homes, when this is unusual.[18] Women support him financially out of their own means.[19] Jesus allows a woman to anoint his feet and head with oil prior to his crucifixion, using valuable oil, and defends and honors her for her actions.[20]

When a woman is brought to Jesus for adultery and is about to be stoned (without the man, in a common double standard of the day), Jesus challenges the men present, saying whoever is without sin should throw the first stone.[21] He confronts the men for lust in their hearts rather than blaming women for men's sexual impurity, as the culture does then.[22]

Jesus with the woman taken in adultery, perhaps in the women's court of the temple.

Jesus has his longest conversation in the Bible with a woman, the Samaritan woman.[23] This is when Jewish men are especially discouraged from speaking with foreign women in public.[24] When the apostles find Jesus conversing alone with the Samaritan woman at the well, they are "astonished" at his trespass of their customs.[25] Jesus reveals to her the great truth that God is Spirit and is to be worshiped in spirit and in truth, and she becomes an evangelist to her village.

When asked about divorce, in a time when a man could easily divorce his wife and leave her with nothing,[26] Jesus goes back to the principles in creation.[27] He says God created male and female, and for this reason a man is to leave his father and mother, be united to his wife, and they will become one flesh. This is the opposite of his culture. The woman is to leave her family to go to the man's power base, and the "one-flesh" principle is often overridden by male dominance and easy abandonment.[28] Jesus says that anyone who divorces his wife, except for marital unfaithfulness, and marries another commits adultery, surprising even his own disciples who say it is better then not to marry![29]

When Jesus is asked whose wife a woman will be in the resurrection if she has been married to seven different brothers one after the other, he replies that people will not marry then.[30] This would be astonishing in a time when usually a father or husband has control over a woman,[31] and some Jews believe that a woman finds covenant with God only through a circumcised man. But Jesus' statements could certainly be seen as implying she would not need either of these. She would have her own direct relationship with God.

Jesus never endorses circumcision and says it comes from the ancestors, not Moses.[32] He tells his disciples to baptize people in the name of the Father, Son, and Holy Spirit, not to circumcise them.[33] (And Paul clarifies later that in Christ circumcision is not needed.[34]) In Christ, all, both male and female, can be baptized.

Baptism in Christ is for male and female

WATER BAPTISM

In a time when some rabbis teach that the father should be honored more than the mother, Jesus says both are to be honored and does not give favor to the father.[35] When a woman cries out that Jesus' mother was blessed for giving him birth and nursing him, Jesus refutes her.[36] He sets a broader standard for women than their prime function in that day of giving birth, especially to sons, when he says that blessed rather are those who hear the word of God and obey it.

When Jesus is talking to a crowd and is told his mother and brothers stand outside wanting to speak with him, he stretches out his hand to his disciples and replies that whoever does the will of his Father in heaven is his brother and sister and mother. Kenneth Bailey says that in the Middle Eastern culture, a speaker can gesture to a crowd of men and say here are my brother and uncle and cousin, but he *cannot* say, "Here are my brother *and sister and mother.*"[37] Yet Jesus does, pointedly including the women.

Ben Witherington III is one of the top Bible scholars today and author of probably the definitive work on Jesus and women in English. He says Jesus' attitude toward a woman's right to be a disciple of a religious leader and receive religious training would have been "shocking" to the Jews.[38]

BEN WITHERINGTON III

> **It would have been "shocking" to the Jews that Jesus taught women and included them as disciples.**

Witherington also concludes that Jesus was teaching in the women's court in the temple, where both men and women could hear him.[39]

It has been pointed out that Jesus chooses twelve male apostles. But this is a time when only men would normally be received as public speakers, and this would be needed from the apostles.[40] Also, Jesus says a woman (the Queen of Sheba) will rise in judgement against that generation, when women's testimony is not usually deemed reliable even to testify in court.[41] Jesus also appears first to women after his resurrection, commissioning them first, in spite of their supposed unreliability, to tell the apostles he is risen.[42] He could easily have just appeared to the men, as he does later. Then he rebukes the men for not believing the report (that came from the women).[43] After his resurrection, Jesus appears to more than 500 "brothers and sisters," reportedly a more accurate translation than just "brothers," as some versions say.[44]

Recently, some scholars have tried to downplay the significance of Jesus' treatment of women.[45] Some have said women were indeed educated and traveled with male teachers, but these scholars often fail, says a highly respected scholar, to state that these were exceptions.[46] Others have tried to formulate negatives about women in Jesus' ministry, with some stretching Bible passages and even the character of God to do so.[47]

There is no doubt among respected scholars, however, that Jesus is born when his culture considers women as a group inferior.[48] And the Bible is clear that Jesus does not treat them that way. As their creator, he treats them with a naturalness, respect, and inclusiveness, and he violates religious taboos to do so.[49] He never makes negative remarks about women compared to men.[50] He never speaks to a group with male-only terms of address such as "men of Israel."[51] He normally uses the inclusive Greek word for "mankind" in his teachings instead of just the word for "men," as often translated.[52] And he never preaches a doctrine of male leadership or women's subordination to men. Rather, he contends for an attitude of servanthood by all of his followers.

What effect would his treatment of women have on the early Christian church?[53] We turn to that next.

5

Early church and women . . .

The disciples watch the resurrected Jesus ascend to heaven and praise God with great joy. Then 120 men and women, including Jesus' mother, join together in continual prayer to await the power from on high he promised them.[1] It comes on Pentecost, with a wind from heaven and tongues of fire that rest on all of them.[2] They go out to the street and speak of the glories of God in other languages they do not know. The crowd gathered in Jerusalem for the great festival is astonished.[3] And thousands of new believers come to the Lord.

Many scholars have concluded from these verses that the women who had been praying for the power from on high are part of the "all" who are filled with the Spirit that day too.[4] They also prophesy and declare the wonders of God publicly. Peter's words would confirm this when he says to the crowd that this is what the prophet Joel had prophesied, that God would pour out his Spirit on all flesh, and both men and women would prophesy.[5] Thus the church is birthed that day by the Holy Spirit with the involvement of women, in dramatic contrast to the culture.

Women then continue to participate quite visibly in the new church, unlike the common experience of Jewish women and women of other faiths. Sometimes the women minister with their husbands, sometimes as individuals.

One outstanding couple, Priscilla and Aquila, are mentioned seven times. In five of the seven, Priscilla's name is given first.[6] This is unusual in that time, if a woman's name is mentioned at all, and multiple scholars have concluded that this is a strong indication of Priscilla's importance.[7] Her name is given first even when she and Aquila expound the truth to the great speaker Apollos. Here the Greek word for "expound" is the same one used for Paul giving his daily teachings in the synagogue.[8]

In addition, it has been stated that Luke, who wrote the verse about Priscilla and Aquila teaching Apollos, normally mentions the dominant member of a pair first, so Priscilla may be taking the lead in instructing Apollos here.[9] The widely used King James Version of the Bible, though (written in 1611 with frequent instances of male bias),[10] reversed the order of Priscilla and Aquila's names from the original when they instruct Apollos. The translators were apparently unhappy that Priscilla would be given the prominence of being listed first when the couple was teaching a man, especially the great Apollos.[11] In contrast, a famous German theologian proposed in 1905 (and some scholars still believe) that Priscilla may be the unnamed author of the book of Hebrews.[12]

Paul describes another woman in the early church, Phoebe, as a *diakonos*.[13] Here he uses the same word that he calls himself, and others, and is often translated as "minister." Some translations, however, with apparent gender bias, simply call Phoebe a "servant." Paul also calls her a "*prostatis*," sometimes just translated as a "helper," when elsewhere it is used a "leader" or "benefactor."[14] This same word has been used to describe Moses, temple rulers, and in the later church, bishops.[15] It has been said that benefaction and leadership went hand in hand in the Greco-Roman world.[16]

Kenneth Bailey, renowned not only for his study of Jesus but also of Paul, and an expert in their original languages, concludes from the terms Paul uses that Phoebe is the leader of the church at Cenchrae.[17] Evidently, Paul's introduction of her with such strong terms is important for her to be received with respect, especially as a woman in that culture. As the bearer of his letter to the Romans, she would need to know his intention with it, might read it in the Roman congregations, and be called on to explain elements if questions arose.[18]

Phoebe carries Paul's letter to the Romans.

Paul gives strong praise to another woman in the early church, Junia, whom he calls outstanding among the apostles.[19] Reportedly, a translator in the 13th century was so offended that a woman could be called an apostle that he changed her name to a male form, Junias, which did not even exist in Paul's time.[20] (It was later changed back.) Even Chrysostom, the renowned fourth-century bishop of Constantinople, wrote of her: "Oh how great is the devotion of this woman that she should be counted worthy of the appellation of apostle!"[21] Other well-known church fathers, including Origen and Jerome, wrote of her as a woman too.[22]

JOHN CHRYSOSTOM

"How great is the devotion of this woman [Junia] that she should be counted worthy of the appellation of an apostle!"

Some translations say, perhaps with bias against Junia as a woman, that she was well-known *to* the apostles rather than outstanding *among* them. Numerous respected scholars disagree. A common Greek idiom has reportedly been used here, indicating that Junia was outstanding "among" the apostles, not "to" them. [23]

Several women have house churches in their homes.[24] At that time, the churches met in homes and, socially and legally, the host was the leader.[25] Normally a male was the leader of a household at that time, but sometimes a wealthy widow or businesswoman (such as, probably, Lydia) would have the resources to have a large home and host a church in it. Paul also uses the same phrases to describe Chloe and Nympha that he does to describe the house churches of Aristobulus, Narcissus, Stephanas, Onesiphorus, and Priscilla and Aquila.

Paul says two women, Euodia and Syntyche, contended "at his side" for the Gospel.[26] He also greets Tryphena and Tryphosa, calling them women who work hard in the Lord.[27] He uses the same word for their work that he does for his own and that of Timothy, Barnabas, and others. This Greek word translated "work very hard" was used regularly by Paul to refer to the special work of the Gospel ministry, including his own.[28] One of the early church fathers even calls some women of the early church "more spirited than lions!"[29]

Luke refers to women 31 times in Acts,[30] when it was rare to even mention women in literature, especially positively.[31] He says women believed, were baptized, and imprisoned for their faith. Christian women were also publicly martyred, and this was normally reserved for known leaders.[32]

Luke says the evangelist Philip has four unmarried daughters who all prophesy.[33] Luke tells of the woman Lydia, a dealer of purple cloth, who becomes the first convert in Europe after God gives a vision to Paul and calls him to Macedonia where she lives. She is followed by others in her household, perhaps becoming a house church.[34]

Paul talks about women when they pray or prophesy, which he ranks as a high function in the church, describing their head coverings when they do.[35] Ben Witherington says prophecy is addressed to the whole church and has a teaching purpose.[36] Paul also greets 10 women in Romans 16, an astonishingly high number for that time out of the 29 co-workers he lists.[37]

Paul says to entrust his teachings to reliable people, selecting, as the careful writer that he was, a Greek word meaning both men and women (*anthropos*), rather than the one meaning only men (*andros*).[38] Again, he chooses the same inclusive word when he says that Jesus ascended on high and gave gifts to his *people*.[39] Three verses later, continuing the same theme of gifts, he says Jesus gave some to be apostles, prophets, evangelists, and pastor-teachers.[40]

Paul proclaims that through faith in Christ, we are all redeemed from sin, new creations in Christ, reconciled back to God. He says there is not male and female and we all are one in Christ.[41] Jesus becomes the high priest for women too, who enter into the new covenant with him through faith and baptism, rather than circumcision.[42] Women need no longer be considered "unclean" due to bodily functions for childbearing or menstruation, unable to enter into God's presence or minister for him.

Some passages use a male-only address such as "men of Judea."[43] Scholars explain this was a common form of address then in public speaking and did not exclude women from being present.[44] Also, some English Bibles refer to the "brothers" in the church, but some scholars have stated that "brothers and sisters" is often more faithful to the original Greek.[45] That is why some highly respected translations have changed to this wording.[46]

A. J. Gordon, one of the most influential evangelical leaders in the late 1800s and founder of Gordon-Conwell Seminary (still vibrant today), was upset when a successful woman missionary returned home to the U.S. to give a report of her work and was not allowed to do so to a gathering of male leaders in her denomination. So he researched the Scriptures on women himself and wrote a paper on his findings in 1894. In it he cited "unfair translation" and "traditional bias." He pointed out then that Phoebe was called a "servant" (one of the possible translations), when the same word is translated "minister" for Paul and Apollos.[47]

Unbiased translation would call Phoebe a "minister" instead of a "servant."

A. J. GORDON

An overall look at women in the early church, especially in context of God's sovereign actions and the culture then, is quite remarkable. The Holy Spirit births the church on Pentecost, empowering both men and women to testify publicly in other languages of the glories of God. Peter rises up on that day, "filled with the Spirit," and says publicly that this is what the Old Testament prophet Joel had forecast, that both men and women would prophesy. Luke repeatedly includes the work of women for the Gospel in his accounts, honoring their impact and sacrifices such as imprisonment. Women pray and prophesy in the church gatherings (where prophecy would take place), expound the word, and are emissaries for Paul.

Paul, once a zealous Jew steeped in Judaism and his culture's limits on women, now affirms them as leaders and teachers. He does so publicly in his letters to the churches and uses the same words to describe them as himself. He says they contend for the Gospel at his side, with no indication of their being under his leadership. It has been stated that like Jesus, Paul presents a transformed vision of the old patriarchy and a new place for women.[48]

So do some passages by Paul limit women in leadership, as often reported? We turn next to these.

6

Women silent in church?

> *1 Corinthians 14:34–35*
>
> *"Women should remain silent in the churches. They are not allowed to speak, but must be in submission, as the Law says. If they want to inquire about something, they should ask their own husbands at home; for it is disgraceful for a woman to speak in the church."*

In Paul's time, meekness and shyness were generally seen as honorable for a woman, and silence "adorned" her.[1] It was considered disgraceful in most cases for a woman to speak publicly to a man other than her husband.[2] Famous philosophers Cato and Plutarch said a woman should ask her questions of her husband at home, rather than running around in the streets, and she should not question or disagree with him in public.[3]

So does Paul repeat this approach by saying women have to be silent and it is disgraceful for them to speak in church?[4] Would he do this just a few chapters after he describes head coverings for women when they prophesy?[5] And would he quote "Law" that women are not allowed to speak and must be in submission, when the Old Testament has no such law, but Jewish oral law, which he often rejects, does?[6]

Scholars have said this passage is difficult to interpret, especially given Paul's statements elsewhere affirming women.[7] Alice Mathews, long-time professor and academic dean at a prestigious seminary, says few expositors today take this passage at face value.[8] If they did, women would not be able to recite Scripture or even sing in church. So interpreters must explain the difference between what it says, and what they think it means. The theories vary widely.

Few expositors today take these verses at face value.

ALICE MATHEWS

One theory is that women were interrupting the services by asking uneducated questions.[9] Because the only type of speech mentioned in these verses is asking questions, some propose that the context may be the testing of prophecies mentioned just a few verses earlier. (It should be noted that, perhaps in a case of translation bias, the Greek word for women being "silent" in some translations is the same for the prophets who are to be "quiet" if there is no interpreter.[10])

In the culture then, listeners to speeches regularly interrupted lectures with questions.[11] But it was considered rude for uneducated people to do so, and women were far less educated in the Scriptures then than men were.[12] Also, it was seen as shameful in that society, driven by values of honor and shame, for a woman to ask questions publicly of a man other than her husband.[13] So the husbands, who would have had more training, could inform their wives privately at home.[14] Husbands did not normally devote much time to such teaching, so an encouragement along this line could be seen as a breakthrough for the wives who wanted to learn.[15]

Another theory about these verses is that Paul is quoting a view of some participants in this church and then rejecting it.[16] He did this numerous times in this letter. It is not always clear, though, when he is quoting someone, because ancient Greek had little punctuation. Sometimes, Paul quotes various sources that are recognizable, such as Old Testament Scripture, the words of Jesus, and proverbs. He also references various viewpoints by the Corinthians who received this letter.

It is interesting that verse 34 is similar to the words of the famous Jewish rabbi Josephus when he refers to the law and women's lower status: "The woman, says the Law, is in all things inferior to the man."[17] Verse 35 is similar to Cato and Plutarch, who said a woman should ask her husband questions at home, and Jewish tradition then called for women to be silent in the synagogues (though there were some exceptions). In addition, Paul's phrase the "churches of the saints" in the prior verse normally referred to Jewish Christians.[18] So there may have been a desire by some Jews to carry these perspectives forward into some of the new Christian churches.

It should be noted that virtually all the ancient manuscripts place this phrase, "as in all the churches of the saints," at the end of the prior verse, reading: "For God is not a God of disorder but of peace, as in all the congregations of the saints."[19] Some translations today, though, move it to the next verse, changing the meaning, in apparent gender bias, to: "As in all the congregations of the saints, women should be silent. . . ."

Paul immediately follows verses 34 and 35 about women being silent in church with a word of rebuke: "Did the word of God originate with you? Or are you the only people it has reached?" Such quoting and then rebuking resembles a pattern elsewhere in this letter. So it could be interpreted that Paul is not silencing women, but rather the critics of women who are asking questions. A strength of this interpretation is that it would not conflict with Paul's statements elsewhere that acknowledge women praying and prophesying.[20]

A third theory is that Paul did not write these verses that women should be silent. Scholars are aware that readers of ancient manuscripts wrote notes in the margin, and some of these were mistakenly drawn into the text in later hand-written copies.[21] Gordon Fee, author of one of the most respected commentaries on this book of the Bible, and a leading expert in assessing ancient versions of the New Testament,[22] believes this is the case here.[23]

Believes these verses were margin notes, not original text.

GORDON FEE

Our Bibles today do include some verses that scholars have concluded were originally such margin notes. They are not considered extensive, nor have they been thought to affect major tenets of the faith.[24] Some are even footnoted in our Bibles today that the earliest manuscripts do not include them.[25] In 1987, Gordon Fee wrote that he was driven to consider this possibility for verses 34 and 35. He cited the problems with interpretation (even with the above theories), as well as inconsistencies with Paul's style.[26] He also pointed out that these verses appear in two significantly different places in ancient manuscripts, a "radical displacement" that does not happen anywhere else in the New Testament.[27]

Fee explained that our earliest manuscript of most of the Bible goes back only to about AD 350. (Prior Bibles were lost or burned or degraded with time.) That leaves centuries for a comment to be added in the margin during copying and then inserted incorrectly into the text of a new copy at a later time.[28] In fact, a well-known backlash against women in leadership after the early church, and some time before AD 350, may have prompted such a margin note that eventually became verses 34 and 35.[29]

Then some research into an ancient Bible supported what Fee had been saying. The earliest surviving Greek Bible (from about AD 350) is considered the most important of all early manuscripts due to its excellent text quality and other factors.[30] Since the 1400s, it has been held at the Vatican as a protected treasure.[31] Then after centuries, the Vatican made it available for limited study by some scholars from outside the Vatican.[32] Paul Canart, the Vatican's world-renowned expert on this ancient Bible, invited Philip Payne, a Cambridge-educated expert in early New Testament texts, to examine it with him.[33]

PAUL CANART   **PHILIP PAYNE**

Together they looked at verses 34 and 35, whether women should be silent in church. They knew that in ancient times, when a scribe hand wrote a new copy of a Bible, the scribe would first examine multiple manuscripts to find the oldest and most original text. If some of the manuscripts included certain text but others did not, a scribe of integrity, such as the one for this ancient Bible is believed to have been, would not omit that text. Instead, the scribe could put symbols by it on the new copy that were used in various types of documents then to indicate questionable text.[34] Canart and Payne found such markings by verses 34 and 35 in the ancient Bible at the Vatican, and in its original apricot-colored ink. In the year 2000, they published their groundbreaking findings together.[35]

PAGE FROM THE "CODEX VATICANUS"

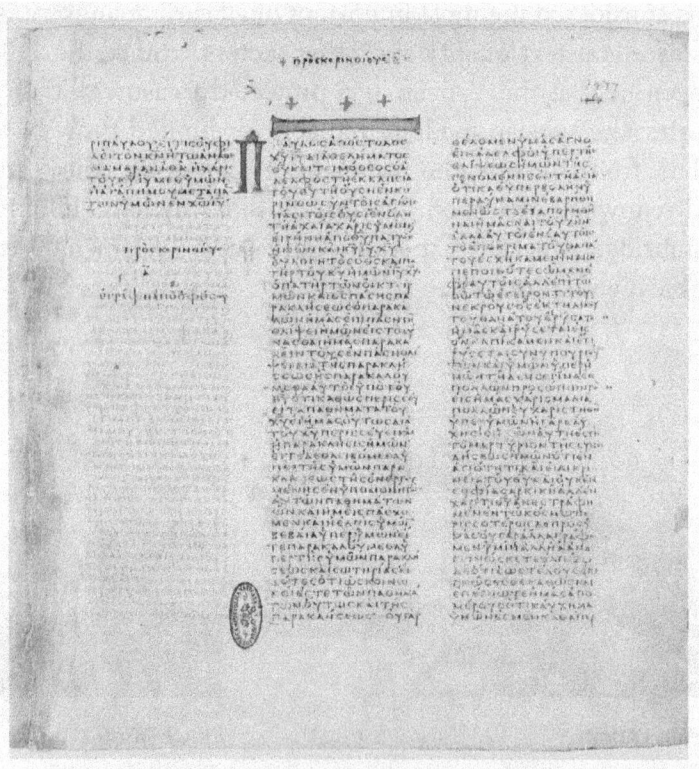

Vat. gr. 1209 (p. 1477) © [2024] Biblioteca Apostolica Vaticana. Reproduced by permission of Biblioteca Apostolica Vaticana (the Vatican Library), with all rights reserved.

The world's oldest Greek Bible is held at the Vatican.

As a follow-up (after Canart's passing), Payne examined fifteen places in this Bible's New Testament that virtually all modern translations agree were not in the original text. He found the same markings indicating doubtful text by every one of them that also appear by verses 34 and 35.[36] Payne has also pointed to two other old manuscripts that indicate a problem with these verses.[37] In addition, he notes that the apostolic fathers gave no sign of awareness of verses 34 and 35, even though this letter was the most quoted one by Christian writers in that time.[38]

Today, the majority of academic commentators on this book of the Bible reportedly believe these verses were not in Paul's original letter.[39] Dozens of textual studies have come to the same conclusion.[40] Some scholars, though, continue to debate the above theories and research.

Few people today, however, take these verses literally. Women now are often as well educated as men, most cultures do not consider it shameful for women to speak publicly, and these verses would violate Paul's affirmation elsewhere of women praying and prophesying in the churches.

Next we turn to what Paul meant when he said man is the "head" of woman.

7

Man as "head" of woman?

> *1 Corinthians 11:3–5, 11–12*
>
> *"Now I want you to realize that the head of every man is Christ, and the head of the woman is man, and the head of Christ is God. Every man who prays or prophesies with his head covered. . . . Every woman who prays or prophesies with her head uncovered. . . . In the Lord, however, woman is not independent of man, nor is man independent of woman. For as woman came from man, so also man is born of woman. But everything comes from God."*

Paul loved puns, cleverly using the same word with different meanings.[1] And that is what he did in this passage with the Greek word for *head*. In his day, this particular word usually meant just an actual, physical head. This would fit with Paul's discussion here of head coverings for men and women when praying and prophesying. But the word could also have metaphorical meanings, as when Paul says that man is the "head" of woman. What does he mean here? Several meanings are possible in the Greek, and context is important for understanding Paul's intent.[2]

At that time, head coverings sent important signals, and Jews, Greeks, and others in the Corinthian church had different customs.[3] Jewish women covered their hair in public and could be divorced if they did not.[4] Female prostitutes and slaves would have their hair uncovered and loose in public.[5] Some well-to-do women (apparently not Jewish) had begun to style their hair up elaborately in the latest styles and not always wear head coverings.[6] In the cults, some women let their hair down loose to prophesy in a wild manner.[7] On men, long hair could signal an invitation to homosexual liaisons.[8] New Christians may have tried to import some of these customs into the Corinthian church, with volatile results.

Apparently for the sake of the Gospel, Paul encourages modest head coverings rather than personal freedoms. Earlier in his letter, Paul appeals to the Corinthian church not to have divisions but to be united.[9] He begins his discussion about appropriate head coverings with a statement that may have been intended to be a unifying principle.

Paul says that the "head" of man is Christ, the head of woman is man, and the head of Christ is God.[10] What does he mean here by "head"? Does it mean "leader" or "authority" as it often does in English or Hebrew, as in the head of a company or tribe? Scholars debate this point, but in the Greek this meaning would reportedly be very rare.[11] In fact, some scholars have found that the ancient Greek dictionaries covering that time period give dozens of meanings for the Greek word Paul uses for "head" (*kephale*), but none are for a meaning of "authority" or "leader."[12]

Scholars also point out that this word for "head" is not the one normally given in the New Testament to indicate a leader or an authority.[13] This Greek word is almost never used this way in the Greek version of the Old Testament that was quoted by Jesus and Paul and widely used by the early church.[14]

So what is Paul saying here? Cyril of Alexandria, an early church father and native Greek speaker, reportedly provides us with the earliest known consistent interpretation of this metaphor.[15] He believes that *head* here (*kephale*) means "source," as in the head or source of a river, a meaning that can be found in old Greek dictionaries.[16] Cyril writes:

> "Because head means source . . . man is the head of woman, for she was taken out of him."[17]

CYRIL OF ALEXANDRIA

Paul says man is woman's "source."

Other church fathers also reportedly wrote about "head" in this passage as meaning "source."[18]

Why would Paul emphasize man as woman's source? In that culture, origins and ancestry were very important.[19] They were to be treated with honor.[20] So Paul may be calling men and women to head coverings that honor one another, and God. Just a few verses later, he repeats a theme of mutual respect and "source" when he says that men and women are not independent of each other, but come from each other, and everything comes from God.[21] A few chapters earlier, Paul uses similar wording when he says that Jesus came from God the father, and all things come from God.[22]

A meaning of "source" would also fit in the same verse about man as the "head" of woman when Paul says the "head" of man is Christ—as man's creator,[23] and the "head" of Christ is God—the Godhead from whom the incarnated Christ came.[24] Also, the order Paul gives for the "head" of man–woman–Christ would work chronologically for creation sources, but not for a supposed hierarchy.[25] In addition, the passage itself is primarily about head coverings in worship, not about authority.[26]

Anthony Thiselton, who wrote an in-depth commentary on 1 Corinthians, says the Greek word for "head" here does not seem to denote a relation of "subordination" or "authority over."[27] Another recent commentary in a highly respected series concludes that the evidence for a meaning here of "leader" in the usual English sense is "weak and limited."[28]

Gordon Fee writes in his commentary on 1 Corinthians that almost certainly the only meaning that the Corinthian people would have recognized here for "head" is "source," especially the "source of life," not "authority."[29] Catherine Clark Kroeger, a longtime professor of classical and ministry studies at a prestigious seminary,[30] explains that paintings and sculpture were of great importance then, and some showed the physical head as the source of life and water. These include a painting of a sphinx with a fountain emerging from its head and Athena springing from the head of Zeus.³¹

Kroeger also states that the ancient Greek writers Homer and Galen wrote of the source of a body of water as its "head."³² Aristotle said the physical head was the source or beginning of life. It was believed then that human sperm was created in the head and traveled down the spinal cord to procreate the human race.³³ Artemidorus of Ephesus wrote that as the physical head was the source of light and life for the whole body, so a father was the source of life for his son.³⁴ Photius, a ninth-century scholar renowned for his knowledge of classical authors, created a lexicon stating that "head" (*kephale*) was a synonym for "procreator" (a producer of offspring) or "progenitor" (an ancestor).³⁵

Artwork and literature of antiquity present the physical head as the source of life.

CATHERINE CLARK KROEGER

All things considered, numerous leading scholars have concluded that the Greek word for "head" in this passage (*kephale*) implies "source" or "origin," not "authority."³⁶ Some scholars, however, lean toward a meaning of "prominence," literally, "topness," as in the head is the top of the body (though other scholars question this).³⁷ And some scholars, especially those who have long advocated for male leadership, continue to promote a meaning of "authority" or "leader" here, even though the studies used to back up such meanings have been strongly criticized for faulty methodology and interpretation.³⁸

Two other verses in this chapter should also be noted. In verse 10, some translations say a woman ought to have a sign of authority over her head in order to prophesy. The original language, however, as affirmed by numerous respected scholars, indicates that the woman has authority over her own head to prophesy and ought to exercise it.[39] In fact, this is the only time a Greek word meaning "authority" (*exousia*) is mentioned in this passage. And this particular Greek word normally carries the sense of the active use of authority, here by the woman, rather than authority imposed by another.[40] Scholars who conclude that the text indicates the woman has her own authority include F.F. Bruce, the preeminent scholar who wrote respected commentaries on many books of the Bible.[41] He also concludes that "head" in this passage means "source."[42]

Paul says woman has authority over her own head to prophesy.

F.F. BRUCE

It should be added that in verse 9, some versions say that woman was created *for* man. A better and more accurate translation, says Kenneth Bailey, the highly esteemed scholar who lived in the Middle East and was fluent in several ancient languages, is that woman was created *because of* the man, not *for* him.[43] Bailey also says the phrase that she is the "glory of man" can mean "the glory of humankind . . . created as the final climax of the creation story."[44]

Bruce Metzger, chair of the translation committee for the NRSV Bible,[45] says with admirable humility that plays on words can "defy the ingenuity of the translator."[46] A play on words with the use of "head" (*kephale*) and other words in this complicated passage have long challenged translators and readers. This is especially true when incorrect assumptions from the English language, and traditionalism, have prevailed.

Perhaps Kenneth Bailey, beloved by many for the high quality of his work, his depth of understanding of ancient languages, and the Christlikeness of his life, can guide us best.[47] Toward the end of his life's work, he wrote an acclaimed book about Paul and 1 Corinthians through Mediterranean eyes. In it, he chooses the word *origin* to describe "head" in verse 3, not "authority."[48] Bailey also says that Paul emerges "as a compassionate figure who boldly affirms the equality and mutual interdependency of men and women in the new covenant."[49]

Bailey states that we need to have some "ancient barnacles" scraped from our understanding of men and women in leadership, so that Paul's "original intent can shine forth with grace and power."[50] "I hear Paul saying in this passage," Bailey writes:

> *"Men and women have gifts that they share together, and prophecy is among them (Acts 2:17–18). Those with these gifts should participate together in the leadership of worship. When doing so, do not dress in a manner that leads to misunderstanding or in any way detracts from the task of bringing the faithful into the presence of God. Both women and men are created in the image of God. Let the focus be on God, not on yourselves. In the Lord you are equal and mutually interdependent. Let the angels rejoice once again."*[51]

Angels then were said to rejoice when worship was glorifying to God.[52] Such worship would surely be Paul's desire, and he appears to be offering a unifying theme of head coverings on prophesying men and women that honor God and one another.

Next we examine passages about submission and the husband as the "head" of the wife.

8

Submission?

Ephesians 5:21–23, 25, 6:1, 5

> "*Submit to one another out of reverence for Christ. Wives submit ["submit" here is not in the original Greek but is drawn from the prior verse] to your husbands as to the Lord. For the husband is the head of the wife as Christ is the head of the church. . . . Husbands, love your wives, just as Christ loved the church and gave himself up for her. . . . Children, obey your parents. . . . Slaves, obey your earthly masters. . . .*"

The letter to the Ephesians describes the relationships that probably would have been on display in the early house churches.[1] Scholars believe that most of them met in the atriums of large villas owned by Christian believers.[2] These atriums were semi-public and could hold about 40 to 50 people. The public could come and go into them to conduct business with the villa and presumably attend a house church. Those who actually lived in the villa included extended family with grown children and their families as well as slaves.[3]

Culturally, and often legally, the owner of a villa (usually a man) generally had absolute rule over everyone in the household, including the power of life and death.[4] He was to be honored and feared, and those who benefited from his patronage and kinship were to lay down their lives for him.[5] The letter to the Ephesians, however, presents a very different model.

Paul sets an overarching theme, calling believers to be like Christ and filled with the Spirit. He encourages them to speak to one another with psalms, hymns, and spiritual songs, giving thanks in everything, and submitting to one another out of reverence for Christ.[6] The concept of submitting to one another has been called a "startling idea" for Paul's time.[7] Pope John Paul called it an "innovation of the Gospel."[8]

Katharine Bushnell, a brilliant medical doctor in the 1920s who learned Greek and Hebrew to study the original Scriptures about women, published a book still quoted for its groundbreaking research.[9] She points out that Paul liked to use words in new ways to explain life in Christ. She says he does so here with *submission* to describe a relationship peculiar to believers. The true sense of the word, she writes, does not speak of impassable ranks, superior and inferior, but rather the "Christian grace of yielding one's preferences to another," where principle is not involved, rather than asserting one's own rights.[10]

KATHARINE BUSHNELL, M.D.

Paul used submission in a new way as a Christian grace.

Paul also applies the word *submission* to marriage, and this too was new.[11] Greek and Jewish marriage contracts varied but often required wives to *obey* their husbands, or wives could be left destitute.[12] Generally, wives were considered inferior and husbands, except in cases where the wife stayed under the father's authority, were to rule them.[13] But Paul never says this.[14]

Right after calling for believers to submit to one another, Paul encourages wives to submit to their husbands (not obey as children and slaves are told). The word submit, though, does not appear here in the original Greek.[15] Rather, it reads "wives to their husbands," meaning to refer back to the verb right before it.[16] What comes before it is "submitting to one another out of reverence for Christ." So, the wives' submission appears, literally, within the context of the mutual submission of all believers.[17] Some translations place mutual submission and submission in separate paragraphs, because ancient Greek does not have paragraphs, but this is misleading.

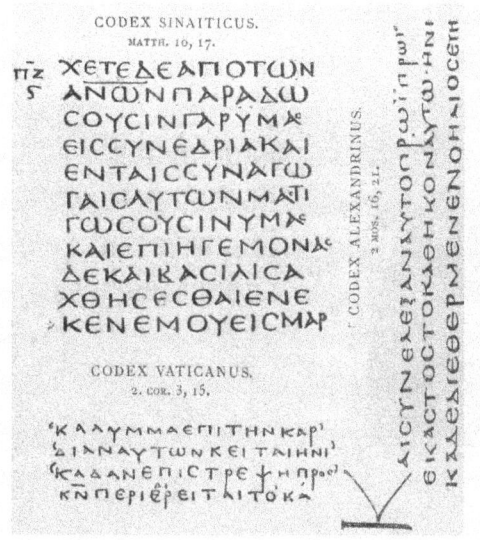

Ancient Greek has no spaces, paragraphs.

4TH AND 5TH CENTURY GREEK BIBLES

Some say mutual submission does not relate to husbands, but many scholars believe it does.[18] Lynn Cohick, author of a major academic work about this letter, says it would be almost impossible culturally and legally for Paul's audience to understand if he said that husbands should submit to their wives. In terms of actual practice, though, Paul does ask husbands to submit in the command that they love their wives as Christ loved the church and gave himself up to death that the church might live.[19]

Craig Keener agrees. He is an expert on the cultural background of the New Testament, author on Paul's writings about women, and past president of a prestigious society of scholars. Keener writes that Paul was well aware of the persecution of Christians, writing this letter as he did from prison. And he was "smart," says Keener.[20] Paul does not remove the common ancient ideal of the wife's yielding to her husband. Rather, he "adds the requirement that the husband join her in it."[21]

Paul invites husbands to join wives in submissiveness.

CRAIG KEENER

Paul speaks to husbands in a much stronger way than to wives. And it was unusual at that time to talk of husbands loving their wives.[22] But Paul uses a command verb in the Greek to tell them to do so, even to the point of self-sacrifice, again the opposite of his culture.[23] It has been stated that the wife's submission to the husband "as to the Lord" limits the submission to what a holy God would ask of his followers.[24] Also, some translations say a wife should respect her husband, but it has been pointed out that the grammar of the original is best translated that the husband must love his wife *so that she respects him*.[25]

When Paul calls the husband the "head" of the wife, this is not one of the usual Greek words for "ruler" or "leader."[26] Rather, this is the same word described in the prior chapter (*kephale*). It normally means a physical head but can occasionally mean functions of that head as the ancient Greeks perceived them. This could include the head as the source of life and provision, which a privileged householder certainly was.[27] (As discussed in the prior chapter, the evidence for a meaning of "leader" or "authority" is weak and limited.)

Paul goes on to develop further his meaning with the word *head*. He calls the husband the head of the wife as Jesus is the head of the church, his body, savior. Here *savior* is in a grammatical format where it explains "head."[28] At that time, "savior" normally meant "provider/protector."[29] (Paul would certainly not be saying that the husband is the spiritual savior of the wife!) Therefore, numerous scholars have concluded that Paul is calling the husband in such a household to use his position of prominence to be a source of life, provision, and love for the wife, rather than simply take from her as the culture prescribed. And this is to be done sacrificially, as Christ did.[30]

Paul is said to have been the first to use the word *head* for a husband (and does so only this once).[31] Apparently he was calling the husband to be a life giver, rather than a ruler, then the cultural norm.[32] In fact, Paul never tells the husband to rule or lead the wife,[33] or calls him the leader in Greek words indisputably meaning that.[34] The only literal command Paul makes to the husband is to love his wife self-sacrificially. It should also be noted that Jesus never says anything about marriage with a hierarchy. Rather, he cites the creation account where man and woman were to be one.

Paul says elsewhere that wives should submit to their husbands, so that no one will malign the word of God, and slaves should be subject to their masters to make the teaching of God attractive.[35] Peter, who knew Paul's work, also addresses the three sets of relationships in a privileged household. He comforts slaves through harsh beatings (not condoning slavery!). He then addresses wives, including those with unbelieving husbands, who had to be especially careful.[36] Clearly, neither Peter nor Paul is endorsing slavery or oppressive marriages. Rather, as scholars have concluded, each is encouraging slaves and wives in how to conduct themselves in the midst of such.[37]

Peter also calls the wife a "joint heir" in a time when wives rarely had such privileges. He tells the believing husband that his prayers will be hindered if he does not treat his wife considerately.[38] Peter cites Sarah as an example of submissiveness, with some translations (in apparent bias) saying she "obeyed" Abraham.[39] But this same word is given elsewhere in the New Testament as "listen to," "hearken," or "heed."[40] Scholars say this is the equivalent of the word in Genesis when Abraham "listens to" or "agrees with" what Sarah says.[41]

Was Paul actually telling wives to do "everything" the husband wants?[42] Many probably had to in that culture. But such actions could go against other passages of Scripture, including lying, breaking the law, engaging in illicit sexual activities, being beaten rather than cared for, etc. The Bible was even used in earlier centuries to justify wife beating and slavery.[43] But today, wives and their husbands would be held accountable individually for their actions, both legally and before God, and wives have every right to say no to any such activity.[44] Multiple scholars point out that Christ would never ask them for anything wrong, and he is the model for this passage.[45]

It should also be noted that neither the New Testament or the Old Testament says a wife is to *obey* her husband. In fact, in Paul's longest discussion on marriage (1 Cor. 7), he identifies the same rights and responsibilities for husbands and wives in twelve key areas and never implies leadership by the husband or different roles.[46] Kenneth Bailey says this granting of equal rights and powers to each partner in that time is "nothing less than amazing."[47]

Even the fact that Paul addresses the normally subordinate wife directly, and first, rather than just the man, gives her a dignity the culture did not.[48] In that time it was unusual for "subordinates," including wives, children, and slaves, to even be addressed. And Paul never uses command forms in the Greek when he addresses wives (they are simply encouraged to submit). But the husband is told multiple times in the command verb form to love his wife. And it was he who had the social standing to change the marriage relationship.[49]

In a time when the wife usually left her home to be married, Paul quotes Genesis that a man is to leave his family.[50] When men were often unfaithful, Paul quotes that a man is to cleave to his wife.[51] Paul even elevates the discussion of the union of man and wife, and the likeness to Christ and the church, to a "profound mystery."[52]

So was Paul trying to confirm submission by a wife, with the man as the unquestioned leader, the standard in his culture? Or was he establishing a new standard where the husband and wife are loving and submissive to each other with Christ as the model?[53]

Paul calls the Ephesians to live a life of love.

PAUL WRITES TO THE EPHESIANS

Ben Witherington has written several major academic works on Paul's rhetoric, how he communicates and persuades. Witherington says Paul's emphasis here is on changing the behavior of the householder to a loving and Christian manner. The "trajectory" of the passage is toward a "significant equalizing of the relationships in Christian marriage." Witherington concludes that Paul is deliberately trying to reform the patriarchy of his day. Paul's purpose with this passage is not to promote the subordination of wives.[54]

Howard Marshall, called a "gentle giant" of New Testament scholarship, says a more promising approach is for the Christian husband not to make demands on his wife that reduce her to submission. Rather, they should seek God's will for their married life together.[55] Marshall concludes:

> "One-sided submission becomes impossible, for Christian love by the husband requires him also to respect and submit to his wife. . . . Mutual love transcends submission."[56]

I. HOWARD MARSHALL

Mutual love transcends submission.

9

Teaching and authority over a man?

1 Timothy 2:11-15

> "A woman should learn in quietness and full submission. I do not permit a woman to teach or dominate a man, she must be silent. For Adam was formed first, then Eve. And Adam was not the one deceived; it was the woman who was deceived and became a sinner. But women will be saved through childbearing—if they continue in faith, love and holiness with propriety."

Scholars debate this passage more than any other in the Bible. Its translation and interpretation are challenging due to a rare key word, special Greek connectors, and possible references to myths. And it is this passage that has primarily affected whether many women teach men or have leadership in churches and homes.

Paul is said to have written this letter to Timothy in Ephesus.[1] At the time, it was a major center of worship to the goddess Artemis.[2] Her temple there was so large that it was considered one of the Seven Wonders of the Ancient World. When emerging Christianity threatened her supremacy, Paul was nearly caught up in a riot with a two-hour chant of "Great is Artemis!" and the "whole city" in an uproar.[3]

Artemis was said to be the founder of Ephesus and guarded it. In return, Ephesus was to guard her honor.[4] Women were taught to pray to Artemis to come safely through childbirth, or suffer her vengeance.[5] Artemis, as woman, was supposedly formed first and then helped with the birth of man. So she and her female followers could be considered superior to men.[6]

TEMPLE OF ARTEMIS IN EPHESUS

One of the Seven Wonders of the Ancient World

Some other myths also said Eve was created first, and it was man, not woman, who was originally deceived.[7] Paul's words from Genesis—that man was formed first and woman was deceived, would specifically counter those teachings.[8] Paul's words about childbirth, then a major cause of death for women, could be reassuring that prayer to the goddess was not necessary and "the" childbirth of Jesus would save them.[9]

At the beginning of his letter, Paul urges Timothy to command certain persons not to teach false doctrines or devote themselves to myths.[10] He warns Timothy to have nothing to do with godless myths and old wives' tales.[11] He focuses at least half of his letter on the problem of false teaching.[12] So, in the above passage Paul may have been correcting some of these beliefs and dismantling a sense of superiority (as with the Artemis influence)[13] on the part of some of the women.[14]

Scholars point out that without an alternative explanation, some of Paul's statements would be illogical.[15] For example, being born first does not always indicate superiority in the Bible, as with David. Also, women in general are not more easily deceived than men in the Bible. And Adam is faulted for sin multiple times in the New Testament.[16]

It is significant that Paul uses a rare word when he refers to a woman "dominating" a man and that it appears only this once in the New Testament (*authentein*).[17] Also, Paul does not use the word he normally does for having authority (*exousiazo*).[18] Until World War II, most of the main translations give this rare word as "dominate/domineer" or "take/usurp authority."[19] After that, some changed it to "have authority," implying that Paul was forbidding the exercise of any type of teaching or authority by women over men. Some translations, including the most widely used one, have since moved away from such a translation. But this is not well known, and old translations are often still followed that women should not have authority over men.[20]

This rare Greek word (*authentein*) was studied in a database of ancient Greek writings soon after it was compiled in 1988. Only a handful of uses of this word were found near Paul's time. The study concluded that these few uses indicated a dominating, unhealthy form of authority.[21] Then several hundred years later, the word could also mean simply exercising authority.[22] (It still could mean "domineer," though, as early church father Chrysostom used it.)[23] Some scholars, however, misinterpreted the results of the study and concluded that *authentein* meant normal authority earlier, in Paul's day.[24] The respected author of the study called this a "grave misunderstanding" of his work, but he continues to be misquoted.[25]

Also, it is not well known that Paul uses special Greek connectors between "teach" and "dominate" that have no exact counterpart in English. These connectors *(ouk/oude)* are used in the Greek, reportedly in the overwhelming majority of cases, to combine two verbs to create a new concept.[26] This can be missed in English translations, though, because they often translate literally word for word.[27]

An ancient source can be helpful here. Origen of Alexandria, considered the most important biblical scholar of the early church and expert in biblical Greek, combines the two verbs "teach" and "dominate" into a single prohibition. He says the passage concerns woman "not becoming a ruler over man in speaking."[28] Accordingly, some scholars today have proposed that this verse should be translated as one idea rather than two, such as *"teach a man in a dominating way."*[29]

ORIGEN OF ALEXANDRIA

Teach and dominate are combined into one new concept.

Another of this rare verb's meanings, and its actual roots *(auto + entes)*, meant to be an originator or author of something.[30] So Paul may be using this verb with a double meaning to say that he does not permit a woman to teach that woman is the originator of man (as in the Artemis myth).³¹ If so, this meaning would flow well with the next verse—that Adam was formed first.³²

Scholars also point to Paul's statement that "I do not permit" a woman to teach. This was a particular phrase he used when he wanted to give personal advice for a situation that is not universal.³³ Scholars have also pointed out that this was an "occasional letter," written primarily to address the needs of the occasion.³⁴ It does not make a general address to the Ephesians, the church, or to Timothy to share it with the church, as elsewhere.³⁵

Walter Liefeld (co-author of a massive work about "daughters of the church"³⁶) also points out in his commentary on this letter, as have numerous scholars, that Paul's statement to women is not in the command form in the Greek. The only command form in the passage is to let the woman learn, a significant change for that time,³⁷ and an antidote to the false teaching Paul laments.³⁸

Paul also says a woman is to learn "in quietness and full submission." This was a known phrase of the day meaning the attitude of a good student.³⁹ Aida Besancon Spencer (author of a pioneering work about women in ministry⁴⁰) explains in her commentary on I Timothy that the Jews especially revered these qualities as important for a good student.⁴¹

Learning in quietness and submission meant being a good student.

AIDA BESANCON SPENCER

Also, the word used here for "quietness" is the same one earlier in the passage that describes living peaceful and quiet lives. It is not one of the Greek words indicating total silence.[42]

Leading scholar Walter Kaiser agrees that Paul is not silencing the women. Kaiser says Paul gives instructions in this letter for both men and women when they pray publicly. The men are not to be angry, and the women are not to wear certain attire.[43] Kaiser points out that a Greek word meaning "in like manner" introduces the verses about women immediately after the men, and the grammar ties the two statements together.[44] Therefore, because Paul is discussing women praying here, he is not silencing them altogether in the meetings.[45]

Some scholars believe Paul is correcting a certain segment of women, specifically the younger widows he mentions later in the letter who are idle and going house to house.[46] Some translations say they were gossiping, but Gordon Fee says the Greek word here (*phylario*) does not mean that. Rather, it relates to identifying teachings or philosophies opposed to the truth.[47] If the young widows, or anyone else, were spreading the Artemis myth of the superiority of women and bringing that into the church, that certainly could have caused anger in the men and upset the church.

Whether an Artemis influence is involved or not, various scholars have concluded that Paul's prohibition relates either to false teaching by women, or their teaching in an inappropriate manner, not their teaching men at all.[48] Howard Marshall says in his massive commentary on Paul's pastoral letters that the context here makes it clear there was something wrong with the content of the teaching by the women. Also, he says, a reference to authority would exceed the scope of the discussion begun in verse 11 about a woman learning. He says it is more likely that the nature of the teaching is being addressed, not the role of women in church leadership in general.[49]

Ben Witherington, currently one of the world's leading scholars, suggests Paul is correcting abuses by both men and women in worship. He concludes that nothing in this material suggests a permanent ban on women engaging in the ministry of the word.[50] Leading scholars Gordon Fee and Douglas Stuart point out that women are found teaching and prophesying elsewhere in the Bible, so it is altogether likely that this passage speaks to a local problem.[51]

F.F. Bruce, called the dean of evangelical scholarship, concludes that Paul is merely making a statement of practice at that time. He says Paul makes no distinction between men and women among his fellow workers, and anything that might seem to run contrary to this must be viewed critically in context of the main thrust of his teaching. Bruce also says this passage should be interpreted in light of Galatians 3:28, that in Christ there is neither male nor female, not the other way around. (He states that some have tried to say this statement is just about baptism, but the text does not make this restriction.) Bruce concludes that Paul does not limit women in leadership or teaching in the church and society.[52]

David Scholer, who taught a seminary course for 36 years on women in the New Testament, believes Paul's prohibition is against "some abusive activity," not the appropriate exercise by women of teaching and authority in the church.

DAVID SCHOLER

The prohibition is against some sort of abuse activity, not women teaching and having authority in the church.

Scholer says this text must be put in balance with other biblical texts, including that: both women and men are new creations in Christ, Jesus includes women among his disciples and witnesses, the Holy Spirit comes upon both sons and daughters on Pentecost, and Paul includes women in his circle of co-workers.[53]

In summary, this passage has a rare word whose meaning is still debated, a grammatical structure that does not exist in English, and is sent as a personal letter to Timothy, not a formal letter of instruction to the church. As sometimes translated to restrict women in general, it would violate Paul's support elsewhere of women in leadership and teaching.[54] And this is the only time such a statement appears in the Bible.[55]

At the end of a long and distinguished career, preeminent scholar Roger Nicole wrote about this passage. He says that because of the many difficulties with it, and Paul's strong affirmations of women in ministry elsewhere, he follows the principle: "Do not doubt in the darkness what you have seen in the light."[56] He concludes:

> *"We are not at liberty to imagine that St. Paul condemned in Timothy what he had sanctioned in Romans."*[57]

10

Church leadership?

After the Holy Spirit fills 120 men and women on Pentecost to prophesy publicly of the glories of God, thousands come to faith in Jesus. The believers then continue to meet, mainly in homes.[1] For the first 200 years in the life of Christianity, these are the churches.[2]

Both men and women have churches in their homes.[3] Scholars tell us that the homeowner, usually a man but sometimes a woman, would be the leader of the church in that home, both legally and socially.[4] In accord with Jesus' teaching, though, there is no evidence of authoritarian control by these leaders.[5] Rather, leadership appears to be plural and inclusive,[6] with a new kind of authority defined by servanthood.

As the apostles, Paul, and others travel to spread the good news, the churches multiply. The churches are then encouraged and taught by letters and emissaries from Paul and others.

Participation in these early churches has an inclusive feel. In the Corinthian church, for example, "everyone" has a hymn, or a word of instruction, a revelation, a tongue, or an interpretation.[7] We know that women prophesy in church because Paul describes head coverings for them when they do.[8]

And when Paul discusses spiritual gifts, he never limits them just to men, using instead a word for both men and women, contrary to what some translations say.[9] When Paul says Jesus gave gifts to mankind, Paul uses a gender-inclusive Greek word, not just the one for men, with some as apostles, prophets, evangelists, pastor-teachers.[10] Ben Witherington concludes that women and men were not just allowed to exercise their gifts in early Christian worship, they were expected to do so.[11]

LETTER FROM PAUL BEING READ TO THE CHRISTIAN CHURCH IN ROME

Women and men together in the early church

The Bible does not describe a pastor conducting a service such as we have today (which does not negate the value of such a model).[12] In all cases, says Gordon Fee, leadership was plural.[13] Presumably women, who were named singly as having churches in their homes and identified by Paul and others in strong ministry capacities, would have been part of such leadership teams. Walter Liefeld says this plural leadership then led the whole church in decision-making processes.[14]

Paul describes characteristics of a godly "overseer." Some scholars believe this is the host of the house church, some that it is an elder. When Paul says that anyone who wants to be an overseer desires a good thing, he uses a generic Greek word for *anyone*, rather than a word indicating just men.[15] In fact, in the list of qualities for overseers, the word *man* does not appear as a standalone at all in the original, as some translations state, nor are there any male pronouns.[16]

One phrase does include the word *man*, that an overseer should be a "one-woman man." Scholars explain that this was a saying of the day meaning marital fidelity, in a time when unfaithfulness was common among men and divorce was rampant.[17] Paul uses a similar phrase for widows, that they should have been faithful to one man.[18] If the phrase "one-woman man" is taken literally to describe only men, that would mean that even single men could not qualify, including Paul, Timothy, and Jesus. Paul also says overseers should manage their homes well when elsewhere, he encourages younger widows to remarry and manage their homes, so he would not be excluding women.[19]

Character qualities are also described for "deacons," and women are mentioned specifically. Some translations say "their wives," implying the wives of male deacons. The Greek word used here, though, (*gyne*) can mean either "women" or "wives." But no possessive "their" is included in the original. Also, Paul calls Phoebe a deacon. This term was also used then for civic and religious leaders.[20]

Historical records and archeological findings show numerous examples of women deacons, ministers, and even bishops (some translate as "overseers") in the early centuries of the Christian church.[21] Even the Roman government was aware of Christian female deacons by AD 112, torturing them for their faith as was done with impactful Christian leaders.[22] Multiple early church fathers also mention women deacons.[23] At this writing, most of the recent major scholarly commentaries have concluded that Paul is referring to women deacons, not wives.[24]

Scholars say the Bible does not define offices as clearly as they are in many churches today.[25] Linda Belleville, highly respected for her academic publications about women in the New Testament, points out that the early church followed Jesus' teaching and did not buy into the prevailing style of leadership with force of will. The main concern, she says, was not offices, but godly character.[26] Ministry was the job of the whole congregation, and "respect and submission were earned by hard work, tender loving care, and an exemplary life."[27]

The early church's main concern was godly character, not offices.

LINDA BELLEVILLE

About fifty years after Paul's death, though, major changes occurred. A church leader named Ignatius was awaiting death by lions in the Roman Coliseum and wrote seven hurried letters to different churches that became quite influential.[28] Apparently concerned about a possible church split, he increased the power of an overseer (later called "bishop"), giving one person sole authority to rule the congregations in an area. From then on, Ignatius wrote, no activities were to be valid without this person's permission. This included baptisms and communion.[29] At the time, officers in civil government were generally male, and apparently the bishops followed suit.[30] As a result, many women, and male lay leaders, were marginalized.³¹

Women were also impacted in a major way when Emperor Constantine legalized Christianity in the year 313. Scholars tell us that church leaders wanted to be seen as respectable, so they began to conform even more with Greco-Roman values rather than those of Jesus or Paul.³² Christians began constructing church buildings, some grand like the old marble temple in Jesus' day. These had raised pulpits and altars, formalized services, and an increasingly male priesthood.³³

About that time, important gatherings of male religious leaders began taking away the ministry of women.³⁴

EMPEROR CONSTANTINE CONVENES BISHOPS

Council decided women should not preach or baptize (AD 398)

This included preaching in an assembly of men or baptizing.[35] It also came to be considered unthinkable for a woman to preside over communion during her period. This followed the Old Testament priestly guidelines for cleanliness, rather than the liberating work of Jesus.[36] In the sixth century, the large Christian cathedral at Constantinople reportedly had forty deaconesses, but a leadership gathering decreed that women could no longer be deaconesses "due to the weakness of their sex."[37] Women were even stopped from singing in church. In some places this continued until the 1800s, because women were supposed to be "silent" in church.[38]

Yet throughout church history, women have been bright lights for the Gospel and the Word of God.[39] In the fourth century, two educated noblewomen, Paula and Marcella, were reportedly credited by Jerome, the most important scholar of his time, for working with him on a major translation of the Bible into Latin.[40] In the late 1800s and early 1900s, women from different countries translated the Bible. This included Americans Julia Evelina Smith in 1876 and Helen Barrett Montgomery in 1924, and Pandita Ramabai of India in 1922.

PANDITA RAMABAI

Early Bible Translators

HELEN BARRETT MONTGOMERY

Ramabai was raised in a poor but priestly Hindu caste, found Jesus, was acclaimed for her humanitarian work, and translated the Bible for the uneducated poor. (She was later commemorated by a stamp in India.)[41]

Today, one of the most popular Bible teachers internationally, Beth Moore, is a woman.[42] And one of the world's largest mission agencies (Youth With A Mission) includes women who have reportedly pioneered and led some of their most important works for God, in some of the hardest places.[43]

Millard Erickson writes in his respected textbook on Christian theology that because of what God has done, women have been in positions of leadership throughout biblical history. He believes that any restrictive passages relate to particular local situations, and the greater evidence supports the full access for women to church ministries.[44]

MILLARD ERICKSON

Women have been leaders throughout history, because of what God has done.

Preeminent scholar F.F. Bruce agrees. He says both of the main passages that appear to limit women have many problems in interpretation and should be viewed in light of Paul's statement that there is not male and female in Christ.[45] Paul does not clearly establish a pattern of male-only leadership.[46] Rather, Paul cites the involvement of women in the work of the Gospel in strong ways.[47] F. F. Bruce concludes: "There can be no reason a Christian woman should not exercise her priesthood on the same terms as a Christian man."[48]

In the Old Testament, priesthood was male-only, with the Old Covenant marked by male circumcision. In contrast, the New Covenant has a royal priesthood of male and female, with water baptism for all.[49] In Jesus' time, only the priests, who were male, could enter the inner courts of the temple. Women had to stay in the outermost court—the Women's Court, and not proceed inward to the Court of the Israelites, or the Court of the Priests, or the innermost Holy of Holies.[50]

But when Jesus was crucified, as Aida Besancon Spencer points out, the earth shook and the curtain barring entrance into the Holy of Holies was torn in two from top to bottom.[51] As a result, all believers, both male and female, may enter the Most Holy Place, approach the throne of grace, and draw near to God. And all believers, male and female, are a holy priesthood, offering spiritual sacrifices acceptable to God.[52]

Today, many churches are including the leadership and teaching gifts of women for the whole assembly.[53] They are basing this on the new covenant Jesus inaugurated, his profound inclusion of women in spiritual matters, a better understanding of the few verses that appear to limit women, and the strong examples of women in the early church.

11

What the Bible does not say . . .

Based on what we have seen so far, the theories below that are sometimes taught are not clearly stated in the Bible:[1]

1. **The Bible does not say that man's leadership was established from creation.** God creates male and female and gives "them" dominion over the earth.[2] No reference to male rulership appears until after sin enters in.[3] Then God *predicts* in the original Hebrew verb usage, not *commands*, that man will rule over woman.[4]

2. **The Bible does not say that woman was created as a subordinate helper to man.** "Helper" and "helpmeet" are reportedly not the best translations of the phrase in the original Hebrew. A more accurate translation is said to be "a strength corresponding," with a word that repeatedly describes the kind of help God gives.[5]

3. **The Bible does not say that woman is more easily deceived than man.** Eve is deceived by the serpent, then Adam sins knowingly and is said to be responsible for sin entering the earth.[6] Eve is mentioned twice in the New Testament for being deceived, but this is not generalized to all women. Also, one instance states that Eve was deceived not Adam, and here Paul may have been correcting a myth in Ephesus that Adam was the one deceived rather than Eve.[7] The other instance warns the Corinthian church

not to be deceived as Eve was.⁸ Also, the Bible gives numerous examples of wise and godly women.⁹

4. **The Bible does not say men should be the leaders because man was created first**. This is based on one verse (in the same highly debated passage cited above) that says Adam was formed first, then Eve, but this could be countering a myth that woman was created first.¹⁰ Also, it is not a biblical principle that the firstborn is always the leader. Joseph, David, and Solomon were born after their brothers and became rulers over them.¹¹

Older brothers bowing down to Joseph

5. **The Bible does not establish a pattern that only men should teach or lead men.** This theory is based on only one verse (in the same controversial passage cited above) that has a key rare Greek word whose meaning is unclear and Greek connectors without an English equivalent.[12] For multiple reasons, including examples of women in the Bible, many scholars have concluded that Paul was stopping false teaching, not prohibiting all women from teaching or leading men.[13] Also, the Bible says all Scripture is God-breathed and useful for teaching, and this would include the inspiring passages from Deborah, Elizabeth, and Mary.[14]

6. **The Bible does not state that only a man can be an overseer or pastor or elder.** Paul does say an overseer is to be a "one-woman man," a known phrase at the time meaning marital fidelity that could probably apply to either men or women.[15] But no other statements indicate that only men are to be overseers, even though some translations use the word *man* repeatedly, making it appear that way. In addition, the Bible provides multiple examples of women leaders.[16]

7. **The Bible does not say the husband is to be the leader of the wife and family.** The Bible says in one verse only that the husband is the "head" of the wife, but the Greek word for "head" here did not often mean "leader" as it does today in English.[17] That is why the most respected Bible translations do not use the term "leader." In the Greek, "head" normally meant the physical head, but it could be used to describe the source of life and sustenance, as the head was for the body, the husband was for the wife in that culture, and Jesus is for the church. Therefore, many scholars have concluded that Paul is calling the husband to use his position in that culture to love and care for his wife, rather than expect her to lay down her life for him, the norm in that day.[18]

8. **The Bible does not state that marriages are better if men are the leaders of the home.** To the contrary, Paul affirms equal

rights in marriage that were radical for that time,[19] and Jesus provides an example of love and service that would apply to both mates. Substantial research shows that satisfaction in marriages is much higher when husbands and wives have equality in decision making.[20] Some research also shows, soberingly, that violence is higher in patriarchal marriages where traditional roles are followed.[21]

9. **The Bible does not say that wives are to obey husbands.** Wives culturally then were to obey, but Paul tempers this to "submit," a voluntary cooperation, and does so, in the original Greek grammar, in the context of mutual submission.[22] Paul also describes reciprocal rights in marriage that were unheard of in his time.[23]

10. **The Bible does not say a woman needs a spiritual "covering" by a man.** This theory is based on a disputed translation that a woman needs a sign of authority over her head in order to prophesy.[24] Sometimes this is interpreted to mean that a woman needs a male in authority as a figurative "covering" over her. Multiple highly respected authors, however, state that the original says a woman has her own authority over her head.[25]

11. **The Bible does not say that men and women have certain roles.** This is a theory developed in the 1970s in response to societal changes. By that time, many men and women would no longer tolerate the long-held belief that men should be the leaders because women are inferior to men. So one Bible scholar developed the theory that men and women are equal, but have different roles—men are to be the leaders and women the followers.[26] The Bible does not generalize like this, and interpretations of the Scriptures used to undergird this theory have been strongly challenged (and are addressed in this book).

12. **The Bible does not endorse stereotypes for men and women.** Rather, it describes strong leaders such as Deborah, Miriam,

Priscilla, Phoebe, Paul, and Peter, and more sensitive temperaments such as Mary and John. Stereotypes for male and female reduce people to generalizations, but Jesus demonstrated an openness to the God-given uniqueness of each individual, whether male or female.²⁷

JESUS AND THE SAMARITAN WOMAN

Jesus treated everyone as an individual

13. **The Bible does not say that a key principle is for the husband to love his wife and the wife to respect her husband**. This theory is based on a debated translation of one verse. Some scholars have pointed out that a little Greek word in the sentence is translated repeatedly elsewhere in Scripture as "so that." Therefore, they

say, the translation should be that the husband should love his wife *so that* she respects him.[28] Kingdom principles would mean that both husbands and wives are to love each other and treat each other respectfully.

14. **The Bible does not say that man is the authority over woman as father God is the authority over Jesus**. The idea that Christ is eternally subordinated to God the father was deemed heresy by the early church fathers. Some have tried to use this idea today to justify the subordination of women but have been strongly rebuked by respected church leaders.[29] Also, Jesus did not say anything about male leadership and went against his culture repeatedly to be inclusive and respectful of women.[30]

15. **The Bible does not say that because Jesus and his apostles were male, only men should be the leaders**. Only men could teach in the synagogues then, as Jesus and the apostles needed to do. But Jesus commissions women first to say he was risen, in a time when women's word was generally considered unreliable.[31] Also, Jesus describes himself on earth with the inclusive Greek word for "human being," rather than the one for just a "male." Ultimately, in risen form as part of the godhead, Jesus transcends gender.[32]

12

What remains...

What have we seen so far from top scholars, and what remains?

Jesus paid the price for sin, including any original sin in the Garden by man and woman.[1] For anyone who chooses to receive his sacrificial gift, the power of original sin is broken. Jesus reconciles us back to God and to the creation plan for male and female, when they walked with God in the Garden, unashamed.

Both had been created in God's image, and woman was created a "strength corresponding" to the man.[2] Both were given dominion over the earth.[3] No roles or hierarchy were established between them. When both sinned, God informs them (not commands) that man will rule over the woman.[4] But God says one will come who will crush the head of the enemy.[5] That was Jesus.

When on earth, Jesus identified kingdom principles in stark contrast to his culture. He restated God's original plan that a man is to leave his mother and father and cleave to his wife.[6] He said we are to lay down our lives for one another.[7] We are not to lord it over others.[8] We are to love our neighbor as ourselves.[9] And Jesus made no exceptions for gender or marriage. Rather, he treated women with a respect and inclusion highly unusual for his time. He inaugurated a new covenant with water baptism that is for both male and female, rather than the old covenant sign of male circumcision.[10]

The church was launched on Pentecost with the Holy Spirit empowering both men and women to prophesy.[11] The early churches had women who prophesied, taught, and ministered.[12] The church was a community of male and female believers who were all responsible to share their spiritual gifts as they worshipped God.[13]

Paul teaches that when we receive Christ, we become a new creation.[14] And our identity in Christ is not trumped by gender.[15] All believers are now priests to a holy God.[16] And all believers will reign with Christ in the new heaven and earth.[17]

Paul also affirms women in ministry in unheard of ways for his time.[18] Some of his teaching, however, is difficult to translate and understand. One passage seems to imply that Paul is quoting the law that women should be silent in church, but scholars believe he may have been quoting Jewish law, or did not write this passage at all.[19] Highly respected British theologian Morna Hooker asks, "Could there have been a greater distortion of the spirit of Paul, who insisted that religion was not a matter of law, than to turn him into a great lawgiver?"[20]

MORNA HOOKER

It is a distortion to turn Paul into a lawgiver.

Paul also uses plays on words that can be difficult to understand. His word for *head* for a man does not often mean "leader" in the Greek as it does in English. It can mean the "origin" or "source" of something, and many scholars believe that is Paul's intent here, that man was woman's source in creation.[21] Paul also uses a rare Greek word in a phrase that is sometimes translated women should not teach or have authority over men. But this is a poor translation given the grammatical components, and the Bible does not say this elsewhere. Numerous scholars have concluded that Paul is dealing here with false teaching or domineering teaching, not stopping women from teaching or having authority over men in the churches at all.[22]

Paul calls for radical changes in marriage. At the time, the norm was that a wife was to obey her husband and lay down her life for him. But Paul calls for the husband to lay down his life for her, as Jesus did for us.[23] Paul's statement that a wife is to submit to her husband (not "obey") is based grammatically in the prior statement that Christians are to submit to one another out of reverence for Christ.[24] And this mutual submission is part of being filled with the Spirit.[25]

Jesus said his followers are to love others, prefer others, not lord it over others, and he gave no exception for marriage.[26] Jesus becomes the "head" of the household, as Gordon Fee says, and all follow him for God's leading in their lives.[27] The Holy Spirit is available to guide both the husband and wife, so they can press in with prayer, both together and individually, for decisions based on what pleases God.[28]

Both are responsible to bring life to the marriage and their own spiritual walk through prayer, Bible reading, and worship.[29] Both are responsible to use their God-given gifts, contributing to their strength and joy individually and as a team.[30] Out of love for one another and Christ, they also share the practical work of a home and family life.[31]

Originally, the only direct instruction given to the man about the woman was to cleave to her. And through Jesus, what was lost in the Garden of Eden begins to be restored. One-sided submission yields to mutual submission in awe of Christ's sacrificial love.[32] And what is done in marriage behind closed doors is an indication of one's walk with God.[33]

Jesus never assigned roles or endorsed stereotypes for men and women. Rather, he shattered these in the way he treated people.[34] He never defined masculinity and femininity. Rather, he embodied qualities of both, even likening himself to a mother hen who desires to gather her chicks.[35] He never promoted male leadership in the home or society. He included women in his ministry in revolutionary ways for his time.[36]

Manfred Brauch, who writes eloquently about the problem of abusing Scripture, says we are to interpret everything through the cross of Christ. And Jesus' words and actions are to set our norms. "Whatever withers in light of the cross," he says, does not reflect God's will and way. But "whatever blossoms in light of the cross" has "transcendent, abiding authority."[37]

MANFRED BRAUCH

Whatever blossoms in light of the cross has abiding authority.

F.F. Bruce said we need to be influenced by the guidance of the Spirit as we receive the Spirit's liberating word to men and women today. And we need to avoid turning the New Testament into a book of rules. To use Scripture aright, Bruce says, is to hear what the Spirit is saying to the churches of the twentieth century, as well as what the Spirit said to those of the first.[38]

Gordon Fee and Douglas Stuart call for "enlightened common sense" to find the correct interpretation of Scripture. This requires the Holy Spirit's help and brings "relief to the mind, as well as a prick or prod to the heart." Then we leave the rest in the first century.[39]

Beloved seminary professor Howard Hendricks says (in speaking of the Bible in general) that our English text leaves us a long way from a complete understanding. So we have to use our minds to interpret it accurately and perceptively. Our faith is not "taking a deep breath, shutting our eyes, and believing what we know deep down inside is absolutely incredible." We need "sanctified common sense."[40]

Loren Cunningham, cofounder with his wife Darlene of what many consider the world's largest Christian missions agency (Youth With A Mission), has ministered from the Bible in every nation on earth. He writes that Scripture never contradicts God's character. If a verse of the Bible seems to make God unjust, such as not allowing women to exercise their gifts fully, then the problem must be with our interpretation. God and God's Word, Cunningham says, are infallible, but our interpretation is not.[41] (Highly respected scholar I. Howard Marshall makes this same point.)[42] Youth With A Mission itself works successfully around the world in teams, often with both male and female, some led by men and some by women.[43]

One of the long-time leaders of the successful college campus ministry InterVarsity, that works with male and female leadership teams, has published doctoral-level research on what makes mixed teams work well.[44] Through the Gospel of Jesus, he shows, mature men and women *can* work together in joyful leadership teams as brothers and sisters in Christ. These sanctified communities help usher in God's plans for bringing people to God.[45] And they represent God's original plan to give male and female dominion over the earth together.

Today, many churches organize small groups that meet in homes to learn and grow together. These reflect the early church, where ideally everyone, male and female, can bring a word, a song, a hymn, with the joy of sensing God among them. In the public churches, worship that brings glory to God (not just human performance) can bring a touch of God's majesty that uplifts and comforts. And particularly skilled Bible teachers can bring increased understanding for living in ways that God blesses. In many churches, a deeper study of the Bible verses about women has resulted in mature and gifted women of God bringing their teaching, worship, and leadership too.[46]

Centuries of gender bias in Bible translation and misunderstanding now need correcting. This requires teams of both male and female translators for every language. Biblical teaching needs to be based on Jesus-like behavior in marriage and ministry, rather than entitled behavior. Those who would inject bias into translation of the Bible, or teach about male-female behavior without due care, are responsible for any type of abuse that might cause, and need to be called into godly ways.[47]

Congregations today are filled with many people who have been taught from biased Bible translations regarding women. Some men, and women, would be threatened at the idea of shared leadership in the home and church. But teachers in the Christian world have an obligation to correct misunderstandings of Bible passages with courage, love, and wisdom, following Jesus' model.

N.T. Wright, considered by many the world's leading New Testament scholar today, believes we have "seriously misread" the New Testament passages about women. He says that worldly attitudes have crept into Christianity, and we need to make sure we do not conform to the stereotypes the world offers. Rather, he says, we need to follow "the healing, liberating, humanizing message of the Gospel of Jesus."[48]

Evangelist Billy Graham boldly broke a stereotype for women in 1974 when he organized a historic gathering of Christian leaders from around world. The norm then was for only men to be delegates to major conferences. But Billy Graham called for ten percent of the delegates to be women, and this has increased at succeeding conferences.[49] Women were also in leadership for his crusades (at least his latter ones). I know, because I was one of these and asked by his staff to be an officer on the top leadership team for his last San Diego Crusade.

BILLY GRAHAM AT HIS 2003 SAN DIEGO CRUSADE

Photo courtesy of Billy Graham Evangelistic Association.
Used with permission. All rights reserved. www.billygraham.org

Included women in leadership

Was Billy Graham following Jesus' bold example by including women where they had not been previously, breaking stereotypes and limitations? And what does that say to us today about the inclusion of women in leadership, rather than a model of male-only leadership?

To know for ourselves, we have studied afresh. Now may we trust God to guide us in how to respond, living a life saturated daily with prayer, worship, and service.[50] And may we find ways to work side by side with our Christian brothers and sisters with integrity, finding there the joy and blessing of God.

"And now I commit you to God and to the message of His grace, which is able to build you up and to give you an inheritance among all who are sanctified."

Acts 20:32[193]

Notes

For all of these Notes, each work cited is listed alphabetically by the author's last name in "Works Cited," along with the publisher and year of publication.

About this book

1. Jane L. Crane, "History of the Partnership of Men and Women in the Lausanne Movement," and "A Map for Gender Reconciliation." [See "Works Cited" for full citation.]
2. I aimed to include mainly scholars from leading seminaries, such as those with doctoral programs, or, in some cases, scholars who were highly respected for their academic publications in this field.
3. Two other books with study guides are (1) *God's Women Then and Now* by Deborah Gill and Barbara Cavaness, and (2) *Is Women's Equality A Biblical Ideal?* Mimi Haddad and Sean Callaghan, Contributors. A more recent book (2021), written in an academic style, gives a broad collection of essays on the issue by various scholars: *Discovering Biblical Equality: Biblical, Theological, Cultural & Practical Perspectives.*
4. Howard Hendricks and William Hendricks say to recreate the culture to study the Bible; "only then will the text come alive." They call literary, historical, cultural, geographic, and theological context key to understanding. Craig Keener states that "virtually all scholars . . . acknowledge the importance of taking cultural context into account." Ben Witherington believes that "any biblical book, passage, or verse needs to be interpreted in light of its various original contexts," including narrative, literary, historical, rhetorical, social, and linguistic. He says that the more we "bring to the surface internal clues about their [the biblical writers] intentions and meanings, the better." Hendricks and Hendricks, *Living by the Book*, 231–234, 247. Keener, *Paul, Women, and Wives*, xiv. Witherington, *Reading and Understanding the Bible*, 96, 112, and *Conflict and Community in Corinth*, xiii.
5. This has come to be called "the Spirit of Lausanne," and comes originally from the historic gathering of Christian world leaders that Billy Graham and John Stott assembled in Lausanne, Switzerland, in 1974, and is still carried forth as a principle by the Lausanne Movement today. www.lausanne.org. Respected scholar Manfred Brauch says we need to practice "the biblical call to humility" and "refuse to dictate in advance what Scripture reveals about any particular aspect of God and God's dealing with human life." We do need to contend for the truth, he says, defending and proclaiming "theological certainties at the core of the Christian faith," but we also need to reject pride

and arrogance, "with a grace-filled spirit that refuses to demonize and judge those who do not share those certainties with us." Brauch, *Abusing Scripture*, 117-118.

Chapter 1 – What does the Bible really say?

1. Numerous scholars have described this problem of errors by copyists. Seminary professor Victor Walter says, "The best of scribes occasionally inadvertently made errors in copying a text." Mark Norton, managing editor of the *New Living Translation Bible*, lists both unintentional and intentional errors by Old Testament scribes. Walter, "Versions of the Bible," 319. Norton, "Texts and Manuscripts of the Old Testament," 178–9.

2. Neil Lightfoot's bestselling and easily readable book, *How We Got the Bible*, tells the fascinating story. Lightfoot was a Distinguished Professor of New Testament at Abilene Christian University.

3. Neh. 8:8 tells how the people needed translators to understand the reading of the book of the law of God. (Also see Neh. 13:24.) Karen Jobes and Moses Silva state that the Pentateuch was translated into Greek, "probably all within a short period, in the third century BCE," and the rest of the Old Testament probably by the middle of the first century before Christ. Jobes and Silva, *Invitation to the Septuagint*, 34–5.

4. For an overview of the Septuagint, see Jobes and Silva, *Invitation to the Septuagint*.

5. Norton, "Texts and Manuscripts of the Old Testament," 178.

6. Walker, "Biblical Languages," 220. A few parts of the Old Testament were written in Aramaic, a similar language to Hebrew. Metzger states that "the Hebrew Scriptures contain several hundred words that have not been found in any other literature, and are therefore difficult to translate." Metzger, *The Bible in Translation*," 187.

7. These scribes, the Masoretes, worked in Tiberias on the Sea of Galilee from about AD 500 to 900 and their version is called the Masoretic Text. Philip Comfort states that the primary Hebrew text used by scholars continues to be the *Biblia Hebraica Stuttgartensia*, "an edition of the Masoretic Text of the Hebrew Bible as presented in the Leningrad Codex" (the oldest complete manuscript of the Hebrew bible, reportedly dated AD 1008). He says it is "generally recognized that this text needs correction in some places according to the evidence of other Hebrew manuscripts, some early versions, and various manuscripts among the Dead Sea Scrolls." Comfort, "Afterword, Recent Developments," 334, 341.

8. Larry Walker says that prior to the work of these scribes, in the original Hebrew script, "vowels were simply understood by the writer or reader." Peter Flint states that "many words could thus be read in more than one way, leading to different meanings;" in English, *dg* could be *dig*, *dog*, or *dug*, depending on which vowels are used. "As Jews dispersed to many areas in the early centuries of the Common Era [AD], different understandings of many

consonantal Hebrew words arose." To standardize the biblical text, these scribes "added vowel signs and other components, which fixed the meaning of each group of consonants." Walker, "Biblical Languages," 222. Flint, *The Dead Sea Scrolls*, 37.

9. Walter Kaiser.

10. The Dead Sea Scrolls precede the Masoretic Text (when vowels were initiated) by approximately 1000 years, starting from about 250 BC to AD 135. These scrolls have helped with understanding some difficult passages, but as with other ancient documents, some uncertainties remain. The NIV states that the more significant of the uncertainties have been cited in its footnotes (though there is not significant footnoting regarding the debated passages about women). Abegg et al., *The Dead Sea Scrolls Bible*, xviii. Flint, *The Dead Sea Scrolls*, xxi. *Holy Bible*, New International Version, 1986, ix.

11. Elliott, "Bible Translation," 243. Walker, "Biblical Languages,"236.

12. Walker, "Biblical Languages," 233–4.

13. Elliott, "Bible Translation," 257. Bruce Metzger states that plays on words "defy the ingenuity of the translator." Metzger, *The Bible in Translation*, 189.

14. Metzger, *The Bible in Translation*, 189.

15. Larry Walker says that "no translation can replace the original languages of the Bible in primary importance for conveying and perpetuating divine revelation." Walker, "Biblical Languages," 217.

16. *Holy Bible*, New International Version, 1986, viii.

17. Scholars state that new translations can be prompted by major occurrences such as the discovery of ancient Bible manuscripts, significant new research into original word meanings, and changes over time in usage in the receiving language.

18. Karen Jobes and Moises Silva state that the translators "came to the text with the theological and political prejudices of their time" and were influenced, "whether deliberately or subconsciously, by what they believed the Hebrew meant in light of their contemporary situation, which may or may not have been what the author of the Hebrew text intended." Jobes and Silva, *Invitation to the Septuagint*, 3–4.

Chapter 2 – Male and female

1. Gen. 1:27 says male and female he created them. Verse 28 says God blessed them and said to them to rule over the fish of the sea and the birds of the air and over every living creature that moves on the ground. Gen. 5:1–2 repeats that God created them male and female. In Mat. 19:4–5 Jesus quotes that God made them male and female.

2. Bruce Metzger, distinguished seminary professor and chair of the NRSV translation committee, states that "ancient and modern translators have varied widely in their judgment" about where '*adam* changes to Adam. But none he lists precedes Gen. 2:7, and the NRSV currently uses Gen. 4:25 after

the Fall. Old Testament scholar Richard Hess states that "Old Testament Hebrew has no common term for 'humanity' other than '*adam*,'" and that "Adam" as a personal name does not clearly indicate the man until after the Fall (agreeing with Metzger at Gen. 4:25). Scholar Linda Belleville explains that when gender is intended, the Hebrew *zakar* is used for the male and *neqeba* for the female, as in the last part of Gen., 1:27, "male and female he created them." She also states that '*adam* as "a gender-inclusive term is clear from the repeated references to '*adam* as 'them' (Gen. 1:26-27; 5-2)." Metzger, *The Bible in Translation*, 189. Hess, "Equality With and Without Innocence," 79-80. Belleville, *Women Leaders and the Church*, 102.

3. Scholars have stated that a translation of "rib" is not correct; this is a different word in Hebrew, and the translation of "rib" probably relates to an ancient Jewish fable. Richard Hess states that the word here in Gen. 2:22 is *tsela*, meaning "side," a term "also used for the sides of the ark and of the tabernacle." Hess, "Equality With and Without Innocence," 86-7.

4. Gen. 2:20.

5. Kaiser et al., *Hard Sayings of the Bible*, 94.

6. Philip Comfort says the Hebrew text used for the King James Version (the Masoretic Text) was "adequate, but their understanding of the Hebrew vocabulary was insufficient." Neil Lightfoot, author of the bestselling *How We Got the Bible* and distinguished professor of New Testament at a Christian university, says the King James Version came from an inferior medieval text containing a number of scribal mistakes and includes "many archaic words whose meanings are either obscure or misleading." Comfort, "History of the English Bible," 282. Lightfoot, *How We Got the Bible*, 186-8.

7. Walter Kaiser says it appears that sometime around 1500 BC, two different Hebrew roots were merged. One meant "to rescue, to save," and the other "to be strong." The result was "almost certainly" a wrong translation as "helper." Kaiser, *Hard Sayings of the Bible*, 93.

8. An example is Ps. 121:1-2, where the Psalmist looks up to the hills, with his help coming from the Lord.

9. Walter Kaiser et al., *Hard Sayings of the Bible*, 93. Also see Walter Kaiser, "Correcting Caricatures: The Biblical Teaching on Women," http://www.walterckaiserjr.com/womenpage2.html. Scholar Aida Besancon Spencer points to the 1907 Lexicon of Hebrew and English in the Old Testament by Brown, Drive, and Briggs as providing the meaning of "corresponding" for part of this phrase. She also says that when the Hebrew text was translated into Greek around 250 BC, in the Septuagint, the translators used the Greek word *kata* followed by the direct object, which signifies "horizontal rather than perpendicular direction." Millard Erickson writes in his textbook on Christian theology that the expression "helpmeet" translates two Hebrew words; the second word means "corresponding to" or "equal to" him and the first word, rendered "help," is "used of God in several places in the Old Testament." Linda Belleville points out that the New Revised Standard Version translates this phrase as "partner." According to Martin Abegg et

al., a respected Dead Sea Scrolls translation has "partner." Spencer, *Beyond the Curse*, 25. Erickson, *Christian Theology*, 499. Belleville, "An Egalitarian Perspective," 198. Abegg et al., *The Dead Sea Scrolls Bible*, 7.

10. Aida Besancon Spencer explains that English translations may leave out the phrase "with her" (*'mmah*) in Gen. 3:6, because it can be "difficult to translate." However, the King James Version does include it. Spencer, *Beyond the Curse*, 31.

11. Gen. 3:16. Walter Kaiser references changes to "the interlinear Hebrew vowel signs which came as late as the eighth century of the Christian era." He describes the correct meaning as relating to an "ambush" or "lying in wait" that is described fourteen times in Joshua. Kaiser, *Hard Sayings of the Bible*, 96–7.

12. Kaiser, *Hard Sayings of the Bible*, 96-7.

13. Rom. 5:12–14 says that sin entered the world through one man and Adam sinned by breaking a command. 1 Cor. 15:21–22 says that death came through a man and in Adam all die. The use of Adam in these passages conveys the proper name (rather than all of humanity), according to *Thayer's Greek-English Lexicon of the New Testament*, No. 76.

14. Gen. 3:16b. Walter Kaiser says the Hebrew reads: "You are turning away [from God!] to your husband, and [as a result] he will rule over you." Kaiser, *Hard Sayings of the Old Testament*, 35.

15. Walter Kaiser credits Katharine Bushnell, a brilliant physician in the early 1900s who learned Hebrew and Greek to study the Bible in its original languages, with the first research into this word in the ancient translations and church fathers. She provides a listing of this word in the various ancient translations in Katharine Bushnell, *God's Word to Women*, Lesson 18, 61–64. Kaiser says that the preferred way to handle the same Hebrew words for "turning" and "rule" in Gen. 4:7 is to make a question: "Sin is crouching at the door, unto you is its turning; . . . but you, will you rule over it?" Linda Belleville states that the Hebrew term *tesuqa* is "found only two other times in the Old Testament and neither is an exact parallel." She explains that "the pronoun is the neuter *it*, not the masculine *he*," and Gen. 4:7 provides a parallel only if the pronoun in 3:16 is translated "it": "Your yearning will be for your man and *it* [not he] will rule over you." She says traditionalists argue that the woman's desire is to dominate her husband, but this "imports an idea that is alien to the context." Belleville also says Eve's desire was "to be wise like God," not to dominate her husband. Further, the husband's rule does not reappear in the Old Testament. Kaiser, *Hard Sayings of the Bible*, 98-9. Belleville, "Women in Ministry," 33, 198.

16. The Septuagint was considered quite an accurate translation of the Hebrew, when more was known about Hebrew than at any time since.

17. Walter Kaiser, *Hard Sayings of the Bible,* 97–8. Kaiser says the translation of *teshuqah* as "desire" dates "to the Middle Ages when a sexual nuance was introduced for the first time." Kaiser, *The Promise-Plan of God*, 43, endnote

13. Also see is discussion in Kaiser, *Hard Sayings of the Bible*, 98, and Kaiser, *Hard Sayings of the Old Testament*, 33–7.
18. Walter Kaiser says the Hebrew grammar for Gen. 3:16b will not allow a construction of "he shall rule over you"; that would "make the statement mandatory with the force of a command." Rather, "the verb contains a simple statement of futurity," with no "hint of obligation or normativity." To argue differently, he says, "would be as logical as demanding that a verb in verse 18 be rendered, 'It *shall produce* thorns and thistles.'" If so, Kaiser says, then "all farmers who used weed killer would be disobedient" to God, that the ground must have thorns and thistles. Manfred Brauch, a former professor of biblical theology and seminary president, says the statement that man will rule over woman is not to be understood "as *prescriptive* (what should be) but as *descriptive*, revealing the human condition when separated from God." Brauch says it is the fall that precipitates the man's rule over the woman, and this "power-over relationship" is to be "understood as a distortion of God's creative design." In contrast, "God's redemptive work" points followers of Jesus beyond "this power-over relationship and toward the reaffirmation and re-actualization of God's created intention." Kaiser, *Hard Sayings of the Old Testament*, 35. Brauch, *Abusing Scripture*, 64, 80.
19. Nicole, "Biblical Concept of Women," 1177. Roger Nicole was president of the Evangelical Theological Society.
20. Gen. 3:20. Linda Belleville states that in biblical times naming was "a way to memorialize an event or to sum up a distinctive personal trait." She references research on naming then by scholars George Ramsey and Anthony Thiselton. Richard Hess states that naming was not considered an indication of power over a person. Belleville, *Women Leaders and the Church*, 102. Hess, *The Old Testament*, 41.
21. Gen. 4:1.

Chapter 3 – Old Testament and "Days of Mingling"

1. Job also gives an inheritance to his daughters, along with their brothers, after his great suffering (Job 42:15).
2. Craig Keener says some rabbinic sources expanded the list of women prophets to include Sarah, Hannah, Abigail, and Esther. Keener, *Acts, An Exegetical Commentary*, 883.
3. Joel 2:28–29.
4. Witherington, *Women in the Ministry of Jesus*, 7.
5. This is also called the intertestamental period.
6. Harrison, "Old Testament and New Testament Apochrypha," 88.
7. Craig Keener, an expert in ancient Greco-Roman culture, says ancient Israelite roles for women "often mirrored those of surrounding societies." They conformed to norms around them and "were regulated by Greek rather than Judean practices." Keener, *Acts, An Exegetical Commentary*, 614.

8. Larry Walker called this a major, "epochal event." "Biblical Languages," 232.
9. David Scholer says the negative picture of women in Judaism at this time "was greatly shaped and influenced by Greek and Greco-Roman androcentrism [focus on men] and misogynism [hatred and prejudice against females]." He also says it has been argued that "women's place in Israel began to decline [prior to Greek influence] with the emergence of a bureaucratic monarchy." Scholer, "Women," 881.
10. *Aristotle, Volume XIII*, 4.3 (767b 4–8) and 2.3 (737a 25–30).
11. Keener, *Acts, An Exegetical Commentary*, 610.
12. Kenneth Bailey states, "With the passage of time and the rise of the rabbinic movement, the position of women by New Testament times was, on all levels, inferior to men." Lynn Cohick writes that culturally, women "as a group" were seen as "inferior to men." Craig Keener says that women were considered weaker "physically, emotionally, intellectually and socially." Ben Witherington writes that it is fair to say that a low view of women was common before, during, and after Jesus' era. Bailey, *Jesus through Middle Eastern Eyes*, 190. Cohick, *Women in the World of the Earliest Christians*, 67. Keener, *Acts, An Exegetical Commentary*, 610–11. Witherington, *Women in the Ministry of Jesus*, 10.
13. The first appearance of strong negativity about women in the writings of the rabbis is reputedly the book of *Ecclesiasticus*, written in the "days of mingling," about 250 BC or somewhat later. *Ecclesiasticus* was reportedly written by a Jewish scribe, Ben Sirach of Jerusalem, and is part of the Apochryphal books still used by the Catholic Church, Orthodox Church, and others. *Ecclesiasticus* speaks quite negatively about the wickedness of women, says they should be silent, and attributes the start of sin to woman. Kenneth Bailey confirms that a deterioration in the place of women "seems to have taken place in the intertestamental period as seen in the writings of Ben Sirach," an aristocratic scholar. R.K. Harrison states that the Book of Ecclesiasticus "adheres closely to Jewish orthodoxy." Craig Keener writes that the rabbis "clearly had it in for Eve," and "her sinful act was often rehearsed in rabbinic literature." Ben Witherington says that "by the first century of the Christian era a negative assessment regarding women was predominant among the rabbis." Roger Nicole says the rabbinic outlook regarding women developed after the close of the Old Testament canon and "does not do justice to the ennobling elements presented in the Hebrew Scriptures." Manfred Brauch says that during the Intertestamental Period (ca. 300 BC to AD 100) an ominous note arose in Judaism that widened the status and authority between men and women within Jewish patriarchal culture; this included seeing women as "chiefly responsible for humanity's fall," more susceptible to temptation, and "temptresses to sin because of their sexual attractiveness." Brauch provides an appendix with a sampling of such writings. Bailey, *Jesus Through Middle Eastern Eyes*, 189–90. Harrison, "Old Testament and New Testament Apochrypha," 87. Keener, *Paul, Women and Wives*, 114. Witherington, *Women in the Ministry of Jesus*, 10. Nicole,

"Biblical Authority and Feminist Aspirations," 43. *Ecclesiasticus* 25:26. Brauch, *Abusing Scripture*, 65, 261–5.

14. Ben Witherington explains that women were excused from certain feasts (though not all) and periodic prayer and did not make daily appearances in the synagogue, as men did, to make quorum. Men were to recite the daily *Shema*, but not women, and only men were expected to make pilgrimages to Jerusalem for the feasts of Passover, Pentecost, and Tabernacles. Lynn Cohick states that women were "active" in their religious communities but "not always identified by leadership titles." Craig Keener says women held leadership roles in some synagogues in Asia Minor, probably "a minority approach that mirrored the social prominence of women in some of these cities." He says some were apparently wealthy "and probably benefactors of the synagogues, which was also how men typically achieved the same office." Witherington, *Women in the Ministry of Jesus*, 8. Cohick, *Women in the World of the Earliest Christians*, 23. Keener, *Acts, An Exegetical Commentary*, 628, 608, and *Acts*, New Cambridge Bible Commentary, 346.

15. Some believe this is because Jewish women could not engage in all the spiritual activities Jewish men did. Sociologist Alvin Schmidt states that this prayer is one "that the Hebrews apparently borrowed from the Greeks," with Plato (fourth century BC) as possibly first formulating it. David Scholer writes that according to the rabbinic Tosefta (possibly reflecting first-century AD tradition), "a Jewish man prayed three benedictions each day, including one in which he thanked God that he was not made a woman (*t. Ber.* 7.18)." Schmidt, *Veiled and Silenced*, 199. Scholer, "Women," 880.

16. Deut. 31:12 and Josh. 8:35 specifically mention including women.

17. Ben Witherington says a separation of women and men in the Temple and synagogue was introduced after Old Testament times. Aida Besancon Spencer describes the different courts of the Temple, including the Court of Women. Witherington, *Women in the Ministry of Jesus*, 8. Spencer, *Beyond the Curse*, 44.

18. Ben Witherington says it would be "wrong to assume that a Jewish woman had no respect or rights" in Jesus' time. For example, he says, a mother was to be honored along with the father, and the Talmud instructed a man to "love his wife as himself and respect her more than himself." At home, she was to prepare the dough offering, light the Sabbath lamp, say the eighteen benedictions and table blessings, and maintain the Mezuzah on the door of the home. Witherington, *Women in the Ministry of Jesus*, 4, 7–8.

19. Ruth Tucker and Walter Liefeld reference the noted Rabbi Eliezer in an infamous quote where he writes that it was better for the words of the Torah to be burnt than given to a woman; Torah study was required for Jewish boys but not Jewish girls; some exceptions of women studying Torah are known, usually a wife/daughter of a rabbi. Aida Besancon Spencer explains that women could attend synagogue, called the "House of the Book." However, they did not participate in the "House of Study," called *andron*, meaning "of males." She says women could hear the Scriptures but not "study fully." Both

NOTES – Chapter 3

Spencer and Craig Keener state that some of this was apparently due to a concern for immorality if there was a mixing of the genders. Keener also says that "as a rule" the rabbis forbade women from teaching even children and "a Torah scroll written by a woman was considered invalid." Tucker and Liefeld, *Daughters of the Church*, 60. Spencer, *Beyond the Curse*, 49-50, 61. Keener, *Acts, An Exegetical Commentary*, 633, 636.

20. Ben Witherington says "certain views about propriety appear to have taken away a woman's theoretical right to read the Scriptures in synagogue in Jesus' day." He states that there are no known examples of women reading in the synagogues during Jesus' time. Aida Besancon Spencer writes that, technically, women could read the Torah aloud before the congregation at synagogue, but the Talmud said they should not "out of respect for the congregation." In more recent research, Keener says there is "slender evidence" that some women read the Scriptures in synagogue, but "the evidence against the practice is more explicit," and "we may gather that in most locations men were the more usual readers." He also points out that women could hear Scripture, though, in synagogue, and elsewhere. Lynn Cohick says "we cannot say definitely whether women read Scripture or prayed publicly," but she suggests that "evidence points to at least some women performing religious duties." Witherington, *Women in the Ministry of Jesus*, 7–8. Spencer, *Beyond the Curse*, 49. Keener, *Acts, An Exegetical Commentary*, 637, 633. Cohick, *Women in the World of the Earliest Christians*, 218.

21. Aida Besancon Spencer points to rabbinic teaching that if a Jewish woman spoke to a man in public other than her husband, "she could be divorced without having her dowry repaid." Craig Keener says that "very conservative circles might consider it offensive for a man to speak with a woman under most circumstances." Spencer, "Jesus' Treatment of Women in the Gospels," 128, footnote 9. Keener, *Acts*, New Cambridge Bible Commentary, 388, footnote 1592.

22. Craig Keener says most of Jesus' Jewish contemporaries "held much less esteem for the testimony of women than that of men," reflecting a "broader Mediterranean limited trust of women's speech and testimony" that was also in Roman law. Keener says that "apart from significant exceptions, women's testimony, when accepted, normally carried much less weight than men's in both Roman and rabbinic law." Ruth Tucker and Walter Liefeld quote Josephus as saying that no evidence should be accepted from women due to the "levity and temerity of their sex." Aida Besancon Spencer says Roman law treated women as "weak" and "light-minded," that rabbinic tradition generally "disqualified women as witnesses," and that "according to Jewish law, only certain Jewish men could testify officially about a person." Keener, *Historical Jesus of the Gospels*, 331, and *Acts, An Exegetical Commentary*, 600, 607. Tucker and Liefeld, *Daughters of the Church*, 63. Spencer, "Jesus' Treatment of Women in the Gospels," 139–40, and *Beyond the Curse*, 62.

23. Tucker and Liefeld, *Daughters of the Church*, 42.

24. Roman matrons in the upper class, for example, had much more freedom

outside the home, ate with the husband, etc. Women in the countryside also generally had more freedom than those in the cities. Bruce Winter states that "pivotal legal and social changes" allowed some Roman women to have "a measure of financial independence," occupy civic posts (some with the title of magistrate), and influence "commercial, civic, and provincial affairs." Winter believes that this greater freedom for Roman women contributed to the spread of Christianity. Craig Keener states that there was considerable variation from one region to another and within class. Winter, *Roman Wives Roman Widows*, 38, 204, 4. Keener, *Acts, An Exegetical Commentary*, 605.

25. David Scholer cites the Jewish queen, Salome, who reigned after her husband from approximately 76 to 67 BC, and the story of Judith, a Jewish widow who reputedly used her beauty and charm to destroy an Assyrian general and save Israel from oppression. Craig Keener states that "in the Diaspora, even some formal synagogues gave titles to well-to-do women, often donors." Scholer, "Women," 881. Keener, *Acts*. New Cambridge Bible Commentary, 346.

26. Aida Besancon Spencer discusses the Eastern cultural setting. Lynn Cohick says that in the cultural arena "women as a group were inferior to men;" also, "women who spoke in public were seen as invading male space and were often ridiculed." Craig Keener contends that even those who acknowledged women's intellectual equality did not "advocate destroying 'the public/private partition' that separated most traditionally masculine from most feminine activities." Spencer, *Beyond the Curse*, 52. Cohick, *Women in the World of the Earliest Christians*, 67, 244. Keener, *Acts, An Exegetical Commentary*, 635.

Chapter 4 – Jesus and women

1. Bailey, *Jesus Through Middle Eastern Eyes*, 203. David Scholer writes, "As a Jewish male in an androcentric, patriarchal society, Jesus' respect for women as persons of dignity and worth and his inclusion of them as disciples and proclaimers in his life and ministry was very significant in its own first-century context for women." Scholer, "Women," 881.

2. Luke 1:31. Joseph also receives the name in a dream, confirming what Mary had heard (Mat. 1:18-21).

3. Luke 1:18–20.

4. Luke 1:41–42. Luke 2:36–38.

5. Lynn Cohick says women were "vastly underrepresented in ancient literature." Craig Keener states that women were rarely granted public speaking roles in ancient literature. Cohick, *Women in the World of the Earliest Christians*, 201. Keener, *Acts, An Exegetical Commentary*, 635.

6. Mat. 23:37.

7. For example, see Mat. 13:33, Luke 13:20–21; Luke 15:8–10; Luke 4:26; Mat. 15:21-28, Mark 7:24-30; Luke 18:1-8; Luke 7:36-50; Mat. 9:20-22, Mark 5:25-34, Luke 8:43-48; Mark 12:41-44, Luke 21:1-4.

8. Aida Besancon Spencer says "men were encouraged not to converse too

much with women because women were not trained in the Torah." Craig Keener writes that, with some exceptions, many more women than men were illiterate and generally had far less education. Spencer, *Beyond the Curse*, 55-6. Keener, *Acts, An Exegetical Commentary*, 629.

9. Luke 10:39. Paul even references himself this way as sitting at the feet of his teacher (Acts 22:3), as some translations state. Also see Bailey, *Jesus Through Middle Eastern Eyes*, 193. Spencer, *Beyond the Curse*, 58.

10. Keener, Acts, *An Exegetical Commentary*, 601.

11. John 11: 25-27. Mat. 16:16. The other person is Peter.

12. Mark 5:24b-34.

13. Mark 5:24b-34. Jesus also disregards other religious taboos, such as healing on the Sabbath. Ben Witherington discusses Jesus' "rejection of rabbinic ideas of sin and sickness leading to ritual impurity or defilement." Witherington, *Women in the Ministry of Jesus*, 77-8.

14. Luke 13:10-17.

15. For example, see Mat. 15:21-28, Mark 7:24-30; Luke 18:1-8; Luke 7:36-50; Mat. 9:20-22, Mark 5:25-34, Luke 8:43-48; Mark 12:41-44, Luke 21:1-4.

16. Luke 13:16. Ben Witherington says this term is not used for an individual anywhere else in the Bible or rabbinic literature. Witherington, *Women in the Ministry of Jesus*, 70. Also see 79 and 174, endnote 147.

17. David Scholer states that *akoloutheo* (or its compounds) is used more than seventy-five times in the Gospels and "normally means following Jesus in the sense of being a disciple." Scholer says all four Gospels attest to the fact that women followed Jesus; he references Mat. 27:55-56, 27:61-28:1; Mark 15:40-41, 15:47-16:1; Luke 23:49, 23:55-24:1; John 19:25-27, 20:1. Scholer, "Women," 882.

18. Luke 8:1-3. Craig Keener says it would certainly be unusual among ancient rabbis for women to follow Jesus itinerantly along with male disciples, and for some learn at his feet and "inappropriate mixing could violate widespread ancient Mediterranean mores." While the larger Greco-Roman world "knew of traveling philosophers who welcomed women students," Keener says, "even these were a minority." Linda Belleville states that Roman women generally had more mobility, but such independence was quite unusual, "even shocking," for Jewish women. Aida Besancon Spencer points out that women in the cities had less freedom than those in the countryside. (Jewish wives in Palestine village life, for example, could go to the market or well and converse with other women.) Spencer also notes that the women disciples who followed Jesus probably did so "in a group, thereby making it possible for them to appear respectable." Keener, *Acts, An Exegetical Commentary*, 638, 604, 601, 606. Belleville, *Women Leaders and the Church*, 51. Spencer, *Beyond the Curse*, 54-5.

19. Luke 8:3. Only the women are described as doing so.

20. Mat. 26:6-13, Mark 14:3-9, Luke 7:36-50, John 12:1-8. It is not clear whether

the four Gospels are referencing one woman or different women here. It has also been pointed out that the woman is the only one among his disciples who took action regarding his upcoming death and this indicates that she was probably present when Jesus foretold his death to his disciples in Matt. 17:22-23 and Luke 9:21-22.

21. John 8:1-11. Ben Witherington states that the setting for this is the Women's Court in the Temple; there was no other place in the Temple to which the woman could be brought without impropriety. Witherington, *Women in the Ministry of Jesus*, 21.

22. Ben Witherington says the rabbis warned men against looking at a woman (or women looking at a man), lest the man be led astray. (In Rabbinic Judaism it was almost always the woman who was associated with the act of adultery and given responsibility for it.) Witherington says that Jesus was attempting "to liberate women from a social stereotype" and address male responsibility, especially in a male-oriented society where women were weaker. David Scholer states that male writers of that time perceived women as responsible for most if not all sin, "especially for sexual temptation and sin." Witherington, *Women in the Ministry of Jesus*, 20. Scholer, "Women," 880.

23. John 4:4-30.

24. Ben Witherington says Jesus rejected certain rabbinic teachings concerning discourse with women, even foreign and non-Jewish women. Witherington, *Women in the Ministry of Jesus*, 65, 78.

25. John 4:27. Some translations say similar terms such as "surprised."

26. Aida Besancon Spencer states that a woman could be divorced "without any financial settlement;" causes for divorce could include her going out with her hair unbound, or speaking with any man. Ben Witherington says a wife could be divorced for burning a meal, and marriage was "essentially a property transaction." David Scholer refers to the "dominant position that men could divorce their wives for virtually any reason," and cites Josephus in this. In some cases, a Jewish woman could divorce her husband, but only for strict circumstances, and she needed the ability and resources to go to court to do so. Spencer, *Beyond the Curse*, 54. Witherington, *Women in the Ministry of Jesus*, 3, 29. Scholer, "Women," 881.

27. Mat. 19:3-10. F.F. Bruce wrote that Jesus preferred to go back to "first principles," that is, the "original purpose of the commandment." Bruce, "Women in the Church" in *A Mind for What Matters*, 260.

28. David Scholer says Jesus affirms the concept of "one flesh," giving "sexual equality to both women and men." Scholer, "Women," 882.

29. Mat. 19:10.

30. Mat. 22:29. This is an extreme example of levirate marriage where a brother of the deceased husband would marry the widow to provide for her and hopefully impregnate her with a son who could carry on the deceased

NOTES – Chapter 4

husband's line.

31. Ben Witherington refers to the extraordinary control of the father over the daughter with the *patria potestas*. Witherington states that "the laws of inheritance, betrothal, and divorce were heavily biased in the male's favor, with only a few checks and balances." Witherington, *Women in the Ministry of Jesus*, 2.

32. John 7:22.

33. Mat. 28:19–20.

34. 1 Cor. 7:19. Rom. 2:28-29.

35. Mat. 15:3–4.

36. Luke 11:27–28.

37. Bailey, *Jesus Through Middle Eastern Eyes*, 192.

38. Ben Witherington writes that Jesus' attitude toward a woman's right to have religious training and be a disciple of a religious leader would have been "shocking" to the Jews, but not radical to many Romans or Greeks of that day. Witherington, *Women in the Ministry of Jesus*, 126.

39. Ben Witherington believes the setting for the encounter with the woman caught in adultery (John 8:2) is the women's court, where Jesus is teaching the people. Witherington, *Women in the Ministry of Jesus*, 21.

40. This would also apply to the 70 (or 72) he sent out. Numerous scholars believe that the twelve apostles represent the 12 tribes of Israel. Aida Besancon Spencer believes this is because God's original covenant was with Israel and its twelve tribes. She points out that the new covenant, however, is no longer focused on the nation of Israel. She also writes that the apostles in the Gospels include the twelve, and then after Jesus' death and resurrection, the term of "apostle" was broadened to refer to other disciples who had been with Jesus and now were sent off as witnesses to the resurrection, including men and women. Ruth Tucker and Walter Liefeld provide a discussion of why Jesus selected males to be apostles. Spencer, "Jesus' Treatment of Women," 135-7, *Beyond the Curse*, 100. Tucker and Liefeld, *Daughters of the Church*, 46.

41. Luke 11:31.

42. Mat. 28:9–10, Mark 16:9, John 20:10–18. David Scholer points out that the first known pagan written critique of Christianity, by the middle Platonist Gelsus, "builds on the Gospels' report of women as the first witnesses and proclaimers of Jesus' resurrection." Craig Keener reports that in "both Roman and rabbinic law, women's testimony, when accepted, normally carried much less weight than men's." Scholer, "Women," 883. Keener, *Acts, An Exegetical Commentary*, 607.

43. Luke 24:24–26. Ben Witherington says, in a broader context, that Jesus "rejected attempts to devalue the worth of a woman, or her word of witness." Witherington, *Women in the Ministry of Jesus*, 127.

44. 1 Cor. 15:6. The current NIV, for example, uses "brothers and sisters" here.

Aida Besancon Spencer says an "accurate translation" for the word describing the 500 that Jesus appeared to (*adelphos*) is "brothers and sisters." This word was also used in Acts 16:40, taking place in Lydia's house, and Philippians 4:1-2, discussing Euodia and Syntyche. Dorothy Lee explains that the Greek *adelphos* (brother) and *adelphe* (sister) "can be used together in the singular form to represent a brother and sister," as in Mark 3:35. However, when the plural is needed, *adelphoi*, the masculine plural, is often sufficient to represent both brothers and sisters. Gordon Fee says it is clear that from the evidence of 1 Cor. 11:2-16 that in 1 Cor. 14:26 (when everyone has a hymn, word of instruction, etc.) and in Phil. 4:1-3 (where he pleads with Euodia and Syntyche) "that women were participants in the worship of the community." It is therefore "biblically sensitive," he says, to translate this vocative as "brothers and sisters." Jeffrey Miller says that translating *adelphoi* as "brothers and sisters" or something similar, appeared in 1989 in the NRSV; the NLT, CEB, NIV 2011, and CSB have continued this practice. Spencer, "Jesus' Treatment of Women," 138, footnote 38. Lee, *Ministry of Women in the New Testament*, 107. Fee, *The First Epistle to the Corinthians*, 52, with footnote 22. Also see pages 661 and 690. Miller, "A Defense of Gender-Accurate Bible Translation," 486.

45. Craig Keener, however, states that "few evangelicals on either side of the women's ministry debate would dispute that Jesus' acceptance of women in many respects proved unusual in his day." Keener, "Another Egalitarian Perspective," 245.

46. Craig Keener points to this practice by some scholars who "often fail to note" that educated women were the exception. He also says some traveling philosophers had women students, but again these were a minority. Keener, *Acts, An Exegetical Commentary*, 629, 601.

47. One scholar even wrote that the angels with Mary at Jesus' tomb "almost mock her as hysterical" when they ask why she is weeping. Perhaps this scholar was simply trying to be dramatic rather than demeaning, but the result is unfortunate.

48. David Scholer, for example, quotes Josephus, the first-century AD Jewish historian, as stating that "the Law holds women to be inferior in all matters." Scholer, "Women," 880.

49. Ben Witherington says that the way Jesus treated women opened the door for "a more normal and natural basis for relationship," rather than prohibitions. Witherington, *Women in the Ministry of Jesus*, 78.

50. Ben Witherington says Jesus' lack of such negative comments about women is in contrast to various Jewish authors. Witherington, *Women and the Genesis of Christianity*, 237.

51. Unlike some speakers in Acts and the epistles who did use such terms, Jesus did not need to follow cultural norms to maintain his authority and did not do so.

52. An example is Mat. 16:13, Who do people (rather than "men," as sometimes

translated) say that I, the Son of Man (again the inclusive mankind), am? *Thayer's Greek English-Lexicon of the New Testament*, No. 444.

53. David Scholer says that "Jesus' respect for and inclusion of women as disciples and proclaimers of Christ provided the foundation for the positive place of women in the earliest churches and their ministry." Scholer, "Women," 886.

Chapter 5 – Early church and women

1. Acts 1:14 says they joined together constantly in prayer, along with the women and Mary the mother of Jesus, and with his brothers. Acts 1:15 says that in those days Peter stood up among the believers, a group numbering about 120.

2. Acts 2:1 says they were all together on the day of Pentecost, and all of them were filled with the Holy Spirit. Numerous respected scholars have concluded that women were among them. See, for example, Scholer, "Women," 882.

3. Craig Keener says Pentecost was a covenant renewal festival. He also states that "just as Jesus began his public ministry only after being anointed by the Spirit (Luke 4:18; Acts 10:38), so also his followers needed empowerment for their designated ministry." Keener, *Acts*, New Cambridge Bible Commentary, 122 and *Acts, An Exegetical Commentary*, 781–2.

4. Craig Keener writes in his exegetical commentary on Acts that the "all" of 2:1 "must include the Twelve (Acts 1:13, 26; 2:14), the women, and Jesus's brothers (1:14)." Presumably it would include some others as well, given that the total number present some of the time rose to 120 (1:15). Many argue, Keener says, that "we would also have to suppose more than twelve disciples together in 2:1, who will be filled with the Spirit at 2:4." Also, more than twelve languages were spoken (2:5–11), so there would be more than twelve speakers. David Scholer says the women were presumably from the group described in Luke 8:1–3, including some women who were specifically named, and "many" other women. He writes that the female disciples were presumably among the 120 followers "who waited for and received the Holy Spirit on the day of Pentecost, fulfilling the prophecy of Joel." Dorothy Lee says "we should especially note the reference to Mary the mother of Jesus," who by necessity was present at the birth of Jesus and also at the "birth" of the church. Keener, *Acts, An Exegetical Commentary*, 795, 794 (also see endnote 110). Also see Keener, *Acts*, New Cambridge Bible Commentary, 122, 146. Scholer, "Women," 882. Lee, *The Ministry of Women in the New Testament*, 60.

5. Joel 2:28–29. F.F. Bruce writes that "Peter's quotation of this prophecy means that these days, the days of the fulfillment of God's purpose, have arrived." Bruce also writes that "in Old Testament times, when men or women were possessed by the Spirit of God, they prophesied." Craig Keener says Joel's prophecy "declared the eradication of any gender barrier in the Spirit of prophecy." Some women prophesied in the Old Testament, and Luke addresses women and men having this gift. Bruce, *Book of the Acts*, 61, 51-52. Keener, *Acts, An Exegetical Commentary*, 882.

6. Priscilla first: Acts 18:18, 19, 26; Rom. 16:3; 2 Tim. 4:19. Aquila first: Acts 18:2, 1 Cor. 16:19.
7. Ben Witherington states that it would have been "very unusual in a patriarchal culture" to list the woman's name first; it is possible Priscilla was from Rome, of higher social status than her husband, or more prominent in the church, but we may "rightly conclude" that if either was better known for Christian work, it was Priscilla. Craig Keener also states that it would have been unusual for a wife to be named first. Witherington, *Paul's Letter to the Romans*, 385. Keener, *Romans*, 185.
8. Acts 18:26. Spencer, *Beyond the Curse*, 107.
9. Keener, *Acts*, New Cambridge Bible Commentary, 469. Ben Witherington writes that John Chrysostom "was one of the Greek Fathers who commented on Priscilla as a teacher and saw it as noteworthy." Witherington, *Paul's Letter to the Romans*, 385.
10. Jeffrey Miller states that the King James Version uses "unnecessary masculine words" 45 times in Rom. 14, including "man/men," "brother," and "he/him." Miller says many Bibles frequently translate the Greek *anthropos* as "man," when "human being" is the primary meaning. Miller also says the claim that some translations minimize the inherently masculine nature of the New Testament is "misguided." Rather, certain translations, especially the influential King James Version and the pre-2011 New International Version (NIV), have given English Bible readers this impression and "not been faithful to the original Greek text." Miller, "A Defense of Gender-Accurate Bible Translation," 488, 475–6.
11. Lynn Cohick states that Priscilla and Junia held "positions of authority" in the earliest Christian groups. Nijay Gupta speaks to the statement by some that Priscilla and Aquila chose their home rather than a public space to instruct Apollos, but, he says, "their home was the site of their church." Cohick, *Women in the World of the Earliest Christians*, 224. Gupta, *Tell Her Story*, 138.
12. Alvin Schmidt reports that this was the famous German theologian Adolph von Harnack in 1905. This theory is still proposed. Schmidt, *Veiled and Silenced*, 178. Also see Haddad, "Priscilla, Author of the Epistle to the Hebrews?"
13. Rom. 16:1.
14. Rom. 16:2. Spencer, *Beyond the Curse*, 115–6.
15. Aida Besancon Spencer, *Beyond the Curse*, 116-7. Ben Witherington states that "the notions of care as a deacon, and some sort of leadership role in administering that care, benevolence, or patronage, are not mutually exclusive." Witherington, *Paul's Letter to the Romans*, 383.
16. Cohick, *Women in the World of the Earliest Christians*, 190.
17. Bailey, *Paul Through Mediterranean Eyes*, 411. Craig Keener also states that it is likely that Phoebe hosted the house church in Cenchrea. Keener, *Romans*, 182–3.

NOTES – Chapter 5

18. As explained by Keener in *Romans*, 183.
19. Rom. 16:7. Aida Besancon Spencer says some writers have proposed that if Junia is a woman, then she was admired *by* the apostles, not prominent *among* them; however, she says, the preposition used here, *en*, is a common idiom in the ancient Greek signifying "among." Linda Belleville points out that the Latin Vulgate says Junia was notable *among* the apostles. Spencer, *Beyond the Curse*, 102. Belleville, "Women Leaders in the Bible," 55.
20. Aida Besancon Spencer says commentators throughout the years have assumed Junia was a woman, "until Aegidus of Rome (AD 1245 to 1316) simply referred to the two persons Andronicus and Junia as simply 'men.'" Spencer, *Beyond the Curse*, 101.
21. John Chrysostom, "*Homilies on Romans* 31 [on Rom. 16:7]," as referenced in Belleville, *Women Leaders and the Church*, 55.
22. Ben Witherington states that "the feminine name Junia is attested more than 250 times in Greek and Latin inscriptions," but "the masculine counterpart Junias is nowhere attested." Witherington, *Paul's Letter to the Romans*, 378, footnote 13.
23. Aida Besancon Spencer points to this "commom idiom" in the Greek signifying "among." Ben Witherington uses the phrase "notable among the apostles." Spencer, *Beyond the Curse*, 102. Witherington, *Paul's Letter to the Romans*, 378, footnote 13.
24. These include Chloe (1 Cor. 1:11), Nympha (Col. 4:15), Apphia (Phlm. 2), Lydia (Acts 16:14-15, 40), and possibly Stephana (1 Cor. 16:15, 17), which could be a man or woman's name. Some also consider the "elect lady" in 2 John 1 to be a house church leader. Priscilla is also listed with Aquila as having a house church (Rom. 16:3–5 and 1 Cor. 16:19).
25. Ben Witherington gives a discussion of the host of a church also being the leader. Linda Belleville states that a householder in Greco-Roman times was "automatically in charge of any group that met in his or her domicile." Also see discussion in chapter 10 of this book. Witherington, *Conflict & Community in Corinth*, 30-31. Belleville, "Women Leaders in the Bible," (2005), 123.
26. Phil. 4:2-3.
27. Rom. 16:12.
28. Scholer, "A Biblical Basis for Equal Partnership," 9.
29. John Chrysostom, as reported by Witherington in *Paul's Letter to the Romans*, 387.
30. Acts 1:14, 1:14, 2:17, 2:18, 5:1, 5:7–10, 5:14, 8:3, 9:2, 9:36–42, 12:12, 12:13–16, 13:50, 16:1, 16:14–15, 16:16-19, 16:40, 17:4, 17:12, 17:34, 18:2, 18:18, 18:19, 18:26, 21:5, 21:9, 22:4, 23:16, 24:24, 25:23, 26:30.
31. Lynn Cohick states that women were "vastly underrepresented in ancient literature." Ben Witherington suggests that Luke stressed and supported the role of women in the earliest churches because there was "still considerable resistance then to such ideas" and "a case had to be made in some detail."

Witherington also writes that Luke, like Paul, stresses a "transformed vision" regarding women. Witherington concludes that Luke's portrayal of women in various activities in the church shows how the Gospel "liberates and creates new possibilities for women." Cohick, *Women in the World of the Earliest Christians*, 201. Witherington, *Women in the Earliest Churches*, 156–7.

32. See Stark, *The Rise of Christianity*, 110.

33. Acts 21:9. Craig Keener points out that the term translated "unmarried" usually referred to prepubescent or young adolescent virgins, so the Spirit of prophecy includes the young. Keener, *Acts*, New Cambridge Bible Commentary, 513.

34. Acts 16:13–15. Craig Keener says Paul and his colleagues would quickly learn that no synagogue existed in that city. They may have heard, though, that some people practiced Jewish customs outside the city and, in the absence of a synagogue, they would most often assemble near water where they could ritually purify their hands. Keener, *Acts*, New Cambridge Bible Commentary, 387.

35. 1 Cor. 11:5, 13. Craig Keener states that prophecy includes "Spirit empowerment." Keener, *Acts, An Exegetical Commentary*, 603.

36. Ben Witherington says "prophecy is addressed to the whole congregation," including the men. Also, since prophecy involves "authoritative exhortation or a new word of God," then it has a didactic (teaching) purpose. Witherington believes Scripture suggests that women were allowed to engage also in the weighing of prophecy. Witherington, *Women in the Earliest Churches*, 95.

37. Rom. 16:1–15. Craig Keener, who is an expert on the culture of New Testament times, says that the percentage of women colleagues Paul acknowledges is "amazing by any ancient standards." Keener, *Paul, Women and Wives*, 113.

38. 2 Tim. 2:2. *Thayer's Greek-English Dictionary of the New Testament*, 444, anthropos.

39. Eph. 4:8.

40. Eph. 4:11. *Thayer's Greek-English Dictionary of the New Testament*, 444, anthropos. Eph. 4:8 says Christ gave gifts to mankind when he ascended on high; Paul continues his train of thought in the following verses, explaining what "ascended" means, and that it was Christ who gave some to be apostles, prophets, evangelists, pastors and teachers. Linda Belleville explains that a single Greek article comes before "pastors and teachers" and conceptually unites the two nouns, thus, this grammatical arrangement should be translated as "pastor-teacher," meaning that "pastoring is inseparable from the task of teaching." Belleville, *Women Leaders and the Church*, 58, 189, 140.

41. Gal. 3:28.

42. See, for example, Acts 15:5–9. Love Sechrest says Paul substitutes an allegorical genealogy for a physical one, and via baptism offers a solidarity "in the Spirit" that "transcends ethnicity and gender." N.T. Wright states that circumcision marked Jews in a way that automatically privileged males; by

contrast, one can imagine the "thrill of equality brought about by baptism, an identical rite for Jew and Gentile, slave and free, male and female." Sechrest, *A Former Jew*, 211. Wright, *Surprised by Scripture*, 67.

43. For example, Acts 2:14.

44. Craig Keener says this is true for speakers in Acts who address crowds as men of Galilee, Judea, Israel, Athens, or Ephesus. He says this was a common form of address then, appropriate in that era's rhetorical culture, and "did not necessarily exclude female hearers from being present." Keener, *Acts, An Exegetical Commentary*, 867–9.

45. Dorothy Lee explains that the Greek *adelphos* (brother) and *adelphe* (sister) can be used together in the singular form to represent a brother and sister, as in Mark 3:35. However, when the plural is needed, *adelphoi*, the masculine plural, is often sufficient to represent both brothers and sisters. If a text obviously means male siblings only, then "brothers" is the correct translation; if females are included, then "brothers and sisters" is nearer the intent of the text. For that reason, she says, "most modern translations" use "brothers and sisters," not just "brothers," in order to translate more accurately. Gordon Fee says it is clear that from the evidence of 1 Cor. 11:2–16 that in 1 Cor. 14:26 (when everyone has a hymn, word of instruction, etc.) and in Phil. 4:1–3 (where he pleads with Euodia and Syntyche) "that women were participants in the worship of the community." It is therefore "biblically sensitive," he says, to translate this vocative as "brothers and sisters." Lee, *Ministry of Women in the New Testament*, 107. Fee, *First Epistle to the Corinthians*, 52, with footnote 22. Also see pages 661 and 690.

46. Jeffrey Miller says that translating *adelphoi* as "brothers and sisters" or something similar, appeared in 1989 in the NRSV; the NLT, CEB, NIV 2011, and CSB have continued this practice. Miller, "A Defense of Gender-Accurate Bible Translation," 486.

47. Rom. 16:1. Gordon, "The Ministry of Women," 916. Gordon also wrote in 1894: "To many it has been both a relief and a surprise to discover how little authority there is in the Word for repressing the witness of women in the public assembly, or for forbidding her to herald the Gospel to the unsaved. If this be so, it may be well for the plaintiffs in the case to beware lest, in silencing the voice of consecrated women, they may be resisting the Holy Ghost . . . . Let the theologians who have recently written so dogmatically upon this subject consider whether it may not be possible that in this matter they are still under the law and not under grace" (919, 921).

48. Witherington, *Women in the Earliest Churches*, 212.

Chapter 6 – Women silent in church?

1. By Sophocles and quoted by Aristotle, per Philip Payne, *Man and Woman, One in Christ*, 218.

2. Linda Belleville says this was the norm even among the more progressive Romans. Lynn Cohick says it was an "honor/shame culture" that defined

what was honorable for men and women; it publicly praised or shamed those who upheld or rejected these ideals. Craig Keener says women were to leave speaking in public to men, and "respectable women did not typically speak publicly to groups including men." Women were rarely granted speaking roles even in ancient literature. Phillip Payne says "the dominant social perspective throughout Hellenistic, Roman, and Jewish culture" was to keep women in their place; "the normal convention was for women not to speak." Belleville, *Women Leaders and the Church*, 161. Cohick, *Women in the World of the Earliest Christians*, 22–23. Keener, *Acts, An Exegetical Commentary*, 621, 882, 600. Payne, *Man and Woman, One in Christ*, 217, 263–4.

3. Tucker and Liefeld, *Daughters of the Church*, 75-76. Payne, *Man and Woman, One in Christ*, 217–8.

4. It is interesting to note that reportedly the word used in 1 Cor. 14:34 for "assembly" is the same Greek word used for a Greek public meeting, and the normal convention was that women were not allowed to speak. Payne, *Man and Woman, One in Christ*, 217.

5. 1 Cor. 11. Ben Witherington says prophecy is addressed "to the whole congregation, which includes the men." Philip Payne points out that several times in the chapter where head coverings for women when they prophesy are discussed, Paul refers to meeting in the church (1 Cor. 11:17, 18, and 22). Manfred Brauch emphasizes, in the context of discussion of these verses, the importance of being a "faithful interpreter of the whole counsel of God revealed in Scripture." See 1 Cor. 1:5, 14:5, 14:24, 14:26, 14:31, 14:39. Witherington, *Women and the Genesis of Christianity*, 173. Payne, *Man and Woman, One in Christ*, 221. Brauch in Kaiser et al., *Hard Sayings of the Bible*, 613.

6. Gordon Fee quotes the Jewish author Josephus as writing, "The woman, says the Law, is in all things inferior to the man. Let her accordingly be submissive." Walter Kaiser says that in 1 Cor. 14:34, Paul was referring "to the Jewish law found in the Talmud and Mishnah," which taught women should not speak and must be silent, and this was not in the Old Testament. Kaiser says he does not agree, as some suggest, that this was referring to Genesis. Linda Belleville points out that the Old Testament itself did not command submission by wives, but Jewish and Greek legal marriage contracts included "wifely obedience" (but Roman ones typically did not). Ben Witherington says women are not being told here to submit to their husbands, but "to the principle of order" in the worship service and silence and respect when another is speaking. Witherington says that "if one is exercising one's gifts in love, then one will think of the benefit to others first." Kenneth Bailey writes that the command of the Lord here refers to the "royal command of love defined in chapter 13" and has sadly been misused through the centuries "to keep women from the full use of their spiritual gifts in the leadership of worship in the church." Ruth Tucker and Walter Liefeld state that Paul never used the term "law" in this way. F.F. Bruce called Paul the "apostle of the heart set free" and wrote a chapter in his book of the same name entitled "What the Law Could Not Do." Bruce emphasizes that Paul espoused freedom in

Christ as a new creation rather than spiritual legalism. Fee, *First Epistle to the Corinthians*, 707. Kaiser et al., *Hard Sayings of the Bible*, 99. Belleville, *Women Leaders and the Church*, 158-9. Witherington, *Women in the Earliest Churches*, 102-3, and *Conflict and Community in Corinth*, 281. Bailey, *Paul through Mediterranean Eyes*, 418. Tucker and Liefeld, *Daughters of the Church*, 76. Bruce, *Paul: Apostle of the Heart Set Free*, 188-202.

7. Anthony Thiselton writes in his academic commentary on 1 Corinthians that the translation and understanding of these verses are "immensely complex" and presents various theories about them. Thiselton, *The First Epistle to the Corinthians*, 1146.

8. Alice Mathews, *Gender Roles and the People of God*, 107.

9. Some scholars believe that verses 34-35 prohibit women only from disruptive speech or judging prophecies. Philip Payne, however, points out that those interpretations must not be correct "because they permit speech in church that 14:35 prohibits, namely asking questions out of a desire to learn." Payne, *The Bible vs Biblical Womanhood*, 82.

10. Manfred Brauch writes that the Greek word used for women being "silent" (*sigao*) is the same one used when prophets are called to be "quiet" (verse 28), just translated differently. Ben Witherington says the Old Testament speaks of a "respectful silence when a word of counsel was spoken (Job 29:21)," and "it was conventional in the Greco-Roman world to command silence when a religious act was about to be performed." Linda Belleville points out that the command for silence occurs three times, in verses 28, 30, and 34. Brauch, *Hard Sayings of the Bible*, 615. Witherington, *Women and the Genesis of Christianity*, 177, and *Conflict and Community in Corinth*, 285-6. Belleville, *Women Leaders and the Church*, 157.

11. Craig Keener points out that only one kind of speech is explicitly referred to in this passage and it is asking questions. Some have said these verses refer to women chattering too much; Philip Payne says the Greek word used here for the women speaking relates repeatedly in this chapter to "inspired speech," not chattering. He says there are twenty-two uses of the word in this passage, all with the meaning of inspired speech. Ben Witherington states that the word Paul uses for the women speaking has a sense throughout the chapter of "inspired speech." Keener, "Learning in the Assemblies," Third Edition, 150. Payne, *Man and Woman, One in Christ*, 221-2. Witherington, *Women in the Earliest Churches*, 99.

12. Craig Keener says that, customarily, only informed listeners were to ask questions during lectures. He also states that women were far less trained then in the Scriptures and public reasoning than men were. It has been proposed that this may refer to women testing the prophecies, as Paul encourages in verse 29. Keener also points out that it was considered unacceptable for a woman to ask a question of a man who was not her husband; such a practice could have created tension in a church with various cultures present. Keener, "Learning in the Assemblies," Third Edition 150-155, and *IVP Bible Background Commentary*, 483.

13. Craig Keener states that "traditional Romans regarded wives' speaking publicly with others' husbands as horrible behavior;" first-century Romans, including many in Corinth, had generally become more tolerant, "but enough traditional sentiments remained to create tension in the house-church setting, especially with various cultures present." Keener states that from this perspective the key issue would not be gender but propriety in the churches and learning, "neither of which need restrain women's voices in the church today." Philip Payne points out that the same word for the "churches" is also used for Greek public meetings, where "the normal convention was that women were not to speak." Keener, "Learning in the Assemblies," Third Edition, 153, 151, 157–158, 152. Payne, *Man and Woman, One in Christ*, 217.

14. Craig Keener says, however, that Plutarch wrote that "most men did not believe their wives could learn anything;" that would be especially true of Greek men "who were on average a decade or more older than their wives." Therefore, Paul's instruction would be beneficial for the women in encouraging the men to teach them. Keener, "Learning in the Assemblies," Third Edition, 157.

15. Craig Keener says that Paul provides "the most progressive model of his day: their husbands are to respect their intellectual capabilities and give them private instruction." Keener, *IVP Bible Background Commentary*, 483.

16. Anthony Thiselton explores various theories in his commentary and says the view that Paul is quoting a Corinthian slogan or piece of Corinthian ideology, only to reject it, is "not farfetched," for Paul appears to do precisely this in 6:12, 7:1, and 10:23, and perhaps elsewhere, (e.g., 8:1-6)." Thiselton also cites Odell-Scott, who is most associated with this theory, as saying that this passage can be understood "as a strong rebuttal of verses 34–35;" endorsing the "authority of women to speak in the public congregation." Philip Payne points out weaknesses of this theory, including that none of the church fathers give any indication that verses 34-35 are a quotation. Payne also states that many Greek manuscripts place verses 14:34–35 at the end of chapter 14, after verse 40, and would not have done so if they thought that verses 36–38 refuted verses 34-35, nor would verses 36–38 refute text that begins after verse 40. Thiselton, *The First Epistle to the Corinthians*, 1150-1. Payne, "Is I Corinthians 14:34–35 a Marginal Comment or a Quotation?" 24-6, and *Man and Woman, One in Christ*, 224-5, and *The Bible vs Biblical 'manhood*, 84-87.

17. As cited in Fee, *First Epistle to the Corinthians*, 707.

18. Gilbert Bilezikian says the term "saints" designated "exclusively the Jewish Christians of Jerusalem and Palestine (Acts 9:13, 32, 41; 26:10). When the churches were established in the Gentile world," he says, "the Jewish Christians of Jerusalem continued to be called "the saints" (1 Cor. 16:1, cf. v. 3; 2 Cor. 8:4; 9:12; Rom. 15:25, 26, 31)." Later, the designation "was extended to all Christians (1 Cor. 1:2), but it also remained a consecrated name for the Jerusalem Christians (1 Cor. 16:1, v.3)." Bilezikian, *Beyond Sex Roles*, 148.

19. Linda Belleville and other scholars have pointed this out. Belleville also states

that beginning a new paragraph at verse 33b would result in a "redundancy that is quite unlike Paul:" "*As in all the churches of the saints*, let the women *in the churches* be silent." Gordon Fee states that the very early textual evidence in the Western church indicates that this phrase was not considered to be part of verses 34–35. This includes writing by Chrysostom, who joined 33b to 33a. Fee says the idea that verse 33b goes with verse 34 seems to be a modern phenomenon altogether. Philip Payne states that no early Christian author supports a change of speaker at 33b. Belleville, *Women Leaders and the Church*, 157–8. Fee, *The First Epistle to the Corinthians*, 697, also footnote 49. Payne, "Is I Corinthians 14:34–35 a Marginal Comment or a Quotation?" 24.

20. F.F. Bruce states in reference to this passage that it would be "strange" for Paul to silence women after his recognition in verses 11:5 and following of women praying and prophesying. Bruce, *I & II Corinthians*, 135.

21. Philip Payne explains that when scribes were creating a new copy of a manuscript (all hand-written), it was common for them to insert into the main text any words they found in the margin. Payne says that "virtually all biblical scholars" have concluded that this has happened with some passages. Scholars call such a passage an "interpolation" or "gloss." Payne prefers the term "gloss," because some writers define interpolation as deliberate polishing of the body text, but a gloss is text written in the margin and later inserted into the text by copyists. Interpolation also has negative overtones because it suggests deliberately adding to the text, contrary to a scribe's fundamental task, but a gloss is an accidental mistake by a scribe. Payne says an ancient Bible, the Codex Vaticanus, contains twenty instances of small readable old text in the margins of Matthew, and all but three are found in the main text of virtually every surviving manuscript that came after the Vaticanus. Payne also explains a term, "transcriptional probability," as the analysis of what a copyist is most likely to have done, seeking to explain the known variations in surviving manuscripts. Payne, "Is I Corinthians 14:34–35 a Marginal Comment or a Quotation?" 26, 28, and *Man and Woman, One in Christ*, 225, 227-32. Payne and Huffaker, *Why Can't Women Do That?* 115–6.

22. Gordon Fee is considered one of the greatest "textual critics" of the Bible in a generation. "Textual criticism" traces the history of a particular biblical passage by analyzing the earliest manuscripts and ancient translations in the original languages to understand the most likely original readings. The textual critic also looks at the author's normal style and the most common copyist errors, both intentional and unintentional.

23. Gordon Fee states that because the case against these verses "is so strong, and finding a viable solution to their meaning is so difficult, it seems best to view them as an interpolation" (gloss). He says that "since the phenomenon of glosses making their way into the biblical text is so well-documented elsewhere in the New Testament (e.g., John 5:3b–4; 1 John 5:7), there is no good historical reason to reject the possibility here." That these words occur in all existing manuscripts, he contends, "only means that the double interpolation had taken place before the time of our present textual tradition."

He says this could easily have happened before the turn of the first century. Fee, *First Epistle to the Corinthians*, 705, and *God's Empowering Presence*, 272–81.

24. Philip Payne and Vince Huffaker point out there is "no close parallel in any of Paul's letters," so the perspective that verses 34 and 35 are a gloss "does not undermine the authenticity of any other passage" by Paul. Payne and Huffaker, *Why Can't Women Do That?* 115–6.

25. Philip Payne gives examples, including the NIV regarding Matt. 18:11 and John 7:53. Gordon Fee notes John 5:3b–4 and 1 John 5:7. Payne says virtually all textual scholars regard John 7:53–8:11 as the only close parallel. It, too, is added at different places (not transposed), has a specific symbol (a distigme-obelos) accompanied by a gap, exactly where it would begin in Vaticanus, and shares many other features with 1 Cor. 14:34–35. Payne says that additions of similar length also occur at John 5:3b–4 and 1 John 5:7–8. Payne, "Is I Corinthians 14:34–35 a Marginal Comment or a Quotation?" 28. Payne and Huffaker, *Why Can't Women Do That?* 113–4, 116. Fee, *God's Empowering Presence*, 281.

26. Gordon Fee identifies several linguistic irregularities in these two verses that together form "a considerable package": the use of the plural "in the churches," which "occurs nowhere else in Paul;" the appeal to the law in an absolute sense "which is unknown in Paul;" and the appeal to shame in v. 35 as a general cultural matter (quite unlike the appeal to "shaming" one's spouse in 11:5). Fee also says two contextual matters are especially difficult: these two verses "so thoroughly intrude" into the argument of prophecy in the assembly, and they require women to be silent, contradicting "the emphasis on the participation of 'all' throughout the chapter." Philip Payne says these verses "contradict Paul's encouraging women to speak in church, . . . interrupt the flow of Paul's argument, . . . make alien use of vocabulary from the chapter, . . . and conflict with the goal of instruction in church." Also, Payne says, "just as the law says" does not fit Paul's theology or his style of expression. Only the gloss explanation, Fee says, preserves the chiastic structure and integrity of Paul's argument and avoids conflict with Paul's other teachings. Fee, *God's Empowering Presence*, 272–81, *The First Epistle to the Corinthians*, 699–708, and "The Priority of Spirit Gifting," (Third Edition), 259. Payne, *Man and Woman, One in Christ*, 253–65.

27. Gordon Fee explains that in one whole sector of the church these verses are known only at another place in the text. (He provides discussion of these different sectors in *God's Empowering Presence*.) Fee says the verses appear in different places in the Alexandrian/Byzantine text-type manuscripts (after verse 33) and the Western text (after verse 40), and "we are dealing with the entire surviving evidence for the shape of the text in the West before 385 CE." Philip Payne states that moving a thirty-six- to forty-word transposition five verses away with no obvious reason is unprecedented in any Pauline manuscript. Payne says that evidently one early copyist inserted the verses from the margin into one place in the text, and then another inserted it elsewhere. Fee, *The First Epistle to the Corinthians*, 700, "The Priority of

Spirit Gifting," (Third Edition), 258-9, *God's Empowering Presence*, 273-5. Payne, "Is I Corinthians 14:34–35 a Marginal Comment or a Quotation?" 28. Payne and Huffaker, *Why Can't Women Do That?* 115.

28. Gordon Fee says the interpolation could easily have happened before the turn of the first century. B. Ehrman reports that the vast majority of all textual variants originated during the second and third centuries. Fee, *First Epistle to the Corinthians*, 705. Ehrman, *The Orthodox Corruption of Scripture*.

29. Philip Payne states that "every manuscript" containing this passage, or an allusion to it, "comes from after the period of the church's reaction against women in leadership in Gnostic circles." In parallel, he says, "submit" rapidly began to be included in Eph. 5:22 in widespread fashion. Payne, *Man and Woman, One in Christ*, 264, and "Is I Corinthians 14:34–35 a Marginal Comment or a Quotation?" 26.

30. According to Philip Payne, Eldon Epp states: "Vaticanus would be regarded by all as the most valuable uncial [manuscript] of the NT, and by many as the most important of all NT [manuscripts], due to the combination of its early date, its broad coverage of the NT, and the excellent quality of its text." Eldon Epp as cited in Philip Payne, "Is I Corinthians 14:34–35 a Marginal Comment or a Quotation?" 27.

31. Thus, this ancient Bible is called the "Codex Vaticanus." It reportedly contains most of the books of the Greek Old Testament and Greek New Testament.

32. Per Philip Payne, a high-quality color copy has also now been made, allowing more scholars to study the ancient manuscript.

33. Payne had published a paper about 1 Cor. 14:34–35 in this ancient Bible, the Codex Vaticanus. Payne, "Fuldensis, Sigla for Variants in Vaticanus, and I Corinthians 14:34–5."

34. Philip Payne and Paul Canart state that a standard system of dots and lines and other pen strokes was used to indicate textual variants for important documents and was well established even in Sumerian and Akkadian texts. Jewish scribes, Origin's Hexapla, and Bishop Victor of Capua's Codex Fuldensis also employed such symbols. Payne explains that the "obelos" was the standard symbol in ancient Greek literature to mark added text, and the "distigme-obelos" was the symbol particularly associated with glosses. Payne and Canart, "The Originality of Text-Critical Symbols in Codex Vaticanus," 111–2. Payne, *Man and Woman, One in Christ*, 239, 246, and "Vaticanus Distigme-Obelos Symbols."

35. Payne and Canart, "The Originality of Text-Critical Symbols in Codex Vaticanus." Also see "Distigmai Matching the Original Ink of *Codex Vaticanus*: Do They Mark the Location of Textual Variants?" Payne tells the story in Payne, *Man and Woman, One in Christ*, 240–1, and gives visuals of the symbols in *The Bible vs. Biblical Womanhood*, 79-101 and Appendix 1.

36. Payne, "Vaticanus Distigme-obelos Symbols." Payne states that "virtually all scholars" regard John 7:53-8:11, the only close parallel, as not original and points out that it, too, is added at different places (not transposed), has

a distigme-obelos accompanied by a gap exactly where it would begin in the Codex Vaticanus, and shares many other features with 1 Cor. 14:34-35. Payne, "Is I Corinthians 14:34–35 a Marginal Comment or a Quotation?" 28.

37. Philip Payne writes that in about 541 AD, Bishop Victor of Capua, the most renowned expert on manuscripts of his time, had the text of 1 Cor. 14:34-40 rewritten to omit verses 34–35 in "what is considered one of the oldest and most valuable Latin manuscripts of the Vulgate" Bible. Payne says the implication is that a manuscript that omitted 1 Cor. 14:34-35 influenced Victor's thinking. Payne also states that Bruce Metzger made an error regarding Victor's work because Metzger had not seen the actual text and changed his opinion when Payne showed him a copy. In addition, Payne says manuscript MS 88 was probably "copied from a manuscript that omitted verses 34-35." Payne and Canart stated that original-ink-color distigmai marking "the location of textual variants throughout the manuscript prove that the scribe had access to more than one manuscript." Payne, *Man and Woman, One in Christ*, 246-7, 249-50, and "Is 1 Corinthians 14:34–35 a Marginal Comment or a Quotation?" 27-28. Payne and Canart, "The Originality of Text-Critical Symbols," 112. Email from Philip Payne, March 22, 2022.

38. Philip Payne says that this time period was the second century. He also states that Clement of Alexandria reflects a text of 1 Corinthians without verses 34-35. In addition, the earliest known citation of these two verses is from Tertullian, writing about AD 200. Payne, *Man and Woman, One in Christ*, 250-2, 264.

39. Joseph Fitzmyer writes that the "majority of commentators today" (publication date 2008) believe, "with varying nuances," that verses 34–35 are a post-Pauline interpolation. Ben Witherington surveys various theories about these verses and says "an increasing number of scholars" take 1 Cor. 14:33b–36 (or 34–36) to be "a case of interpolation of non-Pauline material into this Pauline letter," based on these factors: the textual difficulties; these verses interrupt the flow of the argument; verse 37 follows nicely with 33a; these verses "blatantly contradict the clear implications of 1 Cor. 11:5;" and peculiarities of linguistic usage. After surveying other theories that the material was indeed written by Paul, Witherington concludes that Paul would simply be redirecting women's questions that were disruptive to another setting, and verses 34–35 "cannot be taken as a prohibition of women praying, prophesying, teaching, or preaching in a worship setting." Fitzmyer, *First Corinthians*, 530. Witherington, *Women in the Earliest Churches*, 90–1, 103-4.

40. Philip Payne writes that "most scholars who have published their analyses" of the early manuscripts agree that these verses are a gloss. He stated in 2009 that at least fifty-five textual studies argue that these verses are a later addition and in 2017 updated that number to 62. Payne, *Man and Woman, One in Christ*, 226–227 (2009), and "Six Ground-breaking Discoveries," (2017).

Chapter 7 – Man as "head" of woman?

1. Raymond Collins says "Paul's rhetorical argument is constructed on the basis of a pun" and plays on the multiple meanings of "head." Anthony Thiselton states that Paul uses the term "head" as a "polymorphous concept." Collins, *1 Corinthians*, 396; 405–6, as referenced in Thiselton, *The First Epistle to the Corinthians*, 820. Thiselton's comment also appears on 820.

2. David Scholer says the "determinative evidence for the meaning of *kephale* is its use and function in particular contexts." Lynn Cohick states in her recent extensive commentary on the book of Ephesians that metaphorical meanings that have been proposed for *kephale* can include preeminence, source, or leader, however, she points out that the ancient Greek lexicons (dictionaries) "do not define *kephale* as 'authority' or 'leader.'" Cynthia Westfall says in her recent in-depth work on Paul and gender that *kephale* "refers to the head of a body and had a range of meaning reflecting Greek beliefs about the function of the head in relation to the body, including the biological functions." Westfall states that as a metaphor, *kephale* can signify "identity, source, life, and provision," but it did not mean authority in "idiomatic Greek" (as it does in English), as evidenced by the lack of definitions as such in Liddell and Scott's *Greek-English Lexicon*. However, in the Hebrew rather than the Greek, "head" was a known metaphor for authority/leader. Scholer, "The Evangelical Debate over Biblical 'Headship,'" 43. Cohick, *Letter to the Ephesians*, 356. Westfall, *Paul and Gender*, 80–1.

3. Ben Witherington says Paul is trying to reform men and women who "continue to take their cues for religious behavior from analogous practices in other religious settings in Corinth" and set up customs for a Christian community. Witherington indicates that some Roman males covered their heads when praying or prophesying. Witherington, *Conflict and Community in Corinth*, 239, 238.

4. Kenneth Bailey says "the Mishnah rules that women should be divorced if they uncovered their heads in public." Mishnah, *Ketubbot* 6:6. Bailey, *Paul Through Mediterranean Eyes*, 300.

5. Bruce Winter writes that it can be "confidently concluded" that "the veiled head was the symbol of modesty and chastity expected of a married woman." Cynthia Long Westfall points out that women slaves may have been part of the house churches, slaves were prohibited from veilings, and prophesying and praying without a head covering or conservative hairstyle could have been an issue. She discusses Paul's possible concern for the dignity of women slaves in the house churches. Winter, *Roman Wives*, 80. Westfall, *Paul and Gender*, 25–34.

6. Bruce Winter describes the phenomenon of the "new woman" who embraced new social mores, including removing the veil. Richard Hays states that the word *veil* is not in the passage, and believes, with some other scholars, that having the head covered "would mean to have the hair tied up on top of the head rather than hanging loose." Ben Witherington states that some in the house churches may have thought they "transcended distinctions of gender

in Christian worship." Winter, *Roman Wives*, xi, 77. Hays, *First Corinthians*, 185. Witherington, *Conflict and Community in Corinth*, 236.

7. Ben Witherington says that in some pagan mysteries women might worship without head coverings and with their hair unbound. Also, Richard and Catherine Kroeger state that "sex reversal was also a significant factor in the worship to Aphrodite, whose temple dominated the Corinthian acropolis," with some men wearing veils or long flowing hair and women shaving their heads. Witherington, *Conflict and Community in Corinth*, 236. Kroeger and Kroeger, "Sexual Identity in Corinth," *Reformed Journal* 28 (1978): 12, as referenced in Tucker and Liefeld, *Daughters of the Church*, 77.

8. Payne, *Man and Woman*, 211.

9. 1 Cor. 1:10.

10. Kenneth Bailey says Paul introduces this homily "with a strong Christological affirmation" in hopes of moving his readers forward to his views. Bailey also states that probably some of his readers were trying "to marginalize woman" as inferior because she was taken out of the side of Adam. Some translations have changed "man" to "her husband" in I Cor 11:3, saying that the head of woman is "her husband." Scholar Linda Belleville, however, says that no possessive exists here in the original Greek and Paul would normally have added one if that were his intention. Bailey, *Paul Through Mediterranean Eyes*, 303, 307. Belleville, *Women Leaders and the Church*, 126.

11. A recent commentary by Lynn Cohick in a highly respected series concludes that the evidence for a meaning here of "leader" in the "usual English sense" is "weak and limited." Cohick, *Letter to the Ephesians*, 356.

12. Lynn Cohick says the 1843 edition of the Liddell and Scott lexicon [considered the most exhaustive lexicon covering Greek literature from about 900 BC to AD 600] listed more than twenty-five entries under *kephale*, including the metaphorical meaning of "source," but no entry referring to "leader" or "authority over." The 1996 ninth edition, she says, likewise does not include these meanings either. Gordon Fee states that one lexicon (BAGD) lists "authority" with examples as a meaning, but one of the references, from Zosimus, dates from the 6th century, many years after Paul, "and most likely refers to 'dignity,' not authority." Fee says the second reference listed for authority does not even appear in the text given for the example. Phillip Payne also explores such lexicon instances with similar conclusions but in more depth. He also states that the LSJ lexicon lists 49 entries for *kephale* but none for leader, authority, or anything related to that. Cohick, *Letter to the Ephesians*, 356, footnote 505. Fee, *First Epistle to the Corinthians*, 502, footnote 42. Payne, *Man and Woman, One in Christ*, 121–2, and *The Bible vs. Biblical Womanhood*, 53.

13. Manfred Brauch says *kephale* is not used anywhere else in the New Testament to designate a figure of authority and if that had been a prominent meaning, it could have served well in numerous places in the Gospels. Brauch, "1 Corinthians," 600–1.

14. This was called the Septuagint (LXX), from the word for seventy, because 70 to 72 Hebrew scholars are said to have translated the Hebrew Old Testament into Greek for the great library at Alexandria, Egypt, around 300 BC. Gordon Fee states: "In the hundreds of places where the Hebrew *rosh* is used in the Greek Septuagint for the literal head on a body, the translators invariably used the only word in Greek that means the same thing, *kephale*. But in the approximately 180 times it appears as a metaphor for leader or chieftain, the translators almost always eliminate the metaphor altogether and translate it *arche* ('leader')." Fee says this indicates that the metaphorical sense of leader is an exceptional usage and not part of the ordinary range of meanings of the Greek word. Berkeley and Alvera Mickelsen state that with Paul's "superb intellectual ability and intense passion to spread the Gospel," he would only have used a word that would convey his meaning clearly to his Greek-speaking Corinthian hearers. Fee, "Praying and Prophesying," 150, and *1 Corinthians*, 503. Mickelsen and Mickelsen, "What Does *Kephale* Mean?" 104.

15. Cyril was patriarch of Alexandria from about AD 412 to 444. Gordon Fee writes that Cyril provides us with the earliest known consistent interpretation of the metaphor in this passage. Fee, "Praying and Prophesying in the Assemblies," 151.

16. Philip Payne writes that "source" is an established meaning listed from the earliest Greek lexicons to the present. Payne, *Man and Woman, One In Christ*, 123.

17. G.W. Lampe says Cyril wrote that man was excellently made through Christ, woman was taken from man's flesh, and Christ is from God according to his nature. Catherine Clark Kroeger writes that Cyril begins the passage by speaking of Adam as the "first head, which is source," and Christ, "the second Adam," also "head, which is source." Gordon Fee says it seems most likely that "something very much like Cyril's understanding was in Paul's mind"; and this supported Cyril's concern not to have Christ "under" God in a hierarchy, "just as it did for Chrysostom." Philip Payne writes that the Greek word here for head is *kephale*, and source is *arche*. Lampe, *A Patristic Greek Lexicon*, 749. Kroeger, "Toward an Understanding of Ancient Conceptions," 6. Fee, "Praying and Prophesying in the Assemblies," 151. Payne, *Man and Woman, One in Christ*, 131.

18. Lynn Cohick cites Cyril and also Athanasius, the fourth-century bishop of Alexandria, who wrote that "the Son is the Head, namely the beginning of all: and God is the Head, namely the beginning of Christ." Cohick also states that both Cyril and Chrysostom write against the position that Christ is a subordinate being to the God the Father. Gordon Fee notes that the early church father Chrysostom totally rejects the idea that the metaphor includes the notion of "rule and subjection." Philip Payne cites other Greek fathers with this view, as well as the Latin father Ambrosiaster. Cohick, *Letter to the Ephesians*, 356–7. Fee, "Praying and Prophesying in the Assemblies," 150. Payne, *Man and Woman*, 136–7.

19. Cynthia Long Westfall states that "the first-century Greco-Roman culture and the ancient Near East were vitally interested in a person's origins in terms of place and family." Westfall, *Paul and Gender*, 80.

20. Gordon Fee says that shame and honor were the "primary sociological value" in this culture. Fee, "Praying and Prophesying in the Assemblies," 148.

21. Gordon Fee writes that verses 11–12 explicitly qualify verses 8–9, so that they will not be understood as setting up a hierarchy. He also says that "to read the text as though it said the opposite of what vv. [verses] 10–12 seem clearly to say is to do Paul an injustice." David Scholer states that "Paul's strong balancing statement in 1 Cor. 11:11–12, introduced by the emphatic adversative *plen*, makes clear that his intent 'in the Lord' is for the mutuality (or equality) of men and women." Cynthia Long Westfall states that these verses are not "arguing for the priority of man based on the order of creation; rather, the creation of woman from man evens out the balance, since every man comes from woman." Fee, *First Epistle to the Corinthians*, 502, 517, 524. Scholer, "The Evangelical Debate over Biblical 'Headship,'" 43. Westfall, *Paul and Gender*, 72–3.

22. 1 Cor. 8:6. Anthony Thiselton states that advocates of "source" might strengthen their case "by pointing out more strongly" that 11:12 "offers precisely the terminology used of 8:6 about God and Christ." He cites the Greek words for "of source" and "of 'mediate' creation." "We have to judge," he says, "whether it is sufficient to make it plausible that Paul *expected* this meaning to be understood by his readers in verse 3, ahead of his argument in verse 12." Thiselton, *The First Epistle to the Corinthians*, 820.

23. Gordon Fee points to 1 Cor. 8:6, stating that all things (including Adam) were created "through Christ"; man then became the source of woman's being, and God was the source of Christ's incarnation. Cynthia Long Westfall points out that Adam is called "the head of humanity" because he was the source of life, but he is "not given supremacy, honor, authority, or reverence by humanity." Fee, "Praying and Prophesying in the Assemblies," 152. Westfall, *Paul and Gender*, 85

24. Australian scholar Kevin Giles, well known for his writings on the Trinity and the Arian heresy of the subordination of Christ to Father God, states that the meaning of "source" works in this passage because Paul is saying that God is the source of Christ in his incarnation. Gordon Fee agrees that this passage is referring to the incarnational work of Christ; it is not about eternal generation. Kenneth Bailey says this passage "can be seen as an affirmation of the divine source from which Jesus has come and thus an affirmation of his divinity." Giles, *What the Bible Actually Teaches on Women*, 113. Fee, *First Epistle to the Corinthians*, 505. Bailey, *Paul through Mediterranean Eyes*, 302.

25. Paul, who is a very careful writer, uses an order that would not work for the idea of hierarchy/authority. The couplets he uses, in this order, are *Christ-man, man-woman, and God-Christ* (that is, Christ-man-God). This order does work for source, though: *man* came from Christ (the creator of all), *woman* came from man (his side), and *Christ* is from/part of *God*. Several

translations have reportedly changed this order to try to make it hierarchical, including the KJV, Phillips, and NEB.

26. Anthony Thiselton, who wrote an in-depth commentary on 1 Corinthians, says the word for "head" here (*kephale*) "does not seem to denote a relation of 'subordination' or 'authority over.'" Ben Witherington says that whether Paul affirms a male human hierarchy in Christ, that is, in the Christian community, "seems doubtful in view of verses 11ff and in view of the fact that he is quite comfortable talking about women as his coworkers, as fellow servants of God, and possibly even as *apostoloi* (Rom. 16:7)." In an earlier book, Witherington addresses why a meaning of "source" fits the text. Gordon Fee points out that the only time authority is mentioned is to describe the woman's authority (*exousia*) over her own head, and Paul never mentions the man's authority. Fee also states that Paul's concern is "not hierarchical (who has authority over whom)," but "relational, the unique relationships that are predicated on one's being the source of the other's existence." Thiselton, *First Epistle to the Corinthians*, 815–6. Witherington, *Conflict and Community in Corinth*, 238, and *Women in the Earliest Churches*, 84–5. Fee, *First Epistle to the Corinthians*, 502, 503.

27. Thiselton, *First Epistle to the Corinthians*, 815–6.

28. Cohick, *The Letter to the Ephesians*, 356.

29. Gordon Fee states that this "seems to be corroborated by vv. 8–9, the only place where one of these relationships is picked up further in Paul's argument." Fee, *First Epistle to the Corinthians*, 503.

30. Gordon-Conwell Theological Seminary.

31. Kroeger, "Toward an Understanding of Ancient Conceptions of 'Head,'" 4–5.

32. Homer, *Odyssey* 9.140, 13.102, 346. Galen, *On the Doctrines of Hippocrates and Plato*, 6.3.21.4. As cited in Kroeger, "Toward an Understanding of Ancient Conceptions of 'Head,'" 4.

33. Aristotle, *Problemata*, 10.57. As cited in Kroeger, "Toward an Understanding of Ancient Conceptions of 'Head,'" 5. Also see Westfall, *Paul and Gender*, for additional references, 83.

34. Artemidorus Daldianus, ed. Roger Pack, *Artemidori Daldiani Onirocriticon Libri V* (Leipzig: Teubner, 1963) 1.2.7. As cited in Kroeger, "Toward an Understanding of Ancient Conceptions of 'Head,'" 5.

35. Photius, *Commentary on 1 Cor.* 11:3, in K. Staab, *Paulus-kommentare aus der griechischen Kirche aus Katenenhandschriften gesammelt und herausgegeben* (Munster: Aschendorff, 1933) 567.1. As cited in Kroeger, "Toward an Understanding of Ancient Conceptions of 'Head,'" 5.

36. This includes the authors of three highly respected academic commentaries on the book of 1 Corinthians: F.F. Bruce, Gordon Fee, and Kenneth Bailey. In addition, Philip Payne states that the majority view in recent scholarship has shifted to understand head in this passage to mean "source," rather than "authority," and gives a substantial list of such scholars. He also provides fifteen

scholarly reasons why source is the best translation here. N.T. Wright states that the word can mean various things, and "a good case can be made that in verse 3 he [Paul] is referring not to headship in the sense of sovereignty but to headship in the sense of source." Bruce, *I and II Corinthians*, 103. Fee, *First Epistle to the Corinthians*, 502–505. (Also see Fee, "Praying and Prophesying in the Assemblies," 145–55). Bailey, *Paul Through Mediterranean Eyes*, 302. Payne, *Man and Woman*, 117–37. Wright, *Surprised by Scripture*, 75.

37. Richard Cervin believes that "topness" is the best implication that is relevant across the board. Gordon Fee, however, states in contrast that there can be no question that Christ as "head" of the church is the most prominent part of the body, but "this can hardly be Paul's point." Richard Cervin, "On the Significance of Kephale ('Head')." Gordon Fee, "Praying and Prophesying in the Assemblies," 153.

38. It should be noted that studies used to back up such meanings have been strongly criticized for faulty methodology and interpretation. In particular, Wayne Grudem published a study in 1985 based on an analysis of 2,336 occurrences of *kephale* in ancient Greek literature and concluded, as reported by Lynn Cohick, that only 2.1 percent meant "authority over" (87 percent meant a physical head). Cohick says the evidence for *kephale* as "leader" in the usual English sense is "weak and limited." Other scholars have studied each of the passages categorized in the 2.1 percent in the Greek that Grudem points to—a total of 49, and dispute Grudem's interpretation that they all mean "authority" or "leader." These include classics linguist Richard Cervin, who says there are only four cases, not 49, where authority is intended; he says three of these are from the Septuagint and all four are "very likely imported, not native, metaphors." Scholar Gilbert Bilezikian also examined all 49 examples in the Greek and disputes Grudem's findings and methodology. Grudem also stated that authority was a well-established meaning for *kephale* in Greek lexicons, but source was not, when, other scholars tell us, the opposite is true. In addition, important information was reportedly omitted. (Gordon Fee and other scholars speak to these issues.) Nevertheless, this study and a follow-up have been quoted repeatedly as factual and helped to spawn a movement promoting the leadership of men over women that continues to this day (The Council on Biblical Manhood and Womanhood). (Another organization, Christians for Biblical Equality, was created shortly afterward present the opposing viewpoint.) Alan Johnson provides a meta-study of the debate regarding *kephale* with key authors and their publications. Grudem, "Does *Kephale* ('Head') Mean 'Source' or 'Authority Over' in Greek Literature?" and Grudem, "The Meaning of *Kephale* ('Head')," as cited in Cohick, *Letter to the Ephesians*, 130, 356. Cervin, "Does *Kephale* Mean 'Source' or 'Authority Over' in Greek Literature? A Rebuttal." Bilezikian, *Beyond Sex Roles*, 215–52. Fee, *First Epistle to the Corinthians*, 502–3, footnotes 42, 44. Johnson, A Meta-Study of the Debate over the Meaning of 'Head' (*Kephale*) in Paul's Writings."

39. Craig Keener says "the only normal way to read the Greek phrase" is that the woman has "authority over her own head," and she "ought" to demonstrate

NOTES – Chapter 7

it. F.F. Bruce states that the veil [head covering] is "not a sign of the woman's submission to her husband's authority . . . [but] a sign of her authority." Bruce writes, "In Christ she received equality of status with man: she might pray or prophesy at meetings of the church, and her veil [head covering] was a sign of this new authority." Bruce also cites the well-known seminal study of 1963 by Morna Hooker, an honored Cambridge scholar, that clarified the physical and metaphorical sense of *kephale* in this passage and stated that verse ten refers not to a sign of male authority over the woman, but rather to her own authority to fully participate in worship. Keener, *Paul, Women and Wives*, 38. Bruce, *I and II Corinthians*, 106, and "Women in the Church: A Biblical Survey," 10. Hooker, "Authority on Her Head: An Examination of 1 Cor. XI.10."

40. Gordon Fee states that there is "no known evidence that *exousia* is ever taken in a passive sense;" rather, "Paul seems to be affirming the 'freedom' of women over their own heads." Philip Payne states that all 103 occurrences of the Greek word *exousia* (for authority) in the New Testament "refer to authority held in someone's own hand." David Scholer, who taught a seminary class for 36 years on women in Scripture, agrees and says Paul uses a word here that "always means the active exercise of authority," rather than a passive sense of having something done to someone. Cynthia Long Westfall states that "as the subject of the sentence, the nominative 'woman' is the subject of the infinitive, the one who has authority." Fee, *First Epistle to the Corinthians*, 513. 519, 521. Payne, *Man and Woman*, 182. Scholer, "A Biblical Basis for Equal Partnership, Women and Men in the Ministry of the Church." 8. Westfall, *Paul and Gender*, 35.

41. Bruce, *I and II Corinthians*, 103. He also states that the connection between a head covering and authority may have suggested itself the more readily to Paul because of an Aramaic word "found in either sense." Bruce, *An Expanded Paraphrase of the Epistles of Paul*, 99.

42. F.F. Bruce says "we are probably to understand" *head* as "source" or "origin," a meaning that is "well attested." Bruce, *I and II Corinthians*, 103.

43. Kenneth Bailey states that the Greek preposition here, *dia*, "appears four times in a row" in verses 9–10 and should be translated consistently each time as "because," not "for." Then Paul would be saying (in verse 9), "For the man was not created *because of* the woman but the woman because of the man." Bailey, *Paul Through Mediterranean Eyes*, 309–10.

44. Bailey, *Paul Through Mediterranean Eyes*, 307. Gordon Fee states that "there is no usage of 'glory' anywhere in Scripture that would suggest that Paul is here advocating a subordinate relationship by means of this word." Fee, "Praying and Prophesying in the Assemblies," 152.

45. New Revised Standard Version.

46. Metzger, *The Bible in Translation*, 189. He says that ordinarily with a translation, "no more than a description and/or transliteration of the textual features can be given in a footnote." Raymond Elliott, author and former member of Wycliffe Bible Translators, agrees. He states that "Greek and

Hebrew occasionally indulge in punning, but it is usually impossible to transfer the same puns into other languages" and it requires "some degree of compromise." Elliott, "Bible Translation," 257–8.

47. The inside cover of Bailey's book about Paul through Mediterranean eyes gives endorsements by outstanding scholars that illustrate Bailey's expertise. Gary Burge, Professor of New Testament at Wheaton College, says Bailey uses "tools unavailable to the average New Testament scholar: twenty-two ancient translations of 1 Corinthians into Arabic, Syriac, and Hebrew, as well as commentaries dating as far back as ninth-century Damascus;" Burge calls Bailey's book "a gold mine of astonishing new discoveries, cross-cultural insight, and sound pastoral wisdom." David Pao, Chair and Associate Professor of New Testament at Trinity Evangelical Divinity School, says Bailey has read 1 Corinthians "through the lens provided by Arabic, Syriac, and Hebrew translations from the fourth century up to the modern period." Anthony Thiselton, author of a respected commentary about 1 Corinthians, writes: "Ken Bailey is already widely known for shedding light on the New Testament 'through Middle Eastern Eyes.' He has taught in Beirut, Jerusalem and other parts of the Near East, as well as in America and Europe. This commentary is more than a conventional, largely repeated exegesis of 1 Corinthians. Bailey shows the relevance of prophetic and rabbinic forms of language, uses Arabic, Coptic and Syriac sources, and rightly stresses the coherence of this epistle, and its theology of the cross. He is alert to intertextual resonances and offers distinctive ideas." Lynn Cohick, author of various respected volumes and commentaries, writes of Bailey's up-to-date scholarship and "unparalleled knowledge of the New Testament in Arabic translation, coupled with his lifetime of experience in the Middle East." Bailey, *Paul Through Mediterranean Eyes*.
48. Bailey, *Paul Through Mediterranean Eyes*, 298.
49. Bailey, *Paul Through Mediterranean Eyes*, 310.
50. Bailey, *Paul Through Mediterranean Eyes*, 313.
51. Bailey, *Paul Through Mediterranean Eyes*, 313.
52. Richard Hays states that the idea that angels were present in worship can be found in the Dead Sea Scrolls. Hays, *First Corinthians*, 188.

Chapter 8 – Submission?

1. Gordon Fee says "the entire passage in Eph 5:21–6:9 assumes the Greco-Roman villa," the household of the "elite or privileged." Fee says it is difficult to imagine our way back into that Greco-Roman culture, given how different it was from today. Lynn Cohick describes the households that included husband/wife, parent/child, and owner/slave and says they functioned "as an economic unit." Fee, "Praying and Prophesying in the Assemblies," 153, and "The Cultural Context of Ephesians 5:18–6:9," 4, 5. Cohick, *Letter to the Ephesians*, 342–3.
2. Gordon Fee says there was a semi-public aspect to the homes of the elite and

privileged, and many from outside of them could come and join the worship. For a description of the villas, including a typical floorplan, see Fee, "The Cultural Context of Ephesians 5:18–6:9," 5-6. Bruce Winter says the room within a home where the church meetings took place was "readily accessible to anyone" so an outsider could easily enter. Winter, *Roman Wives, Roman Widows*, 88-9, 204.

3. Gordon Fee says slavery then was not based on race, but on conquest in war. Slaves had no rights before the law and could not even marry. Lynn Cohick says slavery was widespread in the ancient world, about "ten percent" of the first-century Roman Empire, with "thirty percent" in Rome. Slaves were crucial for the political, economic, familial, and social hierarchy. An owner "could kill his or her slave with impunity and slaves were routinely beaten." Manfred Brauch says a master could have a slave executed or do it himself. Fee, "The Cultural Context of Ephesians 5:18–6:9," 5, 6. Cohick, *Letter to the Ephesians*, 389, 391. Brauch, "Ephesians," 643.

4. Gordon Fee says the *paterfamilias* was the master of his household and under Roman law his rule was absolute "in that none of the others in the household had legal means to redress any grievances." Cynthia Westfall points to the Roman emperor Octavian, who effectively became "the *paterfamilias* of the empire," supported by a traditional view of the *paterfamilias* of the family having "absolute power" over them. Westfall also states that Greco-Roman society and legislation enforced the "proper" behavior of women. Fee, "The Cultural Context of Ephesians 5:18–6:9," 6. Westfall, *Paul and Gender*, 15, 13.

5. In that culture, the one who provided life, identity, and provision was to be served and honored by the recipient. David deSilva and Cynthia Long Westfall describe the power that honor/shame, and patronage held in that culture. deSilva, *Honor, Patronage, Kinship and Purity*. Westfall, *Paul and Gender*.

6. Eph. 5:18–21.

7. Howard Marshall says Paul's teaching of concern for one another and mutual submission in the church was something new, even startling, with the language. Marshall points out that Paul uses the pronoun for "one another" (*allelous*) in Eph 4:2, 25, 32, thus establishing a presumption in favor of its use here for church members in general. This was a new context instead of the one-sided submission that was expected within certain relationships at that time. Lynn Cohick says mutual submission is a "unique phrase found only here in the New Testament" and that Paul intends with it to "highlight a theme he will then develop in the household codes." Manfred Brauch says the mutual submission "enjoined on believers (in Eph. 5:21) is unique in the known literature of the New Testament world." Marshall, "Mutual Love and Submission in Marriage," 197. Cohick, *Letter to the Ephesians*, 340. Brauch, *Abusing Scripture*, 150.

8. Pope John Paul II, "Mulieris Dignitatem," Section VII, 37–8.

9. Bushnell's book is *God's Word to Women*.

10. Bushnell says Schleusner's Greek-Latin Lexicon to the Septuagint states that this verb does not always "convey the thought of servile subjection." Submission is defined as a "voluntary yielding in love" in Bauer, Arndt, Gingrich, and Danker, *A Greek-English Lexicon of the New Testament and Other Early Christian Literature*. 848. Linda Belleville says "obedience" is following the wishes of a superior, "something demanded of someone in a lesser position;" in contrast, "submission" is a "voluntary act of deferring to the wishes of an equal." Bushnell, *God's Word to Women*, Lesson 38, 133. Belleville, *Women Leaders and the Church*, 118, 171–2. "Submission" has sometimes been translated as "subjection," but reportedly this heavier word was not used in translation until the King James Version of Victorian England.

11. Ben Witherington says the verb *submit* (*hypotasso*), as Paul uses it here for all believers and the wife and husband, "seems to have no precedent in the literature." Witherington, *Letters to Philemon, Colossians, Ephesians*, 320.

12. Belleville, *Women Leaders*, 159.

13. When a wife stayed under the father's authority, this was called *sine manu*. Ben Witherington says there was a patriarchal structure from Aristotle until well after New Testament times. Aida Besancon Spencer says Aristotle uses the Greek word *archo* for ruler, describing the language "of one human 'ruling' another." Lynn Cohick says the household codes [definitions of relationships in the household for marrieds, children, and slaves] "go back to the time of Plato and Aristotle" and are "connected to their political reflections on the state." Aristotle said the ruler is not expected to love those he rules, but those he rules are to love him. Witherington, *Letters to Philemon, Colossians, Ephesians*, 320. Spencer, "Leadership of Women in Crete and Macedonia as a Model for the Church," 11. Cohick, *Letter to the Ephesians*, 344, 358.

14. Lynn Cohick says if Paul had wished to use the verb *obey* when speaking of wives, "he could have done so and would have been well in line with his wider culture that viewed adult women as having much in common with children from a legal standpoint and with regards to rational thought." In addition, Paul "does not ask the husband to remind his wife to submit to him or to obey him, as would the ancient philosophers." Sarah Sumner states that there is more dignity in submitting "voluntarily as a peer than to submit obediently as a subordinate." Cohick, *Letter to the Ephesians*, 366, 374. Sumner, *Men and Women in the Church*, 203.

15. Walter Liefeld says "the manuscripts that are generally considered older and more accurate omit the word *submit* in verse 22." Philip Payne states that "virtually all critical editions of the Greek New Testament" have no verb in Eph. 5:22; only later manuscripts add the word *submit*. Payne also cites Bruce Metzger as saying that the shorter reading "accords with the succinct style of the author's admonitions and explains the other readings as expansions introduced for the sake of clarity." Payne says that by the mid-fourth century, scribes "apparently split the original paragraph after verse twenty-one to make Paul's statements about marriage a distinct unit." In addition, each

surviving manuscript prior to AD 350 omits *submit* and every surviving manuscript after AD 350 includes it. Once included, says Payne, no scribe would remove it. Ben Witherington says the omission of *submit* in verse 22 is surely the correct reading. Lynn Cohick says 5:22 "does not have its own verb but relies on 5:21 and its participle." Liefeld, *Ephesians*, 143. Payne, *Man and Woman, One in Christ*, 278–9. Witherington, *Letters to Philemon, Colossians, Ephesians*, 315, also see footnote 167. Cohick, *Letter to the Ephesians*, 334, 341.

16. This grammatical structure is called an "ellipsis." Witherington, *Letters to Philemon, Colossians, Ephesians*, 317.
17. Paul also speaks to the submission of wives in Col. 3:18, with multiple phrases leading up to the concept of submission that are almost identical to those in Ephesians 5 (including speaking to one another in Psalms, singing spiritual songs, giving thanks). Philip Payne says that "the extensive overlap between these two passages indicates that they deal with the same issues and so can shed light on one another." Paul's goal, says Payne, is the actualization of the "new humanity" where "all members are filled with the Spirit and nurtured in Christ." Payne, *Man and Woman, One in Christ*, 271–2.
18. Ben Witherington writes that Eph. 5:21 calls for the "mutual submission of all Christians to each other," which includes marital partners; "humble serving of each other is what is in mind." He says this verse is not specifically directed to marital partners, "but certainly includes them." Richard Hays says that Paul offers a "paradigm-shattering vision of marriage as a relationship in which the partners are bonded together in submission to one another." Markus Barth writes that a wife's subordination to her husband is commanded "only within the frame of mutual subordination." Pope John Paul writes in his famous encyclical on women that the awareness in marriage that there is mutual subjection of the spouses out of reverence for Christ, and not just that of the wife to the husband, "must gradually establish itself in hearts, consciences, behavior, and customs"; further, any violation of equality in the marriage "diminishes the true dignity of the man." Witherington, *Letters to Philemon, the Colossians, and the Ephesians*, 316, and *Women in the Earliest Churches*, 56. Hays, *First Corinthians*, 131. Barth, *Ephesians 4–6*, 610. Pope John Paul II, "Mulieris Dignitatem," 38, 14–5.
19. Cohick, *Letter to the Ephesians*, 352.
20. Keener, *Paul, Women, and Wives*, 139. Keener was president of the Evangelical Theological Society (2020).
21. Keener, *Paul, Women, and Wives*, 87.
22. Philip Payne states that Paul's stress on love in marriage "contrasts sharply with how rarely the concept of 'love' is mentioned in the non-Christian writings about marriage of that time, even within Judaism." Howard Marshall says this instruction to husbands to love their wives is not only "unusual and unconventional in the world of the New Testament, but the sheer intensity of the love demanded is extraordinary." Manfred Brauch writes that Paul "daringly challenges the culture" when he calls upon husbands to

love (*agapao*) their wives. Lynn Cohick says this verb, *agapao*, is "never used in any household codes outside the New Testament" and is modeled on the self-sacrifice of Christ. Ben Witherington explains that the term *agape* is "not used in the Hellenistic literature in relation to households." Payne, *Man and Woman, One in Christ*, 275. Marshall, "Mutual Love and Submission in Marriage," 199. Brauch, "Ephesians," 642. Cohick, *Letter to the Ephesians*, 361. Witherington, *Letters to Philemon, Colossians, Ephesians*, 329, footnote 224.

23. David Scholer points out that husbands are commanded three times in this passage to love their wives (Eph. 5:25, 28, 33), and this was "not typical in first-century Mediterranean cultures." Lynn Cohick explains that "if Paul were consistent with his times, he would have asked for the wife to sacrifice herself (body) for her husband," not the other way around. Scholer, "The Evangelical Debate over Biblical 'Headship,'" 44. Cohick, *Letter to the Ephesians*, 361.

24. Lynn Cohick points out that Paul "does not say the husband is the Lord *of the wife*;" rather, "the wife's submission to the husband is as valuable as if it is done to Christ himself." Nor is Paul saying "that the wife shows her submission to Christ by submitting to her husband, as if her husband were a substitute for Christ or her intermediary with Christ." Howard Marshall states that what is being done in the passage is that both wives and husbands are to submit to one another "as to the Lord." Cohick, *Letter to the Ephesians*, 353. Marshall, "Mutual Love and Submission in Marriage," 204.

25. Eph. 5:33. Walsh and Miller, "Translating Ephesians 5:33." Westfall, "This is A Great Metaphor!" and "Paul and Gender: Highlights and Bombshells."

26. Manfred Brauch says people in authority are frequently mentioned using different Greek words than *kephale*. Philip Payne says that "hardly any dictionaries of Greek usage up to the time of the New Testament list any instance where 'head' means anything like 'leader' or 'authority,' but many include 'source.'" Brauch, *Abusing Scripture*, 138. Payne, "What About Headship?" 160.

27. Manfred Brauch states that in ancient Greek physiology the physical head is the part "from which the rest of the body receives its life." Gordon Fee says the ancient Greeks thought the literal head had a life-giving role in relation to the physical body. Cynthia Long Westfall explains that in Greek culture a progenitor "involved the representation and identity of the family." The progenitor was likened to the physical head and the descendants to the face. As explained in chapter 7, "source" was an established meaning for "head" (*kephale*) in Paul's time. Brauch, *Abusing Scripture*, 142. Fee, "Praying and Prophesying in the Assemblies," 149. Westfall, *Paul and Gender*, 90.

28. Eph. 5:23. When Paul calls the husband the head of the wife as Christ is the head of the church, his body, savior, Robertson's Grammar identifies this as a grammatical form, an "apposition," where "savior" explains "head." Linda Belleville adds that the lack of an article (the) before *head* and *savior* in the original Greek implies that "these two nouns describe rather than define." Philip Payne points out that many English translations obscure the

grammatical structure of the apposition by adding punctuation, changing the word order, and capitalizing savior. Robertson's *Grammar* 399, as cited in Payne, *Man and Woman, One in Christ*, 283–5, and "What About Headship?" 154. Belleville, "Women in Ministry: An Egalitarian Perspective," 100, Endnote 154, where she also refers to the discussion in Zerwick's *Biblical Greek*.

29. Gordon Fee says the more common sense of *savior* then was "provider/protector and was often used to describe the emperor." Ben Witherington states that the meaning of savior of the body here seems to be that Christ is the protector of the body, not in this case the savior of the world who converts and brings change into a new person. Lynn Cohick says Caesar Augustus, who "brought wars to an end and established peace and order" was called "savior." Fee, "The Cultural Context of Ephesians 5:18–6:9," 8. Witherington, *Letters to Philemon, Colossians, Ephesians*, 328–9. Cohick, *Letter to the Ephesians*, 37.

30. Howard Marshall says "the statement that Christ is the Savior of the body favors an understanding of the husband as essentially the provider, the one who cares for his wife," and there is "nothing more to the analogy than that." The wife is "not her husband's body," and the "Christ-church relationship is an analogy or pattern, not a ground for the wife's submission." Marshall also states that the husband then was the person on whom the wife depended, just as the church depends on Christ; wives depended on their husbands as the source of food, clothing, shelter, children. Gordon Fee says Paul's point in using the metaphor of head/*kephale* in Ephesians is that the householder is the "savior" of his wife "in the sense of being the one on whom the entire household is dependent for their well-being." Fee states that Paul's meaning is the Greek anatomical one, that the body is sustained by its relationship to it most "prominent" part [the head]. Cynthia Long Westfall says the wife is "depicted by Paul as dependent on the husband for her life support (food, clothing, nurture, protection and love) in the same way that the body is dependent on the head for food, water, air, and the senses of sight and hearing." Westfall also points out that Paul does not use "head" to describe the masters of slaves, because "head" in the Pauline corpus was not synonymous then with "master" or "authority." Philip Payne says wives depended on their husbands as the source of food, clothing, shelter, and children. Some have said that because Jesus is head over all rule and authority, then the husband as head is in charge of the wife; Manfred Brauch, however, points out that "Christ and the church are not related in a structure of authority and obedience, of ruler and subject;" rather, the church gives itself to Christ "in awe of and in response to his self-giving." Marshall, "Mutual Love and Submission in Marriage," 198-9. Fee, "Praying and Prophesying in the Assemblies," 151–152, footnotes 32, 33. Westfall, *Paul and Gender*, 95, 88. Payne, *Man and Woman, One in Christ*, 288. Brauch, *Abusing Scripture*, 151.

31. It has been pointed out that poor households, and working husband-and-wife teams like Priscilla and Aquila, would not be an exact analogy to Paul's description here. Lynn Cohick says the three household categories are "stylized categories that constitute the family structure but are not descriptive

of everyone's own life." Gordon Fee states that among the larger masses of people, "very few of these relationships pertain at all." The model has "little to do with villas where women served as heads of households," or "married" slaves (legally they could not marry) when the authority over the wife was the householder, or in relationships like Priscilla and Aquila, who had a "clear sense of partnership" in the marriage and business. Cohick, *Letter to the Ephesians*, 348. Fee, "The Cultural Context of Ephesians 5:18–6:9," 4.

32. Markus Barth says there is no proof that Paul repeated a generally accepted opinion, so "the husband is the head of the wife" must be understood as original with the author of Ephesians. Gordon Fee says there is "no known instance where *kephale* is used as a metaphor for the husband-and-wife relationship; this seems to be unique to Paul." Ben Witherington states that there is "no clear evidence" from the Greek literature of the period that "the husband was seen as the head of the wife and the wife as the husband's body." Witherington also states that Aristotle referred to the head of the household, so Paul may have been adapting this term in a new way for the husband. Barth, *Ephesians 4-6*, 618. Fee, "Praying and Prophesying in the Assemblies," 150, footnote 26. Witherington, *Letters to Philemon, Colossians, Ephesians*, 328.

33. John Stott points out that husbands are not told to exercise authority; rather, Stott says, Paul "warns them against the improper use of their authority." Howard Marshall states that "the injunction to husbands is *not* that they exercise their proper authority; rather there is a quite extraordinary emphasis on the total love and devotion that the husband must show to the wife." Walter Liefeld says "it is striking that there is no command here for the husband to rule his wife. His only instruction is to love and care for her;" and the husband "should not claim authority over his wife the way a Roman man used to." Abusive behavior, Liefeld states, would tend "toward pagan rather than Christian moral standards." Gordon Fee says "the male householder is not told to take his proper role as leader of the household—that was the assumed cultural reality that could so easily be abused. Rather, he is told to model the character of Christ in his relations to his wife and slaves." Markus Barth says Paul does "not stipulate a legislative, juridical, and executive power of the male." Philip Payne states that Paul never says the husband has authority over his wife. Nor is Paul saying that the husband has authority corresponding to the authority Christ has over the church ("that would deify husbands"). Stott, *Message of Ephesians*, 219. Marshall, "Mutual Love and Submission in Marriage," 199. Liefeld, *Ephesians*, 142. Fee, "The Cultural Context of Ephesians 5:18-6:9," 4. Barth, *Ephesians 4-6*, 611. Payne, "What About Headship?" 157.

34. See the prior chapter for a discussion of head (*kephale*).

35. Titus 2:5, Titus 2:9. Paul also calls wives to submission in his treatment of the relationships in a privileged household in Col 3:18. Ben Witherington says in his commentary on Colossians that in 3:18–4:1, "one is profoundly struck by not just the Christian elements but also the social engineering that is being undertaken here to limit the abuse of power by the head of the household."

NOTES – Chapter 8

    Witherington, *Letters to Philemon, Colossians, Ephesians*, 184.

36. 1 Pet. 3:1-2. Ben Witherington points out that Peter personally knew Paul and his rhetoric, and Peter's letter was written after Ephesians as an *ad hoc* pastoral document when Christianity was a persecuted minority religious sect with danger of prosecution, torture, and martyrdom. Cynthia Long Westfall says a "major concern" of the authorities was for the proper behavior of women, and it was believed that disorder in the household was "seditious" for the welfare of the empire. Lynn Cohick says household "harmony" included "the wife's worshiping her husband's gods." Howard Marshall says a wife was normally to adopt her husband's religion. Witherington cites Plutarch as saying that the number-one thing in religion was for a wife to follow her husband's lead. Witherington, *Letters, 1–2 Peter*, 22–3, 39, 133, 163. Westfall, *Paul and Gender*, 13. Cohick, *Letter to the Ephesians*, 360. Marshall, *1 Peter*, 98.

37. Howard Marshall says Paul is indicating the way wives should be submissive within a society where such submission was expected, just as he tells slaves how to be obedient in the slave-master relationship [required by law where they were at risk of death for disobedience]. Craig Keener questions whether Peter's letter prescribes "monarchy, slavery, and patriarchal marriage structures," or rather, counsels within such situations. Keener, an expert in the cultural background of the New Testament, then describes the character of ancient social structures as helpful for readers to decide if they should consider such structures as universal or "merely culturally conditioned." Marshall, "Mutual Love and Submission in Marriage," 199. Keener, *1 Peter*, 210.

38. 1 Pet. 3:7.

39. 1 Pet. 3:5–6. Peter also says in verse 6 that Sarah called Abraham her "master" or "lord." This was not the term Peter used for the master of a slave, and it only occurs when Sarah is laughing to herself about the possibility that she and Abraham, both old, could conceive a child. Craig Keener says this was a polite form of address then. Keener, *IVP Bible Background Commentary*, 716.

40. Rebecca Merrill Groothius, a respected writer who has written works on women in the Bible that have been praised by respected scholars, points out that in Acts 12:13 various translations give this same term as "listen," "hearken," and "answer" rather than "obey." In Rom. 10:16 it is translated variously as "heed" and "listen" or "obey." Groothius, *Good News for Women*, 175.

41. Peter Davids explains that the word translated "obey" in 1 Pet. 3:6 is actually used in the Septuagint [the Old Testament translated into Greek] in Gen. 18:6 to refer to Abraham's "listening to, heeding" Sarah. Davids, "A Silent Witness in Marriage," 232, footnote 36.

42. In Eph. 5:24.

43. David Scholer writes that a Bible published in London in 1549 (a new edition of the 1537 Matthews Bible), included notes by Edmund Becke. At 1 Pet. 3:7, he writes of the wife and husband: "And yf [thus] she be not obedient

and healpful unto hym, endeavoureth to beate the feare of God into her heade." Scholer says "the idea that the Bible may justify and even encourage husbands to compel their wives to obey by force is, regrettably, deep within the tradition and life of the church and has shaped a painful reality for countless anonymous women throughout the last two millenia." He calls the connection between the abuse of women and the Bible a "pervasive and constant theme in literature on the sexual abuse of women." In medieval times, Scholer says, "both civil and church law codes permitted wife beating," with church law often stressing that physical punishment should be done "only with reason." In contrast, *The Cape Town Commitment*, composed in 2010 by an international team of theologians in the Lausanne Movement, says, "We deny that any cultural custom or distorted biblical interpretation can justify the beating of a wife." Scholer, "The Evangelical Debate over Biblical 'Headship,'" 28–9, 35–6. The Lausanne Movement, *The Cape Town Commitment*, 63.

44. Ben Witherington says he agrees that a Christian's unconditional and unquestioned "obedience" is reserved for God and the verb *hypotasso*, often translated as "submit," means something closer to "defer" or "respect." Sarah Sumner writes that Matt. 18 is "God's contingency plan" for marriage. For a discussion of cultivating abuse-free faith communities, see *Created to Thrive*, Elizabeth Beyer. For a true story by a former seminary professor on being a battered wife and how her husband used the Bible to justify his behavior, see Ruth Tucker, *Black and White Bible, Black and Blue Wife, My Story of Finding Hope After Domestic Abuse*. Witherington, *Letters, 1–2 Peter*, 131–2. Sumner, *Men and Women in the Church*, 193.

45. Lynn Cohick says "in everything" has the built-in quality of "only what Christ himself would ask of any believer, including the husband." She says the phrase "as to the Lord" "circumscribes submission to that which a holy God would ask of his follower." Philip Payne says "in everything" is specifically qualified by and depends for its verb on "as the church submits to Christ"; therefore, "since Christ never asks the church to do anything wrong," submission to husbands "does not require submission that would entail doing anything wrong." Ben Witherington says what is assumed is the "ideal situation" (the "nature of praise and wisdom in an epidectic piece of rhetoric"), that "the husband will act as he should, modeling himself on Christ, and that he will not ask of his wife anything that Christ would not want him to ask." Cohick, *Letter to the Ephesians*, 358–9, 353. Payne, *Man and Woman, One in Christ*, 289, and "What About Headship?" 157–8. Witherington, *Letters to Philemon, Colossians, Ephesians*, 326 and footnote 205.

46. 1 Cor. 7:2-34. Philip Payne discusses this passage in Payne, *Man and Woman, One in Christ*, 105–8.

47. Bailey, *Paul Through Mediterranean Eyes*, 202–3.

48. Markus Barth points out that, in contrast to the culture, Paul adresses the wives "as persons who are free and able to make their own decisions." Also, the "solemn address directed to women, 'wives' (literally 'the wives'), recognizes

that they stand on the same level as their husbands." Barth, *Ephesians 4-6*, 611.

49. Lynn Cohick says "it is clear from a grammatical standpoint that Paul is not *commanding* wives to submit." If Paul wanted to command this, "he could have used a finite verb in the imperative, much as he does in his command in 5:25 that husbands love their wives. Cohick, *Letter to the Ephesians*, 341, 352.

50. Eph. 5:31; Gen. 2:24.

51. Walter Liefeld says this is "especially striking against the background of a patriarchal society, when the wife could be absorbed into her husband's household" [though some stayed in their father's household even after marriage]. The meaning here, says Liefeld, is that "the husband must deliberately recognize the new entity of marriage by stepping out of his former family unit and forming a new one with his wife alone." Lynn Cohick says "the Genesis quotation explains the husband's responsibilities to his birth family, so that his wife is not relegated to second-class status." Customs then "assumed that the bride left her family," sometimes moving to a new town. Paul's argument about the unity of Christ and the church, she says, "relies on Jesus' conviction about the indivisible bond between husband and wife in this life." Liefeld, *Ephesians*, 149. Cohick, *Letter to the Ephesians*, 370, 371.

52. Eph. 5:32.

53. Paul calls the Ephesians to "live a life of love" in Eph. 5:2. Lynn Cohick says we need to isolate "the ancient culture" and then understand "Paul's affirmation of or challenge to it." She says Paul is introducing oneness in marriage as a sign of the unity of Christ and the church; he is also introducing reciprocity in marriage, subverting the hierarchical framework and nuancing it "according to gospel principles." Gordon Fee says Paul is calling for relationships within the household that are transformed by the Gospel. Manfred Brauch writes that Paul is trying to produce "an expression of the kingdom of God in the church." Cohick, *Ephesians* [2010 New Covenant Commentary], 140, and Cohick, *Letter to the Ephesians*, 343, 370. Fee, "The Cultural Context of Ephesians 5:18–6:9," 8. Brauch, "Ephesians" 644.

54. Witherington, *Letters to Philemon, Colossians, Ephesians*, 314, 322, and *Women in the Earliest Churches*, 55.

55. Marshall, *1 Peter*, 100.

56. Marshall, "Mutual Love and Submission in Marriage," 202, 194.

Chapter 9 – Teaching and authority over man?

1. Many scholars believe Timothy was in Ephesus (see especially 1 Tim. 1:3). Many scholars do not believe, though, that Paul wrote 1 Timothy, but a strong minority reportedly do. This is due to significant issues with vocabulary, syntax, and style that are different from Paul's normal usage in his other ten letters. Commentaries on 1 Timothy usually discuss this concern. Howard Marshall hypothesizes that 1 Timothy was written shortly after Paul's death, perhaps by his associates in his honor, a known practice at that time. Marshall

believes this was done without deception about the actual authorship then, but knowledge of it was lost over time. Marshall references the "tunnel period," from circa AD 70 to AD 100, when little is known about the life of the church, and states that the Pastoral Epistles (1 and 2 Timothy and Titus) might fit in anywhere in this period without serious difficulty. John Stott decides for Pauline authorship and provides in his commentary a list of early references to 1 Timothy that were "probable" (AD 95 to 117) and "indisputable" (ca. AD 200). Gordon Fee says it cannot be simply assumed that Paul wrote these letters. Marshall, *Pastoral Epistles*, 57–92. Stott, *Message of 1 Timothy & Titus*, 21–34. Fee, *1 and 2 Timothy, Titus*, 23.

2. Lynn Cohick says Artemis was a goddess of "great renown," honored with "worship sites in many of the 2,000 towns and cities across the Roman Empire." Her main temple was about two kilometers from Ephesus' city center, "four times the size of the Athenian Parthenon," and "one of the seven wonders of the ancient world." Aida Besancon Spencer writes that Ephesus "had many myths about Artemis." Ben Witherington says there are many names in the Ephesian inscriptions of women who served as priestesses in the temple of Artemis, and the temple of Artemis was famous and honored throughout the province of Asia and beyond. Walter Liefeld says "there is no question that throughout the empire converts to Christianity had acquaintance with" Artemis and other female deities. Markus Barth writes that as a religious and cultural center, Ephesus and its environment were open to all contemporary religious and secular developments; also, the cult of the Great Mother and the Artemis temple stamped this city more than others as a bastion of women's rights. Cohick, *Letter to the Ephesians*, 34. Spencer, *I Timothy*, 25. Witherington, *Letters, Titus, 1–2 Timothy, 1–3 John*, 219. Liefeld, *1 & 2 Timothy*, Titus, 108. Barth, *Ephesians 4–6*, 661.

3. The livelihoods of the silversmiths who fashioned idols of Artemis were also threatened (Acts 19:23–41). Aida Besancon Spencer says Paul was in Ephesus for about three years. Spencer, *I Timothy*, 13.

4. Lynn Cohick says Artemis was considered the founder and protector of Ephesus and the city "took its responsibility to honor Artemis very seriously." Cohick, *Letter to the Ephesians*, 34.

5. Lynn Cohick explains that Artemis was "known as the protector of women in childbirth;" also, Jewish teaching said women who neglected acts of piety were "doomed to die in childbirth." Cynthia Long Westfall writes that "complications from pregnancy and childbirth were the leading cause of death for women" then; "magic, sacrifices, and prayer" were used for help and protection in time of childbirth. Craig Keener says women regularly called upon patron deities such as Artemis or Isis in childbirth. He says that his reading of ancient prayers for safety in childbirth led him to believe that this passage refers to women being brought safely through childbirth; he also writes that "saved" means "delivered" or "brought safely through" more often in ancient literature than it means "saved from sin." Some scholars believe Paul was pointing to the birth of Jesus as the salvation. Cohick, *Letter to the Ephesians*, 35, and *Women in the World of the Earliest Christians*, 196,

NOTES - Chapter 9

footnote 4. Westfall, *Paul and Gender*, 309. Keener, *Paul, Women and Wives*, 118.

6. Linda Belleville explains that Artemis was believed to be the child of Zeus and Leto; she came out of her mother's womb first and then helped her mother give birth to her twin brother, Apollo. Therefore, she had priority over her brother and other male gods. Artemis and "all her female adherents" were "considered superior" to men. Belleville, *Women Leaders and the Church*, 177, and "Teaching and Usurping Authority," 219.

7. Cynthia Long Westfall says there is "sufficient evidence to suggest that" a myth was "circulating among the women in first-century Ephesus that reversed the accounts of the creation and fall, and it was perhaps an antecedent to the gnostic oral tradition." Richard Clark Kroeger and Catherine Clark Kroeger state that Ephesus had a strong contingent of Jews in Paul's time and "certain elements of Judaism, especially the biblical stories, were adopted by the larger society;" this included "strange distortions of the story of Eve in which she becomes the one who gives life to Adam." Linda Belleville explains that in some systems of thought, "women were elevated as the favored instruments of revelation." This may include beliefs in "an early form of gnosticism." Westfall, *Paul and Gender*, 73-4. Kroeger and Kroeger, *I Suffer Not a Woman, Rethinking 1 Timothy 2:11-15 in Light of Ancient Evidence*, 55. Belleville, *Women Leaders and the Church*, 178, and *1 Timothy*, 55.

8. Aida Besancon Spencer states that Bible scholars at least as early as the AD 400s "have been elaborating on the worship of Artemis as background for the New Testament letters." Linda Belleville discusses the influence of Artemis as well as the possibility of incipient Gnosticism. She says it is a "probable explanation that the women were influenced by the cult of Artemis," with "the female exalted and considered superior to the male" [*Discovering Biblical Equality*, Third Edition/2021, 224.] Belleville says "an Artemis influence would help explain Paul's correctives in 2:13-14," especially if the Ephesian women were being encouraged as the superior sex to assume the role of teacher over men. Belleville believes it is a reasonable conjecture that "the women at Ephesus (perhaps encouraged by false teachers) were trying to gain the advantage over the men by teaching in a dictatorial fashion." Roger Nicole writes that "a good case can be made" that there were certain difficulties in Ephesus, such as its worship of Artemis, that called for correction of the wrongful tendency toward domination by the Ephesian women. N.T. Wright believes Paul is saying that women must be able "to study and learn," not take over as in the Artemis cult, "so that men and women alike can develop whatever gifts of learning, teaching, and leadership God has given them." Craig Keener says an Artemis influence would "certainly explain" Paul's correctives in verses 13-14: "While some may have believed that Artemis appeared first and then her male consort, the true story was just the opposite. For Adam was formed first, then Eve (v.13). And Eve was deceived to boot (v. 14)—hardly a basis on which to claim superiority. It would also explain Paul's statement (v. 15) that 'women will be kept safe through childbirth'. Women turned to her [Artemis] for safe travel through

the childbearing process." Walter Liefeld says that "one of the most obvious theological distinctives in the Pastoral Letters is their repeated designation of God as Savior," and Cynthia Long Westfall states that the name Artemis is said to come from words meaning "safe and sound," and one of her titles was "savior." Westfall also says that "if the text is read on its own terms, several points indicate that the creation summary is used to correct the issues that Timothy faced." Howard Marshall believes that verses 13-15 must be understood as an argument against specific aspects of the heresy, "even if precision is not possible." Also, there may well have been a misreading of material in Genesis as part of the speculative use of myths and genealogies practiced by the writer's opponents, perhaps using Gen. 3:20, where Eve is "the mother of all living." In what is "syntactically something of a parenthesis," says Marshall, "the author rejects the women's claims to any superiority over men by insisting that it was not Adam . . . [who] was the first to be deceived (and sin) but Eve. Marshall says "later Gnosticism is not necessary as a basis in view of the foundation that a realized resurrection doctrine might provide." Manfred Brauch points out that Paul does "not quote the biblical passages directly;" rather he gives a particular understanding of those passages, and he is addressing a limited, local situation that calls for "a limited, partial use of the biblical material." Gordon Fee says that when Gentiles were converted, they could absorb their "philosophical and religious" baggage into their new faith in Christ; also, many Hellenistic Jews appear to have supported a religious mixture. Richard Clark Kroeger and Catherine Clark Kroeger have been strong advocates for applying the historical background as a possible explanation for this passage. Catherine Clark Kroeger writes that there were "strong Ophitic tendencies at the time of the composition of the Pastorals," and the development of the elaborate Gnostic system by the second century is not needed to support her theories. Spencer, *I Timothy*, 15. Fee, *1 and 2 Timothy, Titus*, Understanding the Bible Commentary Series, 9, 40, 41, 70. Belleville, "Teaching and Usurping Authority, I Timothy 2:11-15," 219-221, 223 (and Third Edition/2021, 224); *Women Leaders and the Church*, 177-8, "Women in Ministry: An Egalitarian Perspective," 89-91, and *I Timothy*, 61-2. Nicole, "Biblical Egalitarianism and the Inerrancy of Scripture," 9. Wright, *Surprised by Scripture*, 80-1. Keener, "An Egalitarian Perspective: Belleville," 89-90. Liefeld, *1 Timothy*, 29. Westfall, *Paul and Gender*, 310, 296. Marshall, *Pastoral Epistles*, 441, 442, 443, 463, 466, 467. Brauch, "1 Timothy," 669. Kroeger and Kroeger, *I Suffer Not a Woman, Rethinking 1 Timothy 2:11-15 in Light of Ancient Evidence*, and Kroeger, "1 Timothy 2:12 – A Classicist's View," 242. Also see Glahn, "Artemis of the Ephesians in First-Century Ephesus and Ramifications for How We Read 1 Timothy."

9. Also, some cults opposed marriage and childbearing, so Paul may have been reaffirming them. Aida Besancon Spencer says Artemis was considered a virgin goddess and "the heresy at Ephesus included teachings that forbade marriage and promoted abstinence from foods." Linda Belleville points to the presence of the singular "woman" and the article *the* that could refer to the birth of Jesus. Spencer, *I Timothy*, 74-5. Belleville, *1 Timothy*, 56, 62.

10. 1 Tim. 1:3.

NOTES – Chapter 9

11. Eph. 4:7. Richard and Catherine Clark Kroeger state that "in antiquity old women had a reputation for storytelling which sometimes put the gods in an outrageous light" and "kept alive the ancient myths." Kroeger and Kroeger, *I Suffer Not a Woman, Rethinking 1 Tim. 2:11–15 in Light of Ancient Evidence*, 64.

12. Gordon Fee says "the whole letter is a response to the presence of the false teachers." "Everything in it has to do with 1:3," the charge to Timothy to command certain people not to teach false doctrines; this is both the occasion and purpose of this letter." Fee, *1 and 2 Timothy, Titus*, New International Biblical Commentary, 39, and *1 and 2 Timothy, Titus*, Understanding the Bible Commentary Series, 7.

13. Scholars have pointed to another possible Artemis influence on this passage. They say Paul used the same rare word for braided hair that was used to describe the hairstyle of Artemis that was copied by women to honor her. Aida Besancon Spencer says the "braiding of hair was important in some pagan cults, such as the cult of Artemis of Ephesus or the cult of Isis," and hair could be braided with "hundreds of golden ornaments and pearls." Gary Hoag reports that "the same rare word Paul uses in 1 Tim. 2:9–10" is used in an ancient Greek novel, *Ephesiaca*, to describe a hairstyle worn to imitate Artemis; this novel was recently redated to Paul's time by James O'Sullivan, "based on composition analysis and other archeological evidence." Lynn Cohick says the ancients sought the favor of the gods and goddesses and also cites Xenophon's novel *Ephesiaca*, saying it describes an annual festival where the heroine's hair would hang loose "except for a braided portion" to mimick "that of the goddess." Cohick says 1 Tim. 2:9 specifies braided hair using the cognate noun, "which suggests the Artemisian festivals as a backdrop to Paul's injunction on proper Christian prayers." Sumptuous clothing (also mentioned by Paul in 1 Tim. 2:9) was worn in honor of the goddess. Linda Belleville states that in the Greek, "one preposition followed by two nouns connected by the word *and* expresses a single idea," for example, "with gold-braided hair." The next two nouns are separated by *or*, distinguishing "two different ideas" as follows: "gold-braided hair, or pearls, or costly garments." Spencer, *I Timothy*, 57. O'Sullivan, *Xenophon of Ephesus*, 9. Hoag, *Wealth in Ancient Ephesus and the First Letter to Timothy*, 10, 25, 61, 67, 70, 73, 75, 79, 80, 94, and 99. Cohick, *Letter to the Ephesians*, 35, footnote 147, 36. Belleville, *I Timothy*, 50.

14. Sandra Glahn concludes in a recent study of literary, epigraphic, architectural, and visual primary sources, including many newly uncovered inscriptions and artifacts, that Artemis and her cult "were the context in which Paul was instructing Timothy." Glahn points out that Paul uses the titles for the true God in the introduction to 1 Timothy that "directly challenge" the main titles for Artemis "without naming her directly." Glahn believes that Paul uses the statements "Adam was first" and "Eve was deceived" to seek to "restore interdependence in a goddess-first context that emphasizes female preeminence and autonomy." Glahn also explores the possibility that Paul was referring to husbands and wives in 1 Timothy 2 and not just women in general. Ben Witherington submits that women of higher status, likely with

some education, were trying to take over, having probably been misled by the false teachers. Berkeley Mickelsen says Paul was "not writing about *all* women as a class or group;" Paul "knew many women of great Christian maturity who lived godly lives of ministry and service" and called some of them fellow workers. One of them, Priscilla, "had been a teacher of Apollos in this very city." "To suggest that all women of the first century (and today) were guilty of immodesty, unchastity, or exhibition of wealth," he writes, "is preposterous." He concludes there is nothing in this passage to support the silencing of godly women, forbidding their teaching in church, their call to any form of Christian service, or the use of all the gifts God has bestowed upon them. Glahn, *Nobody's Mother*, 38, 117-8, 133-6, 156. Witherington, *Letters, Titus, 1-2 Timothy, 1-3 John*, 231. Mickelsen, "Who are the Women in I Timothy, Part II."

15. Craig Keener, for example, says that in Paul's other writings, the first can be inferior to the second, as in Jesus being the "second Adam" (1 Cor. 15:45–47). Aida Besancon Spencer points out that the firstborn is "not always chosen to rule, as in the example of David." Also, being deceived is not unique to women; Paul says he himself was deceived (Rom. 7:11), and Adam is a prototype for someone who sins, but knowingly, not by deception as Eve is. Walter Liefeld says that "in the Lord", citing 1 Cor. 11, "chronological order is less important." Manfred Brauch writes that rabbinic tradition, not the Bible, has statements that "women were by nature more vulnerable to deception than men." Linda Belleville points out that in the Ephesian community it was two men, not women, who were expelled for false teaching stemming "from personal deception." Keener, "Women in Ministry: Another Egalitarian Perspective," 241. Spencer, *1 Timothy*, 70, 71. Liefeld, *1 & 2 Timothy, Titus*, 110. Brauch, "1 Timothy," 669, 670. Belleville, *Women Leaders and the Church*, 179.

16. Rom. 5:12, 14–19. 1 Cor. 15:21–22.

17. This word was rare even outside the New Testament, complicating its translation. Howard Marshall says he does not believe the verb here conveys a neutral sense of having authority; rather, meanings of "autocratic or domineering abuses of power and authority" appear to be more "naturally linked" with the verb given the meanings of the associated (cognate) nouns. Ben Witherington says it is "reasonable to conclude" that the meaning of "domineer" is the appropriate one for this verse; he points out that the entire context is negative, correcting problems. Gordon Fee also gives a connotation of "domineer." Linda Belleville states that the "mere handful" of five examples that scholars have found of this verb around Paul's time have varied meanings in context (as Greek words can); these include "committing an act of violence," "authoring/delivering a message of something striking," "taking a firm stand," "being a powerful lord," and one planet "dominating" another. Belleville says that grammatically, if Paul had a routine exercise of authority in mind, "he would have put it first, followed by *teaching* as a specific example." Philip Payne agrees that the few examples do not indicate a routine use of authority. He says Knight and Baldwin, who have advocated

for such a meaning, "err procedurally" in ignoring the meanings of the associated noun; he also says Werner has been misquoted regarding one of these passages (about payment by another man's slave on a ferry), and Werner says it should be translated "assume authority to oneself," not "have authority." (Both Payne and Belleville address the debate, positions by other scholars, and misquotations of other scholars' work.) Aida Besancon Spencer says the associated noun (cognate), as "used by Jewish writers contemporary to Paul clearly has negative connotations;" Josephus used it to describe assassins and murderers, and Diodorus of Sicily used it to describe "perpetrators of a sacrilege," and the "author of a crime." She concludes the verb is similar to the "negative type of leadership Jesus portrays for the Gentile rulers." Cynthia Long Westfall states that "the people who are the targets" of this verb are "harmed, forced against their will (compelled), or at least their self-interest is overridden." Marshall, *Pastoral Epistles*, 456-457. Witherington, *Letters, Titus, 1-2 Timothy, 1-3 John*, 228, and *Women in the Earliest Churches*, 121. Fee, *1 & 2 Timothy, Titus*, 73. Belleville, *Women Leaders in the Church*, 175-6, and "Women in Ministry: An Egalitarian Perspective," 78-89, 95-97, and "Teaching and Usurping Authority, I Timothy 2:11-15," 212-9. Payne, *Man and Woman, One in Christ*, 361-97. Spencer, *I Timothy*, 63. Westfall, *Paul and Gender*, 292.

18. Philip Payne says Paul refers to the exercise of authority in many passages, but does not use this rare word in any of them. Aida Besancon Spencer provides a list of twelve Greek words Paul used elsewhere for "authority" that he could have used in 1 Tim. 2:12. Payne, *Man and Woman, One in Christ*, 375. Spencer, *I Timothy*, 64.

19. Linda Belleville provides a list of the translations. The oldest that she lists, the Old Latin and Vulgate, both give the meaning of "domineer." The translations in the 1500s and 1600s, including the Victorian-era King James Version, give a meaning of "usurping" or "taking authority over the man." Translations starting in the 1900s give "domineer," "dictate to," and "take authority." Belleville, "Teaching and Usurping Authority," 209-10, and *1 Timothy*, 59.

20. Prior to 2011, the world's most widely used translation, the NIV (New International Version) said "have authority over a man." In 2011, however, the NIV changed to "assume authority over a man." Some scholars have pointed out that it is still not clear, however, exactly what assuming authority over a man means in practice and whether women teaching men under any circumstances is clearly prohibited. Different churches interpret it different ways. Some say women can teach and preach on the mission field, but not in their home countries. Some say women can teach in Bible studies, or seminaries, but not from a church pulpit. Some say *authentein* refers to "juridical authority in the church or the transmission of the authoritative teaching of the church, but such a view," says Gordon Fee, "assumes a much more advanced structure for the church than actually emerges in these letters." Ben Witherington says the verb here for "teaching" (*didasko*) is "simply a general one for teaching" and "does not in itself (nor from the context) suggest a particular kind teaching" such as authoritative teaching

or preaching. It has also been noted by scholars that this verb can be used to convey negative teaching, not just any kind of teaching, as seen in several other passages of Scripture, including Mat. 5:19a, Titus 1:11, and Rev. 2:14, 20. Fee, *1 and 2 Timothy, Titus,* Understanding the Bible Commentary Series, 77. Witherington, *Letters, Titus, 1-2 Timothy, 1-3 John,* 227.

21. David Scholer reports that in 1988 Leland Edward Wilshire published findings about the word *authentein* as found in a database that had recently been compiled; it was said to include virtually all of the 3,000 ancient Greek authors from Homer to AD 600 and was called the *Thesaurus Linguae Graecae* (TLG). The TLG found only 330 occurrences of *authentein* and its cognates (related forms) in all of these writings, which still makes it a rare word. Scholer reports that "Wilshire's study and summary of the evidence clearly and strongly supports the view that *authentein* carries almost exclusively a negative meaning in Paul's Greek context," supporting the idea of "domineer," "usurp," or "some such translation." Wilshire reportedly stated that the meaning "to have authority over" is "increasingly to be questioned." Linda Belleville also reports on the initial article by Leland Wilshire and that he "subsequently revised" it with a clearly "different conclusion." Scholer, "The Evangelical Debate over Biblical Headship," 45–50. Belleville, "A Complementarian Perspective: Responses," 201.

22. Philip Payne says the first instance of *authentein* that was confirmed to mean "exercise authority" is ca. AD 370 in Saint Basil, *The Letters* 69, line 45: "he [the bishop of Rome] may himself exercise full authority in this matter, selecting men capable of enduring the hardships of a journey." Payne, *Man and Woman, One in Christ,* 374–5.

23. Ben Witherington says that early church father John Chrysostom advises husbands not to *authentein* their wives. Witherington gives the Greek as *me . . . epeide hypotetaktai he gyne authentei* and says it should be translated, "Do not be despotic or domineer the woman (wife)." Witherington also cites Quinn and Wacker as observing that the church fathers even knew the usage of this verb to mean "to tyrannize" or "to act arbitrarily." Witherington, *Letters, Titus, 1-2 Timothy, 1-3 John,* 227.

24. Linda Belleville recounts that Knight has interpreted the verse as "I exercised authority over him" (1984), and this interpretation has been influential in evangelical scholarship. She says the "preposition *pos* plus the accusative *auton* does not bear this sense in Greek;" she states that the range of meanings are "to/towards," "against," and "with" (and less frequently "at," "for," "with reference to," "on," and "on account of." She cites BAGD *pros* + the accusative. Belleville, *1 Timothy,* 55.

25. Five years after publishing his initial study, Wilshire had apparently been misquoted in various studies. So he published a statement that his study differed from that of George Knight III at all crucial points, and it is "a grave misunderstanding" to think that they arrived at the same conclusion that Paul is simply speaking of any kind of authority by women over men. Rather, Wilshire concludes that the word implies instigating violence

and probably refers to the widows of 1 Tim. 5 who were spreading false teaching and instigating violence in the church. Philip Payne also recounts misunderstandings of scholars' work regarding *authentein*. See Scholer, "The Evangelical Debate over Biblical Headship," 45–50. Payne, *Man and Woman, One in Christ*, 365–9.

26. Philip Payne states that Paul uses this construction this way in the "overwhelming majority" of cases; in fact, there is "not a single unambiguous case" where Paul joins two conceptually distinct expressions with *oude* to convey two separate ideas. Payne was reportedly the first scholar to present a thorough analysis on these connectors publicly to a meeting of scholars (1986). According to Linda Belleville, Andreas Kostenberger then replied that based on other examples in Scripture, both terms have to be either negative or positive to be combined, indicating that "teach" and "have authority" should not be combined into one concept. Belleville then responded that Kostenberger's methodology was flawed because both terms function in Greek syntax as "infinitival nouns" and should be combined into one concept. Belleville cites examples in Scripture where *ouk/oude* can pair opposites; she states that the *ouk/oude* construction can serve to define a single, coherent idea and believes that is the best understanding in this verse. Ben Witherington says the "entire context" of the passage is negative, "dealing with correcting problems, and this dictates that we should see 1 Tim. 2:12 as correcting some sort of abuse of power and teaching privilege here." Payne, "*Oude* in 1 Timothy 2:12," Evangelical Theological Society Annual Meeting, Atlanta, GA, Nov, 21, 1986; revised and published as "1 Timothy 2.12 and the Use of *Oude* to Combine Two Elements to Express a Single Idea," NTS 54 (2008):235-53; as referenced in Payne, *Man and Woman, One in Christ*, 337; also see 338, 344, 348. Kostenberger, "A Complex Sentence Structure in 1 Tim. 2:12,"81–103 (as referenced in Belleville, following). Belleville, "Teaching and Usurping Authority," 217–9, "Women in Ministry: An Egalitarian Perspective," 97–8, and *1 Timothy*, 55. Witherington. *Letters, Titus, 1-2 Timothy, 1-3 John*, 228.

27. Ancient Greek is known for the difficulty of translating its verbs. Larry Walker says the Greek verb system is complicated and capable of nuances of meaning that are difficult to express in English. He explains that "each Greek verb has five aspects, . . . tense, mood, voice, person, and number;" and these are "often hard to translate into English." The "time of action and the verb stem's basic meaning (such as whether it takes an object) must be subtly blended with the kind of action into a single idea." He also says that the complex syntax of the Greek language allows intricate word arrangements to express fine nuances of meaning. He adds that New Testament Greek was "free," often "creating its own idiom," with words frequently taking on "new meanings in the context of the Gospel." Walker, "Biblical Languages," 230, 233, 234, 236, 237.

28. Payne, *Man and Woman, One in Christ*, 350–351. Victor Walter says Origen of Alexander (c. AD 185 to 255) is "the greatest textual scholar of all antiquity" and "produced antiquity's most massive Bible, the *Hexapla*," used

by Jerome for his work on the Vulgate. (It later disappeared during war.) Walter, "Versions of the Bible," 319-20.

29. Linda Belleville says this translation would fit well with the next words, that teaching should be done in a calm [not silent] manner. Belleville also says such a translation would solve a grammatical difficulty in the sentence that arises when the two verbs are translated separately. Belleville states that Louw and Nida's lexicon gives another meaning of *authentein* as "to shout orders at" or "bark at." ("Women in Ministry," 85, footnote 126.) It can also mean to "give orders" or "dictate to." Such meanings would also fit well with the following verse that a woman must be calm (not silent). Philip Payne also combines the verbs into one new concept and believes that "to assume authority to teach a man" has the best lexical support and fits the context best. Belleville, "Teaching and Usurping Authority," 219, "Women in Ministry: An Egalitarian Perspective," 82-9, 95-98, and *1 Timothy*, 60. Payne, *Man and Woman, One in Christ*, 395-6.

30. Linda Belleville says the root form (*auto+entes*) literally means to "originate something with one's own hand." Catherine Clark Kroeger writes that *authenteo* is used by the early church fathers "for the creative activities of God." Belleville, "Teaching and Usurping Authority," 212. Kroeger, "I Timothy, A Classicist's View," 230.

31. Catherine Clark Kroeger states that in the late Renaissance era, "scholars studied classical texts more thoroughly than is customary today, and they had materials to which we no longer have access." Catherine and Richard Kroeger say the "widely used" work of Cornelius Schrevel (1823) and the "still-fundamental" *Thesaurus Linguae Graecae* by Stephanus (1831 to 65) gave a meaning for *authentein* as "to represent oneself as the author, originator, or source of something." For example, they say, Saint Basil asked when was he was supposed to have professed himself (*authenton*) to be the author of an anathema against his old friend Dianius. (The Kroegers say this meaning disappeared from dictionaries in the mid-1800s, about the time 1 Tim. 2:12 was being challenged by feminists.) Catherine Kroeger proposes, therefore, that 1 Tim. 2.12 could have the meaning of "I do not allow a woman to teach nor represent herself as the originator or source of man." Linda Belleville states that the *Bibliotheca Historica* of that time (a historical library of 40 books) uses the noun form of *authentein*, which was more common, to describe the perpetrators of a sacrilege. [Teaching that woman was the originator of man would certainly be a sacrilege to Paul and may have been part of his intent with choosing this rare verb in light of the noun's meaning.] Kroeger, "1 Timothy, A Classicist's View," 230-2, and Kroeger and Kroeger, *I Suffer Not a Woman, Rethinking 1 Timothy 2:11-15 in Light of Ancient Evidence*, 102-3. Belleville, "Teaching and Usurping Authority," 212-3.

32. Some scholars have concluded that women are prohibited from teaching or exercising authority because of the creation order. See, for example, Schreiner, "An Interpretation of 1 Timothy 2:9-15." Kostenberger and Kostenberger, *God's Design for Man and Woman*.

33. Gordon Fee says the phrase is Paul's personal instruction, implying specific instructions to this situation. Aida Besancon Spencer explains that "I am not permitting" is in the "first person singular present indicative" and "appears to describe an action Paul is encouraging Timothy to do now." It is not in the imperative as in 1 Tim. 2:11–12. It refers not to commands but allowable acts, as in Jesus saying that Moses permitted divorce. Philip Payne says Paul often chose the first person singular ("I") present active indicative ("am not permitting") "to indicate his own personal advice or position for a situation that is not universal;" he uses the identical grammatical construction four times (in 1 Cor. 7:7, 26, 32, and 40) and again in Phil. 4:2 to express his "current desire or conviction, not a universal demand." New International Biblical Commentary, *1 and 2 Timothy, Titus*, 72. Spencer, *I Timothy*, 61-2. Payne, *Man and Woman, One in Christ*, 320.

34. Philip Comfort distinguishes between literary works, such as the Gospels and Acts, and New Testament "occasional" letters written primarily to address the need of the occasion. Gordon Fee and Douglas Stuart suggest that "recognition of a degree of cultural relativity is a valid hermeneutical procedure and an evitable corollary of the occasional nature of epistles." Comfort, "Texts and Manuscripts of the New Testament," 207. Fee and Stuart, *Reading the Bible for All Its Worth*, 81.

35. Philip Payne gives more than eight reasons why it is more likely that Paul is giving Timothy specific instructions for dealing with false teaching in Ephesus rather than writing "a manual of rules for church order." Payne, *Man and Woman, One in Christ*, 305–10.

36. Tucker and Liefeld, *Daughters of the Church*.

37. Liefeld, *1 & 2 Timothy, Titus*, 109. Walter Kaiser says it was "revolutionary" to have a command that women were to learn, and the English does not have a comparative form, so it sounds like "mere permission." Kaiser, "Correcting Caricatures: The Biblical Teaching on Women," 8.

38. Walter Liefeld writes that the low level of women's education, "especially religious education," would be relevant to the command to learn and the restriction. Liefeld, *1 & 2 Timothy, Titus*, 104, 109.

39. Aida Besancon Spencer says that "in an educational setting, [this concept] refers to the state of calm, restraint at the proper time, respect and affirmation of a speaker." Howard Marshall says the subjection is to teachers, not husbands, and the description here is of men and women, with nothing suggesting just husbands and wives (as some translations say). Ben Witherington says the subordination is not specifically to men; "rather, it seems to be in relationship to the authoritative teaching." Linda Belleville says that "submissively" modifies "learn"—that is, women are to learn "calmly" and "submissively." Spencer, *I Timothy*, 59. Howard Marshall, *Pastoral Epistles*, 444, 454. Witherington, *Letters, Titus, 1-2 Timothy, 1-3 John*, 222. Belleville, *1 Timothy*, 54.

40. Spencer, *Beyond the Curse*.

41. Aida Besancon Spencer gives quotes from rabbis in her book *Beyond the Curse*, 77–80. Also see Spencer, *I Timothy*, 58–60.
42. Spencer, *Beyond the Curse*, 75–7.
43. Linda Belleville says the idea of a respectable, "well-considered demeanor" fits the text better than "modest." Belleville, *1 Timothy*, 51–2.
44. Walter Kaiser says the Greek word is *hosautos*, and some translations do not include the translation for this word, or soften it to "I also want . . . ." Kaiser says Paul is wanting the women to participate with the men in the public service of the church by offering prayers. "There can be no debate over this point," he says, given the presence of *hosautos*. Ben Witherington says this word must be taken seriously and suggests "Paul is envisioning women praying as well, and he wishes them to do so with the same decorum or holiness required of the men." Aida Besancon Spencer says this verse has an ellipsis that would refer back to prayer. Linda Belleville says "the Greek of verses 9-10 lacks a subject and a main verb, thereby tying these verses with what precedes" them. She says the text is literally: "I want to pray—the men . . . likewise the women." Kaiser, "Correcting Caricatures, the Biblical Teaching on Women," 8. Witherington, *Letters, Titus, 1-2 Timothy, 1-3 John*, 224. Spencer, *I Timothy*, 53. Belleville, *1 Timothy*, 53.
45. 1 Cor. 11:5.
46. 1 Tim. 5:13. This also reportedly includes the author of the first study on *authentein* in the computerized database, Leland Wilshire, who is said to have offered a major option that the word implies "instigating violence" and probably refers to the widows of 1 Tim. 5 who were spreading false teaching, and with it, instigating violent reactions in the church. As reported by Scholer, "The Evangelical Debate over Biblical Headship," 45–50.
47. Gordon Fee reportedly cites BAGD's reference to "Josephus," *Vita* 150 with a meaning of "gossipy" an as error; he says that neither occurrence of this word in Josephus can mean "gossipy"; BDAG 1060 also appeals to Plutarch, *Mor.* 39a, but it means "foolish talk," not "gossipy"; 169e, but it means "foolish," not "gossipy"; and 701a, but it means "nonsense," not "gossipy"; nor does LSJ list the meaning "to gossip." Craig Keener writes that Fee has demonstrated to him that a survey of every use in extant Greek literature of the word translated "busybodies" in 5:13 reveals that the word was used for those speaking nonsense; in moral and philosophical texts it typically refers to those spreading false or improper teaching. Fee, "Great Watershed," 37, as cited in Payne, *Man and Woman*, 301, footnote 22. Keener, "Women in Ministry: Another Egalitarian Perspective," 232.
48. David Scholer says a "staggering number of evangelical scholars and writers, many of whom are especially known for their defense and support of biblical authority, have understood 1 Tim. 2:9-15 as a limited text." He also cites an author as early as 1666, Quaker Margaret Fell, who said the passage is "directed only against the deviating women" going house to house as described in 1 Tim. 5:11-15. He also cites authors in the 1800s, including Catherine Booth of the Salvation Army, A.J. Gordon, who began Gordon-

NOTES – Chapter 9

Conwell Seminary, and others, who all argued that 1 Tim. 2:9–15 is "limited to a particular situation." Scholer, "I Timothy 2:9–15 and the Place of Women in the Church's Ministry," 215–7.

49. Howard Marshall also says that because Eve's deception is cited as a parallel, "this strongly suggests the conclusion that behind the present prohibition lies some particular false teaching by some women." Marshall, *Pastoral Epistles*, 458, 460, 455.

50. Ben Witherington says the issue is not women teaching *per se*, or teaching men, in light of Priscilla (who was trained by the apostle himself), but "untrained and unauthorized women" who were "seeking to teach and domineer men" and need to be learning. Witherington says "Rom. 16:1–16 indicates an abundance of women were involved in some form of ministry, and Phil 4.2–3 intimates the same." Witherington, *Letters, Titus, 1–2 Timothy, 1–3 John*, 232, and *Women in the Earliest Churches*, 122, 125.

51. Fee and Stuart, *How to Read the Bible for All Its Worth*, 85. Gordon Fee says elsewhere that the purpose of this letter is not to be a church manual but for Paul to urge Timothy to stop the false teachers in Ephesus. It is "an ad hoc document," he says, "a piece of correspondence occasioned by a set of specific history circumstances." He believes it is a mistake to see Timothy and Titus as model pastors for a local church, because both were itinerants on assignment, not permanent pastors. Fee, *1 and 2 Timothy, Titus*, Understanding the Bible Commentary Series, xiv, 5, 21, 22.

52. F.F. Bruce has written commentaries on every one of Paul's epistles and is the author of more than forty books and nearly two thousand articles and reviews. He says in his commentary on Galatians that Paul states the basic principle in Gal. 3:28, and if apparent restrictions on this verse are found elsewhere in the Pauline corpus, as in 1 Cor. 14:34 or 1 Tim. 2:11, "they are to be understood in relation to Gal. 3:28, and not *vice versa*." In general, Bruce says, where there are divided opinions about the interpretation of a Pauline passage, that interpretation which runs along the line of liberty is much more likely to be true to Paul's intention than one which "smacks of bondage or legalism." Bruce asks, "If a Gentile may exercise spiritual leadership in church as freely as a Jew, or a slave as freely as a citizen, why not a woman as freely as a man?" Bruce, *Epistle to the Galatians*, 189–90. Gasque and Gasque, "Saint Paul, Apostle of Freedom for Women and Men, an Interview with F.F. Bruce," 2, 3, 4. Also see Bruce, "Women in the Church: A Biblical Survey." More about Bruce is also included in the next chapter.

53. David Scholer says that opposition to women in ministry has often been mounted on the basis of just one Pauline text, 1 Tim. 2:11–12. "Whatever that difficult text and context means it must be put in balance with all other biblical texts which bear on the same issue. This shows, in my judgment, that the 1 Timothy text does, in fact, speak to a limited situation." Scholer, "A Biblical Basis for Equal Partnership," 14, 15, 16. Also see Scholer, "Women," 880–7.

54. David Scholer points out that two axioms for Bible understanding have

"wide, general acceptance:" any viewpoint claiming to be "biblical" should be "inclusive of all the texts that speak to that particular issue;" and "clearer texts should interpret less clear or ambiguous texts." Craig Keener states that we should not allow our traditions or "an (at best) uncertain (and most likely mistaken) interpretation of a single passage to deny the calling of women who otherwise prove themselves fit for ministry." Scholer, "1 Tim. 2:9–15 and the Place of Women in the Church's Ministry," 212–3. Keener, "Another Egalitarian Perspective," 248.

55. Craig Keener says "the one passage in the Bible that specifically prohibits women from teaching is addressed to the one church where we know false teachers were effectively targeting women." Ben Witherington suggests that one should look for "positive repeated patterns," and "repetition is the key clue." He also says "there is no shortcut or substitute for doing the hard work of interpretation before one gets to the point of application." Keener, "Women in Ministry: Another Egalitarian Perspective," 232. Witherington, *Reading and Understanding the Bible*, 108, 111.

56. Roger Nicole says that in interpreting Timothy, our understanding of Paul's prohibition has to remain "conscious of what he has permitted." Nicole, "Biblical Egalitarianism and the Inerrancy of Scripture," 7.

57. Nicole, "Biblical Egalitarianism and the Inerrancy of Scripture," 7.

Chapter 10 – Church Leadership?

1. Acts 1:14–15, 2:1. Also see chapter 5.

2. Aida Spencer states that church meetings were not in prominent buildings until after Emperor Constantine's era, around AD 300. Spencer references Eusebius' *Ecclesiastical History*, 10.3-4. Spencer, "Leadership of Women in Crete and Macedonia as a Model for the Church," 5.

3. The Bible references more churches meeting in the homes of women than in the homes of men. See Acts 12:12 (Mary); Acts 16:14-15, 40 (Lydia); Rom. 16:3-5 and 1 Cor. 16:19 (Priscilla and Aquila); 1 Cor. 1:11 (Chloe); Col. 4:15 (Nympha); Phlm. 2 (Philemon, Apphia, "our sister," and Archippus), and possibly Stephana (1 Cor. 16:15, 17), which could be a man or woman's name. Some also consider the "elect lady" in 2 John 1 to be a house church leader.

4. Gordon Fee says first-century sociology makes it most probable that those who were appointed as "overseers" in the early churches (especially since we are dealing with house churches) were in fact the owners of the dwellings where the churches met. He says the little evidence we do have implies that the overseers were from among the earliest converts and "were normally appointed to such positions." Linda Belleville says the patron of the group, who provided the meeting place for a local club or religious organization, "was in charge of the group, including some legal responsibility." Fee, *1 & 2 Timothy, Titus*, 79, 82. Belleville, *Women Leaders and the Church*, 52.

5. Linda Belleville writes that the term "authority" appears more than one hundred times in the New Testament, but not in connection with church

leadership. She says "the closest we come is Titus 2:15," where Paul instructs Titus to "rebuke with all authority," but this is "as Paul's deputy, not as a local church leader." Belleville points out that this statement does not use Paul's normal Greek word for authority, *exousia*, the right to govern, but rather *epitage*, meaning "the right to command;" so a better translation would be "show that you have every right to command when you rebuke." She also states that it is the church, not individuals, that has the authority (Mat. 16:18-20; 18:18-20). Further, "the church's authority derives from the power of the Lord Jesus that is present with believers gathered in his name." Belleville, *Women Leaders and the Church*, 134.

6. Fee, *1 & 2 Timothy, Titus*, 21-2, and "The Priority of Spirit Gifting for Church Ministry," 251.

7. 1 Cor. 14:26.

8. 1 Cor. 11:5. Gordon Fee says Paul is "undoubtedly" referring to the church gathered for worship. Fee, *God's Empowering Presence*, 145.

9. Rom. 12:6-8, 1 Cor. 12:4-11, 1 Cor. 12:28-31, Eph. 4:7-13. Gordon Fee says "the New Testament evidence is that the Holy Spirit is gender inclusive, gifting both men and women." Fee, "The Priority for Spirit Gifting for Church Ministry," 254.

10. *Thayer's Greek-English Dictionary of the New Testament*, 444, *anthropos*. Ephesians 4:7-8 says Jesus gave gifts to mankind when he ascended on high. Paul continues this train of thought in the following verses, explaining what "ascended" means, and then that it was Christ who gave some to be apostles, prophets, evangelists, pastors and teachers. Linda Belleville (with other scholars) explains that a single Greek article comes before "pastors and teachers" and "conceptually unites the two nouns." Therefore, this grammatical arrangement should be translated as "pastor-teacher." In practical terms, she says, this would mean that the task of pastoring is inseparable from the task of teaching. Belleville, *Women Leaders and the Church*, 58, 140.

11. Ben Witherington states that Paul's hierarchy of leadership is determined primarily by calling and gifting from the Holy Spirit, "not at all by gender or cultural background." Witherington, *Conflict & Community in Corinth*, 290.

12. Gordon Fee says the fact that "overseer" is singular in one passage has led some to believe in a single person as pastor, but that is "almost certainly generic" and it is a mistake to see Timothy or Titus as model pastors for a local church, because they were "itinerants on special assignment." Walter Liefeld points out that "the early church had no equivalent to the Old Testament priesthood," nor is there evidence that one person with special authorization "presided" at the Lord's Supper. Further, ordination is "not found in its usual modern sense in the New Testament or in early Christianity;" the practice as we know it did not develop until the third century. In addition, Liefeld says the word *office* itself is "not a New Testament term;" it can be traced to the King James Version but is not in the original Greek. Linda Belleville says the governing authority of a senior pastor is a "modern convention." Fee,

1 & 2 Timothy, Titus, 84, 21. Liefeld, "The Nature of Authority in the New Testament," 264, 267, 268, 261. Belleville, *Women Leaders in the Church*, 151.

13. Gordon Fee says that from the beginning of the Christian churches, leadership was "in the hands of several people who had apparently been appointed by the apostle and his coworkers" (per town, or in larger cities, per house church); "in all cases leadership was plural." Fee also says that for Paul, "the obvious leader" of the churches was the Holy Spirit. Love Sechrest states that, "without question," in Paul's eyes "the Spirit is the primary vehicle for religious conduct." Linda Belleville says "elder" is "consistently plural in form" and "defines a corporate identity (*the elders*) rather than a specific function." Belleville points out that we have no job description for them except that they must be "hospitable, able to refute false teaching, and committed to sound doctrine." Aida Besancon Spencer and William Spencer write that Paul introduces a new concept for the church, "mutual honor and the reciprocating of honor," which takes humility. Also, they emphasize, "Jesus and Paul warn against authority that tyrannizes, dominates, and is self-centered," contradicting "bullying and unwarranted entitlements." Further, the prevention of the misuse of authority rests in the "plurality of leaders" who are being "dependent on God." Fee, *1 & 2 Timothy, Titus*, 21–2, and "The Priority of Spirit Gifting for Church Ministry," 251. Sechrest, *A Former Jew*, 179. Belleville, *Women Leaders in the Church*, 143–44. Spencer and Spencer, *Christian Egalitarian Leadership*, 13, 19.

14. Walter Liefeld says churches founded by Paul at least had plural leadership by elders and whatever role the elders played, and it would apparently be to "lead the whole church in the decision-making process." He points out that the New Testament does not say that individuals or groups possessing an ongoing authority made the decisions. Liefeld, "The Nature of Authority in the New Testament," 263, 266, 267.

15. The generic Greek word *tis* in 1 Tim. 3:1. Spencer, *I Timothy*, 78.

16. Philip Payne says there are not any masculine pronouns or "men only" requirements for the offices of overseer and deacon in 1 Tim. 3:1-12, or elder in Titus 1:5-9. Aida Spencer clarifies that gender in the Greek grammar categorizes words into masculine or feminine for word classes, and the modifier needs to match the gender of the word it modifies. So in 1 Tim. 3:4, 5, the modifier "own" of "household" is masculine, but this is only because the Greek word *household* is characterized as masculine and neither word indicates actual sex or gender. Payne, *Man and Woman, One in Christ*, 445. Spencer, *I Timothy*, 84.

17. Cynthia Westfall states that "one-woman man" was "a catchphrase or idiom" in that time meaning "marital faithfulness (if married)," not a requirement for maleness or marriage. Philip Payne says most scholars, himself included, agree that Paul was excluding polygamy and adultery here, which was legal for Jewish men in that time, not requiring that elders be men. Payne lists eight academic reasons why "one-woman man" does not exclude women from being overseers and notes that the term "overseer" in 1 Tim. 3:1 is never used

NOTES - Chapter 10

with the name of any man. He calls it "bad hermeneutics" to isolate a single word (*man*) from the set phrase (one-woman man) and "elevate that single word to the status of an independent requirement." Gordon Fee concludes that the intent here is for the church's married leaders to live exemplary lives. Aida Besancon Spencer concludes that "one-woman man" probably meant to be faithful in marriage (if married), devoted to and focused on only one woman. She quotes Jewish law that a man could have relations with other women without it being considered adultery, unless it was with another man's wife; a woman, however, had to remain strictly faithful to her husband. Paul's standard of monogamy in marriage, Spencer explains, stood in contrast to Roman and Greek standards when it was acceptable (not considered adultery) for married men to have sexual relations with slaves, concubines, and prostitutes. A one-woman man, Spencer says, would be one who joined fast to his wife and was one flesh with her. Linda Belleville points out that similarly in 1 Tim. 5:9 (RSV), a widow was to be "the wife of one husband." Westfall, *Paul and Gender*, 272. Payne, *Man and Woman, One in Christ*, 445–9. Fee, *1 and 2 Timothy, Titus*, 81. Spencer, I *Timothy*, 80–4. Belleville, *Women Leaders in the Church*, 142.

18. 1 Tim. 5:9.

19. 1 Tim. 5:14. Some have pointed to the verse that overseers are to manage their house well as indicating that this is the role of men, but in the culture of the day, men in general interacted with the public and women managed the home. For example, when Paul encouraged widows to teach younger women to marry and manage their homes, as Philip Payne and others have pointed out, the Greek word here for "manage" is a very strong one meaning to rule their homes, literally, to be "house despots." Payne, *Man and Woman, One in Christ*, 446, 452.

20. Rom. 16:1. Linda Belleville writes that in Greco-Roman culture, "the *diakonos* was an attendant or official in a temple or religious guild." Belleville, *1 Timothy*, 71.

21. Rodney Stark, a respected sociologist of religion, states that there is "virtual consensus among historians of the early church, as well as biblical scholars, that women held positions of honor and authority within early Christianity." In addition, he says "a very significant proportion of martyrs were women;" the majority of men executed were officials, including bishops, suggesting that women were regarded as officials too. Linda Belleville writes that "forty deaconesses were attached to the church of Constantinople." Duties for female deacons in the postapostolic era were "wide-ranging" and included serving communion on occasion, anointing the sick, assisting with the baptism of women, performing last rites, and being doorkeepers for worship (like ushers today). In addition, the Council of Chalcedon (fifth century) detailed "the ordination process for women deacons and placed them in the ranks of clergy." Belleville says there are inscriptions from the fourth through sixth century AD that name women deacons from "a range of geographical locations" including Jerusalem, Italy, Dalmatia, Melos, Athens, and the Asian provinces of Phrygia, Cilicia, Caria, and Nevinne. Aida Spencer states

that evidence has been discovered of many female ministers and deacons in the early church, as well as some elders and bishops. (In addition, she points out that the word in Titus 2:3 sometimes translated "old women" is the word *presbutis*, that can also be translated as "elder.") Ally Kateusz, a cultural historian specializing in the leadership roles of women during the early Christian era and Late Antiquity, says artifacts have been discovered in the twentieth century under the altars of two famous churches (Old Saint Peter's Basilica in Rome and the Hagia Sophia in Constantinople) that date from circa 430 and depict actual scenes in the church with both women and men at the front altar facing the people with communion elements. Stark, *The Rise of Christianity*, 109-10. Belleville, *1 Timothy*, 76, and "Women in Ministry: An Egalitarian Perspective," 48. Spencer, *I Timothy*, 90 (including extensive footnote on that page), and *Beyond the Curse*, 107. Also see Spencer's article on the leadership of women in different cultures: "Leadership of Women in Crete and Macedonia as a Model for the Church." Kateusz, "Women Leaders at the Table in Early Churches."

22. Craig Keener writes in his background commentary for the New Testament that the Roman government was aware of Christian deaconesses (female deacons) by AD 112. Ben Witherington states that Pliny the Elder, a well-known Roman administrator, mentions two female deaconesses in the early second century. (Witherington also states that "in all likelihood, 1 Tim. 3:11 speaks of [women] deaconesses.") Linda Belleville says Pliny the Younger wrote in the early second century about torturing two female deacons. Keener, *IVP Bible Background Commentary*, 613. Witherington, *Letters, Titus, 1-2 Timothy and 1-3 John*, 242, 232. Belleville, *1 Timothy*, 76, and "Women in Ministry: An Egalitarian Perspective," 48.

23. Linda Belleville writes that Clement, Origen, and Chrysostom referred to women deacons, with Origen writing that "even women are instituted deacons in the church" and Chrysostom writing that Paul "added her [Phoebe's] rank by calling her a deacon." Ben Witherington cites Clement, Origen, and Hippolytus as referring to women deacons (with Hippolytus describing a ceremony for the laying on of hands for deaconesses that duplicates exactly the ceremony for deacons), and also possibly Tertullian. Philip Payne gives multiple citations for early church fathers referencing women deacons. Belleville, *1 Timothy*, 75-6, and "Women in Ministry: An Egalitarian Perspective," 61-2. Witherington, *Women in the Earliest Churches*, 199. Payne, *Man and Woman, One in Christ*, 454, also see footnote 34.

24. 1 Tim. 3:11. Philip Payne states that "ancient interpreters nearly universally regarded verse 11 as identifying women in church office, as do most modern scholars." Gordon Fee says most of the recent commentaries in English agree. Howard Marshall writes that "a reference to wives seems less likely than women deacons" and lists his reasons. Linda Belleville provides a list of reasons why "wives" is unlikely here. These include: the lack of the possessive "their" in the original; the term "wives likewise" is lacking for the overseers; and the assumption that wives would possess "the necessary gifting and leadership skills to fulfill a role parallel to that of their husbands." In addition,

there is "nothing in what we know of early church leadership to support this." She also cites early church fathers as referring to women deacons, including Origen and John Chrysostom. Payne, *Man and Woman, One in Christ*, 454. Fee, *1 and 2 Timothy, Titus*, 90. Marshall, *Pastoral Epistles*, 493–4. Belleville, *1 Timothy*, 75.

25. Gordon Fee says we lack "intentional instruction about the early church – its structures, the nature of its leadership, both local and beyond, and its worship, including the various aspects of it, who led it, and its 'order.'" He says 1 Timothy is addressing false teaching, it is not "a manual of church order," and it is "extremely tenuous" to derive church office from this letter. He also says the New Testament does not explicitly teach that only men may lead or serve in certain ways, and nothing that is "merely narrated or described" should be understood to be normative for the church "in all places at all times." For Paul, Fee says, the Spirit is the "obvious leader" of the community in its worship and it would never have occurred to any of the early Christians that they should either describe their worship in full or lay down rules for it at a later time. Fee asks: "How is it, one wonders, that the later church can exercise so much energy in 'getting it right' with regard to leadership, when the New Testament itself shows so little interest in this?" Fee, "The Priority of Spirit Gifting for Church Ministry," 245, 248, 251; *1 & 2 Timothy, Titus*, xiv.

26. Linda Belleville, an author on women leaders in the church, writes that the honor in the first century lay not in the leadership position itself but in serving the church to the best of one's ability. She says there were not offices as we know them today, and the boundaries and relationships among overseer, elder, and deacon are "beyond precise definition" at this early stage in the church's history. She explains that in the culture of the day, overseers and elders were different roles; "elders were found among the Sanhedrin," along with chief priests and scribes, "and in local governing councils;" an overseer was a "community official in charge of public funds and properties" or the administrator of a large household or estate." She points to the term used in 1 Tim. 3 as "overseer" (*episkopoi*), meaning to watch over; she says the translation of "bishop" (as in the King James Version) is poor and assumes "the later development of an episcopal laity." Gordon Fee says the term "elder" (*presbyteroi*) does not appear here or in any of the earlier letters, and believes that when it is used, it likely covers "both overseers and deacons." Belleville, *Women Leaders in the Church*, 136, 141, 147, 145, 182, and *1 Timothy*, 66, 73. Fee, *1 and 2 Timothy, Titus*, 22.

27. Linda Belleville says respect and submission were earned, not mandated through the holding of an office, but acquired through a job well done. When the early church gathered in worship, she says, it was for mutual edification through the sharing of spiritual gifts. Teaching was "an activity, not an office, a gift, not a position of authority" (Rom. 12:7; 1 Cor. 12:28; 14:26; Eph. 4:11), and every believer was called to it, not merely church leaders (Col. 3:16; Heb. 5:12). Belleville says the Greek term for "authority" (*exousia*) is not used of either local church leadership or the activity of teaching, and teaching is subject to evaluation, just like any other ministry role. Belleville states that

some say teaching in 1 Timothy takes on the official sense of doctrine, but she says doctrine "as a system of thought is foreign to 1 Timothy;" there are traditions but not doctrines. The flaw, she says, lies in translating the Greek *hygianouse didaskalia* as "sound doctrine" instead of "sound [good] teaching" (1.10; 4.6; 6.1, 3; 2 Tim. 4.3; Titus 1.9; 2.1). Belleville, *Women Leaders in the Church*, 136, 151, 182, and "Women in Ministry: An Egalitarian Viewpoint," 64–5, 81–2.

28. John Stott, scholar, international evangelical leader, and lead author of the renowned *Lausanne Covenant*, writes that the development of a single bishop who presides over a college of presbyters cannot be dated earlier than Ignatius of Syrian Antioch, circa AD 110. (Stott points out that even Timothy and Titus are not called bishops.) Gordon Fee says concern over matters of church leadership seem to arise at a later time in the church and "can be found in full bloom in the letters of Ignatius from the second decade of the second Christian century." Ben Witherington refers to the debate "whether the Ignatian picture of the monarchical bishop represents a regional concept or one that was widespread." Stott, *Message of 1 Timothy and Titus*, 89–90. Fee, "The Priority of Spirit Gifting for Church Ministry," 253. Witherington, *Women in the Earliest Churches*, 199.

29. New Testament scholar Michael Holmes, respected for his work regarding the early church fathers, states that Ignatius was probably worried about a split in the church at Antioch where he was bishop, which would mean he "was a failure." Holmes also states that Ignatius' letters have been influential to this day. Gordon Fee says the church of the pastoral epistles is "unlike the Ignatian epistles in both spirit and details." Holmes, *The Apostolic Fathers*, 166–70. Fee, *1 & 2 Timothy, Titus*, 23.

30. Craig Keener says "the vast majority of civic administrators were men," and "civic life in the eastern Mediterranean remained primarily a man's world." Keener, *Acts, An Exegetical Commentary*, 608.

31. Sociologist Alvin Schmidt says that "not too long after the apostles were gone, the church reverted to the sexism once practiced by the Greeks, Romans, and rabbis before the days of Jesus and the apostles." Schmidt, *Veiled and Silenced*, 209.

32. Alvin Schmidt says that when Emperor Constantine legalized Christianity, church leaders wanted to be seen as respectable and supportive of Roman culture. Schmidt cites Max Weber, the famous European sociologist, who "noted in his analysis of early Christianity that as church functions became routinized and regimented," the Church "excluded women from leadership roles." Schmidt also cites Brittain and Carroll, who stated that in the Jerusalem Christians "the sexes freely mingled in a pure and noble companionship. But this perfect society was not destined to endure long." Schmidt says the "cultural forces of ancient sexism increasingly gained the upper hand after the apostolic era," and "the church of the second century objected to the prominent position of women in the Apostolic age." Then "in the third, fourth, and fifth centuries the antifeminine views of the Babylonians,

NOTES – Chapter 10

Sumerians, Greeks, Romans, and Hebrews came back in full force, causing the church fathers and others to formulate theological pronouncements that were highly sexist in theory and practice." Ben Witherington says that in the period AD 80-325, one can see "an increasingly non-Christian patriarchal orientation taking over the Church." Schmidt, *Veiled and Silenced*, 211–2, 218–9. Witherington, *Women in the Earliest Churches*, 212.

33. Manfred Brauch writes that the ground was "saturated with centuries-old, deeply ingrained attitudes, mores, and practices that promoted the social and essential inferiority of slaves and women." "Yet the seeds were sown for the eventual abolition of these de-humanizing, demeaning, and marginalizing power-over relationships." But the initial growth, he says, "virtually ground to a halt for centuries, as the old orders of hierarchical power patterns reasserted themselves, and in many ways, persist in our own time within the life, practices, and attitudes of the body of Christ." The tragedy, he says, is that "abusive readings of Scripture have significantly contributed to and perpetuated this state of affairs." Brauch, *Abusing Scripture*, 185.

34. Dorothy Lee says we should assume the presence of female believers at the early church councils, such as the Council of Jerusalem mentioned in Acts 15:1–21. Lee, *Ministry of Women in the New Testament*, 60.

35. The supposed Fourth Synod of Carthage (AD 398). Spencer, *Beyond the Curse*, 63.

36. According to the Old Testament, women would have been considered "unclean" during their time of menstruation. See discussion in Liefeld, "The Nature of Authority in the New Testament," 268, footnote 27. Also see Tucker and Liefeld, *Daughters of the Church*, 111, 131.

37. Ruth Tucker and Walter Liefeld state that this was the Synod of Orleans (AD 533). Ben Witherington says that by AD 325, women's ministry had declined, and they were pushed into a separatist track; in the fifth and sixth centuries, at least three councils mandated that the ordination of deaconesses be stopped entirely, and another seemed to say there should be no more deaconesses at all, not even unordained ones. "In due course," writes Witherington, "principles drawn from the (mis)interpretation of such texts as 1 Cor.33b-36, 1 Tim. 2.1ff., appear to have won the day over other considerations, thus impoverishing the Church of vital female workers from the fourth century onwards." Tucker and Liefeld, *Daughters of the Church*, 131, 133. Witherington, *Women in the Earliest Churches*, 200–1, 209.

38. Alvin Schmidt says that "in spite of all the early, active involvement of women in the apostolic age, by the fourth and fifth centuries, the church's leaders had silenced women and barred them from all significant roles in the church for all practical purposes" in what he calls "the great reversal." In doing so, Schmidt writes, "they unwittingly, contrary to Christ and the apostles, wove the ancient pagan cultural views of women into the church's theology." In the Protestant Reformation, women were permitted to sing in some Protestant churches but not to pray aloud publicly. The Southern Presbyterian Synod of Virginia "did not permit women to sing in a worship service until the latter

1890s." Schmidt, *Veiled and Silenced*, 149, 151–4, 209, 229.

39. Two early writers on outstanding women in the Christian tradition include Julia Kavanagh (1852) and Edith Deen (1959). Also, Ruth Tucker and Walter Liefeld wrote an extensive book in 1987 on "daughters of the church," with an overall history and individual stories. More recently, Lynn Cohick and Amy Brown Hughes wrote about outstanding women in the second through fifth centuries and some of their challenges. Barbara MacHaffie provides an historical overview of women in the Christian tradition. Dorothy Lee says we often speak of the early church fathers, but there were also church mothers, "who either wrote themselves or influenced profoundly the men who did." She says the suppression of women's ministry was "not total in the early centuries and not universally forbidden;" rather, "women's ministry flourished" in some contexts and "women held office in the church, preaching, teaching, and administering the sacraments." Lee explains that more women's ministry and leadership began to reemerge slowly during the Reformation (sixteenth century), including "*ad hoc* preaching and in more formal orders of ministry." Kim Haines-Eitzen, a professor of ancient Mediterranean religions and author on the social history of the scribes who copied Christian texts during the second and third centuries, concludes that women were "involved in the many and various stages of the production, reproduction, and dissemination of early Christian literature." She also quotes Cyril, patriarch of Constantinople, as saying that the book they had of the New and Old Testaments was "written by the hand of Thecla, the noble Egyptian woman." Thecla is also said to have enlightened "many in the word of God." Mimi Haddad writes about early church women who were martyrs, monastics, and mystics, as well as women in the Reformation, various awakenings and movements, missions in the 1800s, activism, biblicism, crucicentrism, and evangelical women today. Many other books have also been written about women's contributions. Examples abound of numerous godly women revered through the centuries, including, for example, St. Nino, who is credited with Christianizing Iberia, now part of Georgia. Kavanagh, *Women of Christianity*. Deen, *Great Women of the Christian Faith*. Tucker and Liefeld, *Daughters of the Church*. Cohick and Hughes, *Christian Women in the Patristic World*. MacHaffie, *Her Story*. Lee, *Ministry of Women in the New Testament*, 166–70. Haines-Eitzen, *The Gendered Palimpset*, 37, 5, 107. Haddad, "History Matters: Evangelicals and Women."

40. This was called the Latin Vulgate, used by the Catholic Church until contemporary times and considered of major importance for Hebrew textual study. Alvin Schmidt writes that Jerome once acknowledged that two women co-authored the Vulgate with him, but "later theologians in the church erased the names of these women and substituted the words 'venerable brothers.'" Elizabeth Clark, known for her study of the early church fathers, says Jerome wrote eulogies of Marcella and Paula and their scholarly pursuits. She includes Jerome's writings that Paula convinced him to read through the Old and New Testaments with her, and when he professed ignorance in response to some of her questions, she would prompt him with questions to "say which of the many possible meanings seemed most likely."

NOTES – Chapter 10

Clark also says that Jerome wrote that Paula memorized the Scriptures and learned Hebrew to the point where she chanted the Psalms in Hebrew with "no trace of the distinctive character of the Latin language." Schmidt, *Veiled and Silenced*, 153. Clark, *Women in the Early Church*, 24, 163–4.

41. Pandita Ramabai of India was born into a poor family and is said to have recited the Hindu Scriptures in public to earn money, eventually becoming known for her extraordinary intellectual ability. After coming to faith in Jesus, and opportunities for higher education, she founded a rescue mission for destitute women, was honored by her government, and felt the call of God to translate the Bible for the uneducated lower castes to understand. Reportedly, she led the first all-women Bible effort, from translation to printing, binding, and distribution. Julia Evelina Smith was reportedly the first American woman to translate the entire Bible. She went to a female seminary in the mid 1800s, had a working knowledge of Latin, Hebrew, and Greek, and spent eight years translating the Bible from its original languages into English (also consulting the Latin Vulgate). She completed her translation in 1855 but would not see it published until two decades later, when she was 84. It is available at this writing in an electronic version on Amazon. Helen Barrett Montgomery was the first woman to have her translation of the Greek New Testament into English professionally published; this was in 1924 by the New York Bible Society as part of its centenary celebration. Montgomery was also the first women elected president of an American denomination, the Northern Baptist Convention. Other early women Bible translators included Louise Swanton Belloc of France (1796 to 1881) and American Elizabeth Cady Stanton (1815 to 1902). Katharine Barnwell from the U.K. lived in Nigeria for four decades and wrote a book that is considered the gold-standard manual for training first-language translators (formerly called mother-tongue translators) the world over. Marion Ann Taylor provides a historical and biographical guide to women Bible interpreters through a large time period. Pandita Ramabai: Bible translation pioneer | Bible Translation | Wycliffe Bible Translators;

    https://library.hds.harvard.edu/exhibits/incomparable-treasure/julia-smith;

    https://www.bu.edu/missiology/missionary-biography/l-m/montgomery-helen-barrett-1861-1934/;

    https://www.cbeinternational.org/resource/article/mutuality-blog-magazine/correcting-caricatures-women-and-bible-translation.

    Katharine Barnwell: https://www.christianitytoday.com/ct/2022/october/linguist-katharine-barnwell-bible-translation-jesus-film.html. Taylor, *Handbook of Women Biblical Interpreters*.

42. Beth Moore was a long-time Southern Baptist but reportedly left that denomination due to its stances regarding women and apologized for being complicit in them.

43. Cunningham and Hamilton, *Why Not Women*, 66.

44. Erickson, *Christian Theology*, 501, 1007. Craig Keener concludes that Paul's

"didactic" passages must be analyzed in light of his whole teaching and practice. Keener, *Paul, Women, and Wives*, 111.

45. F.F. Bruce says some have argued this passage is just about access to baptism, but he says that here Paul "was concerned about practical church life." Bruce says Paul states a basic principle in Gal. 3:28; in contrast, the two limiting passages in (1 Cor. 14 and 1 Tim. 2) are to be understood in relation to Gal.3:28 and not *vice versa*." John Stott says, "When we say that Christ has abolished these distinctions, we mean not that they do not exist, but that they do not matter. They are still there, but they no longer create any barriers to fellowship." Stott writes that men and women in Christ "recognize each other as equals, as brothers and sisters in Christ," resisting by the grace of God "the temptation to despise one another or patronize one another, for we know ourselves to be 'all one person in Christ Jesus.'" Stott writes in his discussion of Gal. 3:23-29: "If we are 'under the law,' our religion is a bondage." Aida Besancon Spencer and William David Spencer write that "Jesus' concept of impartiality influenced early church values and leadership." Therefore, "a Gentile like Titus could become an important leader," "a former slave like Onesimus could become a bishop," and "women could become apostles and ministers." "It is Christ who is seen, not Jew, Gentile, slave, free, male, or female." Bruce, *Epistle to the Galatians*, 189-190, and "Women in the Church: A Biblical Survey," 10. Also Gasque and Gasque, "Saint Paul, Apostle of Freedom for Women and Men, An Interview with F.F. Bruce." Stott, *Message of Galatians*, 100-102. Spencer and Spencer, *Christian Egalitarian Leadership*, 11.

46. Gordon Fee says "the New Testament does *not* explicitly teach that only men may lead or serve in certain ways," and "the issue should more likely be giftedness, not gender." Further, the New Testament evidence, he says, is that the Holy Spirit is gender inclusive, gifting both men and women, and thus potentially setting the whole body free to minister. Fee advocates for a Spirit agenda, with "a plea for releasing the Spirit from our 'strictures and structures' so that the church might minister to itself and the world more effectively." Fee, "The Priority of Spirit Gifting for Church Ministry," 248-9, 252-4.

47. Aida Besancon Spencer writes that "in the later church," the word used by Paul to describe Phoebe, *prostatis*, "was used of civil rulers, ecclesiastical rulers, and bishops." Spencer says Clement calls Jesus Christ the *prostates*, and the related word in the Septuagint, the Hebrew *paqid*, signifies a "commanding officer such as a commissioner, deputy, overseer." It can also be the ruler of the temple. She says those described by this word in the Septuagint include Moses, Joseph, Herod, Caesar, and even God. Lynn Cohick says the literal meaning of *prostatis* is "one who presides" or one "set over others" (and cites Thayer's *Greek-English Lexicon*, s.v.). She says this noun is found "only here in the New Testament, but the masculine form (*prostates*) is employed by Justin Martyr to denote the person presiding at Communion." Paul uses the verbal form in several places, she says, including I Thess. 5:12, when the Thessalonians are "encouraged to respect those who are over them in

NOTES – Chapter 10

the Lord, and in Rom. 12:8, when Paul uses the participial form to describe the gift of leadership." In the pastoral epistles, Cohick explains, the word is "used of church officials who preside over the congregation (1 Tim. 3:4–5, 5:17)." Alvin Schmidt states that Paul used a well-known phrase for male functionaries to describe Phoebe (*diakonos*) that meant "leading officer" in the literature at the time the New Testament was written, similar to a "superintendent today." Catherine and Richard Kroeger write that early church father John Chrysostom called Priscilla a "teacher of teachers." Also, the Old Testament did not teach against women as leaders but rather gave examples of them. Spencer, *Beyond the Curse*, 116–117. Cohick, "Women as Leaders," 644. Schmidt, *Veiled and Silenced*, 181. Kroeger and Kroeger, *Women Elders . . . Called by God?* 15.

48. F.F. Bruce predicates this statement as based on the general belief by evangelical Christians that "Christian priesthood is a privilege in which all believers share." Gasque and Gasque. "Saint Paul, Apostle of Freedom for Women and Men, An Interview with F.F. Bruce," 3. Also see Bruce, "Women in the Church: A Biblical Survey," *Christian Brethren Review*, No. 33, 1982, 12, and in entirety, 7–14. This article was also published in his book *A Mind for What Matters, Collected Essays*, 265.

49. 1 Pet. 2:9. Donald Bloesch says "the most important theological reason" for opening the door to the ministry of women is "the doctrine of the priesthood of all believers." Stanley Grenz writes that if clergy represent Christ, then restricting the clergy to males can "cloud the symbolism of Christ's inclusive humanity." John Wijngaards, a Catholic priest, presents a theological argument for ordaining women in the Catholic church. Bloesch, *Is the Bible Sexist?* 47. Grenz, "Biblical Priesthood and Women in Ministry," 282. Wijngaards, *What They Don't Teach You in Catholic College*.

50. Spencer, *Beyond the Curse*, 44.

51. Mat. 27:50–53.

52. 1 Pet. 2:4–5, 9. Rev. 1:6; 5:10; 20:6. F.F. Bruce says he believes in the priesthood of all believers, and "no distinction in service or status is implied in Paul's many references to his fellow-workers, whether male or female." Stanley Grenz writes that the Old Testament priesthood has been "radically transformed by the new covenant" inaugurated by the Lord; all believers are participants in the "mandate to be ministers of God, and to this end all serve together." Gasque and Gasque, "Saint Paul . . . An interview with F.F. Bruce." Bruce, "Women in the Church: A Biblical Survey," 9, 12. 3. Grenz, "Biblical Priesthood and Women in Ministry," 277–8.

53. Alan Johnson has collected twenty-one essays from prominent evangelicals, including himself, regarding how they have changed their minds to being in favor of women in church leadership. Many churches and organizations, however, still limit what women can do, including whether they can teach "authoritatively" in church, based on the highly debated rare word *authentein* in 1 Tim. 2:12 that appears only appears once in the Bible. Numerous guidelines have been formulated around this idea by one influential

organization in particular, for example, that women can teach the Bible in a secular college but not a Christian one. The seminal 1995 issue of the Council of Biblical Manhood and Womanhood Newsletter (*CBMW News*) identified the list of what women could and could not do in church as related to governing and teaching. Linda Belleville and others have challenged these guidelines as "subjective" and "arbitrary." Craig Keener points out that the moderate "complementarian" view only forbids women being senior pastors, not being pastors at all. Johnson, *How I Changed My Mind About Women in Leadership*. Belleville, *Women Leaders in the Church*, 150-152. Keener "Women in Ministry: An Egalitarian Viewpoint," 110.

Chapter 11 – What the Bible does not say

Note: Some statements in these endnotes for chapter 11 are based on references given in previous chapters/endnotes. Therefore, it is important to read the prior chapters and endnotes for a fuller understanding of this chapter.

1. Some of these theories were espoused in an influential book originally published in 1991, *Recovering Biblical Manhood and Womanhood*, by John Piper and Wayne Grudem. Another book by Wayne Grudem, *Evangelical Feminism and Biblical Truth*, was published in 2004 and updated in 2012. Newer research, however, was not added for the 2012 update. In addition, certain key points espoused by advocates for women's leadership were not addressed and some were overstated.

2. Gen. 1:26-28 states that God said, let us make mankind in our image, male and female, and let them rule over the fish . . . and all creatures. Nothing here restricts ruling to just men. Rather, it includes the male and female in ruling.

3 Gen. 3:16. Chapter 2 explains that the statement that Adam will rule over Eve is a prediction in the Hebrew grammar, not a command.

4. See chapter 2. Also, Katharine Bushnell points out that no following word in the Old Testament supports that men are to govern their wives, except for the pagan king in the book of Esther. Bushnell, *God's Word to Women*, 125.

5. Gen. 2:20. See chapter 2. Also, Linda Belleville points out that the Hebrew in Gen. 2:20 says the man found no "counterpart" (*kenegdo*) "to relieve his aloneness," not that he found no subordinate or helper. Belleville, "*Women in Ministry: An Egalitarian Perspective*," 29.

6. See Rom. 5:12, 14-19; 1 Cor. 15:21-22 for verses about Adam's sin. Gen. 3:6 says that Adam was there when the serpent tempted Eve. Also, Adam had been instructed directly by God, and Eve by Adam. Aida Besancon Spencer explains that English translations may leave out the phrase "with her" (*'mmah*) in Gen. 3:6, because it can be "difficult to translate." However, the King James Version does include it. Spencer, *Beyond the Curse*, 31.

7. For a discussion of 1 Tim. 2:14, see chapters 2 and 9. Ben Witherington points out that Eve's deception is also found in 2 Cor. 11:3, "where Paul is

suggesting it could happen to any of the Corinthians, male or female. "It is unlikely," Witherington says, "that Paul thought falling prey to deception was an inherent flaw in women to which men were not subject." Witherington says it is likely "there is a link here with the false teachers, who are viewed as deceivers." Howard Marshall says that concluding men in general ought not to listen to what women or their wives say because Adam listened to what Eve said is to "go well beyond what the text actually says." Philip Payne concludes that if Paul believed women were more vulnerable to deception than men, he would not affirm women prophesying in 1 Cor. 11:2–16. It should also be noted that Paul says he himself was deceived by sin. Witherington, *Letters, Titus, 1-2 Timothy, 1-3 John*, 229. Marshall, *Pastoral Epistles*, 465. Payne, *Man and Woman, One in Christ*, 410.

8. 2 Cor. 11:3. See explanation in endnote above.

9. See chapters 3, 4, and 5 for some examples.

10. 1 Tim. 2:13–14. See chapter 9.

11. Richard Hess points out that "the norm among the patriarchs is not primogeniture" (priority of the firstborn) "but God's blessing on the second or third born." F. F. Bruce says the "priority of the male in the creation narrative does not bespeak his superiority; any suggestion to this effect might be answered by the counter-argument that the last-made crowns the work." Craig Keener states that the Genesis account does not subordinate Eve because she was created second; "it makes her an equal part of Adam" because "her creation was necessary for him to be complete." Hess, "Equality With and Without Innocence," 84. Bruce, "Women in the Church: A Biblical Survey," 8, 11. Keener, *Paul, Women and Wives*, 116.

12. 1 Tim. 2:12. See an explanation of this passage in chapter 9.

13. See chapter 9. Also, the Bible does not state unequivocably that women should teach only women (or young women), but not men. The Bible also does not say that women can teach men if it is not done authoritatively, as some theorize. The Bible also does not say that women cannot be pastors, as some assume.

14. 2 Tim. 3:16. Roger Nicole makes this point, citing Judg. 5, Luke 1:42-45, 45-46. He asks, "Since God was pleased to incorporate songs and statements by women in Holy Writ . . . , is it improper to think that he may use women in expounding and applying his word?" Nicole points to Paul's statement that "all Scripture is God-breathed" and "useful for teaching," so that the person of God [the inclusive Greek *anthropos* rather than the male-only *aner*], not the "man" of God as often translated, may be equipped for every good work. Nicole, "Biblical Authority and Feminist Aspirations," 50.

15. 1 Tim. 3:12. Cynthia Westfall states that "one-woman man" was a "catchphrase or idiom" in that time meaning marital faithfulness (if married) and not a requirement in this verse for maleness or marriage. (See chapter 10 for more academic references.) It should be noted that some translations go beyond the text, saying that an overseer must be a *man* whose life is beyond reproach.

Howard Marshall says the "more widely held" belief is that "one-woman man" refers to "marital fidelity." Aida Besancon Spencer says "the emphasis in the text is not on overseers being men," but on the type of person who should be in leadership. Marshall, *Pastoral Epistles*, 154. Spencer, *I Timothy*, 83. Westfall, *Paul and Gender*, 272.

16. See chapters 3, 5, 10.
17. Eph. 5:23. See chapter 8.
18. See chapter 7, 8. The Bible also does not say the husband is the "head of the home," the "spiritual leader of the home," or the "priest of the home." Some recent popular paraphrases, including *The Message* (2002 Edition) and *The Passion* (2017), have been prepared by individuals and turn "head" into "leader/leadership" in Eph. 5:23. But the established translations, prepared by teams of respected scholars, have not taken such liberty with meaning and have kept "head." (Ben Witherington states that it is best to choose a translation that is done by a team of scholars rather than a particular individual, which will help eliminate individual bias in translation.) Some translations say in 1 Cor. 11:3 that the head of the wife is her husband, but many respected scholars say that "her husband" is incorrect, with no possessive here, and it should say "man," with Paul's point being that man was the "head," which could mean origin, of woman in the Garden, as the Godhead was the origin of Christ, and Christ the origin of man. Lucy Peppiatt cites early church father Chrysostom as warning "against applying the relation of the Godhead directly to the husband-wife relationship;" when applied to the Godhead, the notions are "too high for us to grasp." Gordon Fee says one of "the more common abuses" of this text is telling modern husbands "that they should assume their proper role as head of their wives" and make the final choice in decision making. "I don't know whether I hear Paul laughing or crying," Fee says, "when that utterly modern reading is superimposed on this text—as though that were actually somehow derivable from the passage itself." Howard Marshall says "the injunction to husbands is *not* that they exercise their proper authority; rather it has a quite extraordinary emphasis on the total love and devotion that the husband must show to the wife." Lynn Cohick also believes this verse in Ephesians is alluding to baptism "as part of Christ's work in creating a radiant church." David Scholer writes that in Eph. 5, "head" (*kephale*) hardly means "authority over," "especially in the leadership and authority-bearing sense for husbands over wives given to it by so many traditionalist and complementarian interpreters;" whatever *kephale* might signify in Eph 5:21–33, Scholer says, "the context makes it clear that it carries for those in Christ no authoritarian sense for men." Craig Keener says household codes then normally covered how the husband was to rule and govern the wife, not how to love; also, "authoritarian leadership on *any* basis conflicts with the teaching and example of Jesus." Numerous scholars, including Linda Belleville, have pointed out that 1 Tim. 5:14 describes younger widows marrying and managing their households, and that the word here for "managing" (*oikodespotein*) is a very strong one related to the English word "despot," better translated "rule their homes." First-

century women were "in charge of running the entire household," including managing the children, Belleville explains, and "even modest households" normally included one or two servants. (Craig Keener states that men traditionally attended to the public domain and women ruled the domestic sphere.) In addition, Belleville points out, a better translation of 1 Tim. 3 is for the overseer to "care for" one's own family rather than "rule" one's own house. Also, "Paul commands the children of his churches to obey their parents not just their father." Katharine Bushnell points out that the Old Testament does not teach that men are to govern their wives; also, Gen. 3:16 should be taught as a prophecy, not a command. F.F. Bruce addresses the reference to husbands' cleansing wives through the washing with water through the word; while some have interpreted this to mean that it is the husband's job to teach her the word and lead her spiritually, Bruce explains that the word for "washing" here occurs only one other time in the New Testament, (Titus 3:5) and the context both times is water baptism. In Paul's time, the wife normally followed the husband's religion; therefore, Paul may be wanting husbands to be supportive of their wives as full participants through their own baptism and confession of faith. Witherington, *Reading and Understanding the Bible*, 246. Peppiatt, *Rediscovering Scripture's Vision for Women*, 75 (citing Chrysostom, "Homily 26"). Fee, "The Cultural Context of Ephesians 5:18-6:9," 7. Marshall, "Mutual Love and Submission in Marriage," 199. Cohick, *Letter to the Ephesians*, 365. Scholer, "The Evangelical Debate Over Biblical 'Headship,'" 43–4. Keener, *Paul, Women and Wives*, 167. Belleville, *Women Leaders in the Church*, 116, 139. Bushnell, *God's Word to Women*, 125. Bruce, *Epistles to the Colossians, Philemon, and Ephesians*, 388–9.

19. See especially 1 Cor. 7, which Ben Witherington calls "a grand exercise in male-female parallelism." Philip Payne says 1 Cor. 7 "never implies the husband's leadership or that husbands and wives should have different roles." Rather, "it identifies exactly the same rights and responsibilities" regarding twelve different issues about marriage, including sexuality, and is Paul's longest and most detailed treatment of marriage. Aida Besancon Spencer points out that men and women are also said to be joint heirs, which they normally were not in that culture. Witherington, *Women in the Ministry of Jesus*, 128. Payne, "What About Headship?" 144–6. Spencer, *Beyond the Curse*, 68–71.

20. Extensive national surveys by distinguished academics have shown that satisfaction is much higher in marriages where husbands and wives have equality in decision making. When both spouses perceive the marriage as more "equalitarian," more than four-fifths say they have a happy marriage. The opposite was also found: more than four-fifths in traditional marriages reported that they are unhappy. Sarah Sumner reports on research showing that "most complementarians" [those who think men are the leaders and women the followers] actually "live in egalitarian marriages;" over 90 percent in the study across 23 states said that "nearly all decisions were made jointly." Olson and Olson, *Empowering Couples: Building on Your Strengths*, 72. Amato et al., "Continuity and Change in Marital Quality Between 1980 and 2000," 1–22. Sumner, *Men and Women in the Church*, 202. Preato, "A Female

Apostle: Was Junia a Man or a Woman?" *Priscilla Papers*, Spring 2003; the substance of this paper was presented at an Evangelical Theological Society meeting on April 23, 2004, under the title: "Empirical Data in Support of Egalitarian Marriages: A Theological Response."

21. Multiple scholarly studies have shown that violence is higher in patriarchal marriages where traditional roles are followed. Studies have also shown that violence can be used to maintain a sense of superiority and control. Crowell and Burgess, "Causes and Consequences of Violence Against Women," 59, 62.

22. Eph. 5:21–22. See chapter 8.

23. See chapter 8. See 1 Cor. 7 for twelve areas of mutually reciprocal rights and duties. Craig Keener suggests that early Christians were on the more progressive edge of gender relationships in their world, given Paul's emphasis on mutual submission. Keener, "Mutual Submission Frames the Household Codes," 10.

24. 1 Cor. 11:5, 10. See chapter 7 for the explanation by some scholars that this passage is indicating that a woman already has authority on her own head, not that she needs it from a man.

25. See chapter 7. Scholars who say that the verse should be translated that a woman has her own authority over her head include F.F. Bruce, who states that the head covering is not a sign of the woman's submission to her husband's authority, but a sign of her own authority. "In Christ she received equality of status with man," Bruce writes. "She might pray or prophesy at meetings of the church, and her veil [head covering] was a sign of this new authority." Bruce concludes that the head covering is the sign of women's "authority to exercise their Christian liberty" to prophesy, "not the sign of someone else's authority over them." Sarah Sumner states that it has "never been orthodox for Christians to believe that all men have inherent authority over all women." Bruce, *I and II Corinthians*, 106, and "Women in the Church: A Biblical Survey," 10. Sumner, *Men and Women in the Church*, 252, footnote 19.

26. The scholar was George Knight; Kevin Giles describes why Knight developed his theory of roles and its impact. Linda Belleville wrote in 2001 that it was not uncommon, as recently as two decades prior, "to hear evangelicals talking about a woman's flawed and self-deceived nature, or her secondary creation in God's image," ruling out any leadership role for her in the church. Now, Belleville says, there are "very few who would go this far, and most who thought this way in the past have changed their minds." Scholars say that theories of men as the protectors, providers, and managers of the family, and women as the nurturers, are based on oversimplified interpretations of a few verses. Sarah Sumner points out that the Bible does not say that men are to be the "leaders, providers, and protectors," or that women are to "affirm" and "receive" the leadership of men. Craig Keener says Paul "gives no instructions on transcultural role differences;" he "merely defines the marriage relationship in terms of mutual service." Lynn Cohick says Paul

"reconfigures the cultural expectations of masculinity expressed within a marriage" between a submissive wife and superordinate husband. Aida Besancon Spencer writes that Adam and Eve are "equal in rank and role" and proposes four advantages of men sharing authoritative leadership with women. Christian psychology professor Cynthia Neal Kimball writes that messages sent to males include performing, providing, and protecting. If these are not "played out successfully," she writes, men can be seen "as failures and inadequate," and "the stress from this can lead to domestic violence, alienation, alcohol and drug abuse, and higher levels of coronary and pulmonary diseases and suicide." Whether we are male or female, she states, "the temptation to evaluate ourselves based on how adequately we meet the expectations of our prescribed roles is strong and hard to resist." Giles, *What the Bible Actually Teaches on Women*, 45-50. Belleville, "Women in Ministry: An Egalitarian Perspective," 21–2. Sumner, *Men and Women in the Church*, 85. Keener, *Paul, Women and Wives*, 166, 168. Cohick, *Letter to the Ephesians*, 362. Spencer, "What are the Biblical Roles of Female and Male Followers of Christ?" 12, 15. Kimball, "Nature, Culture and Gender Complementarity," 476.

27. Lynn Cohick states that Paul's view of believers "does not map masculine and feminine on the spectrum of active/passive or leaders/subordinate." Ronald Pierce writes that the Bible does not define "femininity/womanhood" or "masculinity/manhood," so we should avoid dogmatism, stereotyping, and the making of restrictive lists in these areas. He also states that recent studies show considerable diversity among men, in some cases even more than between men and women (and the same holds true for women). Katharine Bushnell pointed out that gender stereotypes have sometimes influenced Bible translation. For the same Hebrew word, men are "strong" but women are "virtuous"; men are "holy" but women are "pure"; men have "authority" but women have "a veil." Some people use gender brain research to state that men and women are a certain way, but some studies have reported more brain differences within genders than between male and female. Christian psychologist Mary Stewart Van Leeuwen states that "the differences, when they occur, are both smaller and more complex than we thought" and, "in most cases, they are impossible to separate from the effects of learning." "Moreover," she writes, "we cannot invoke biology to excuse our moral failures as men or women." Van Leeuwen also says that when sex differences in psychological traits and behaviors are found, they are always average, not absolute, and "for the vast majority the difference between the sexes is greatly exceeded by the amount of variability on that trait *within* members of each sex." Ben Witherington says Jesus rejected certain common stereotypes, including not putting the burden of responsibility of sexual sin on the female. Aida Besancon Spencer states that the Greco-Roman stereotype was that women were best suited for the "indoor life" and men for public life and statesmanship, but "maleness and femaleness are not derived from roles or tasks." Spencer says that like their Maker, women can be "strong, persevering, reliable, compassionate, comforting," and command and judge. They can also be careful and thorough, "key scholarly traits." Cynthia Long Westfall writes

extensively about male and female stereotypes and how Paul redefines Greco-Roman gender stereotypes in attempting to equip male and female believers to follow Christ. Both men and women needed to make adjustments to their identity and function – women needed to "grow up to maturity" in Christ rather than remaining in immaturity under a guardian; men needed to "recognize vulnerability, nurture other believers, quell aggression, and follow Christ in humility, suffering, and submission." Lucy Peppiatt states "there is little in the Bible that defines and delineates specifically male and female characteristics, temperaments, emotions, or dispositions." The destiny of all believers, Peppiatt says, is to become like Jesus "and participate in his being." Sarah Sumner examines concepts of femininity and masculinity and challenges the church to think about the differences between what we have been taught to think and what the Bible says is true about men and women. She also says that chauvinism is utterly foreign to God's character. Ronald Pierce writes that since "the Bible does not define 'femininity/womanhood' or 'masculinity/manhood', we should avoid dogmatism, stereotyping, and the making of restrictive lists in these areas." Peter Davids points out that Jesus and Paul use the word *gentle*, normally then a feminine expression, to describe themselves and a fruit of the Spirit. Craig Keener states in reference to 1 Cor. 11 that an appeal to nature (as in women having longer hair) was a reference to a standard Greco-Roman argument. Cohick, *Letter to the Ephesians*, 353. Pierce, *Partners in Marriage and Ministry*, 107, 90. Bushnell, *God's Word to Women*, 273-84. Van Leeuwen, *Gender and Grace*, 105, and "Social Studies Cannot Define Gender Differences," 12. Witherington, *Women in the Ministry of Jesus*, 28, 20. Spencer, *Beyond the Curse*, 29, 50, 135. Westfall, *Paul and Gender*, 45–59. Peppiatt, *Rediscovering Scripture's Vision for Women*, 41. Sumner, *Men and Women in the Church*, 100–12, 125. Pierce, *Partners in Marriage and Ministry*, 107. Davids, "A Silent Witness in Marriage," 230. Keener, *Paul, Women & Wives*, 42.

28. Eph. 5:33. See Walsh and Miller, "Translating Ephesians 5:33," and Westfall, "This Is A Great Metaphor!"

29. See chapter 7. This was called the "Arian heresy." Early church leaders speaking against it included Chrysostom, who argued that only heretics read from 1 Cor. 11:3 (father God is the "head" of Christ) that the present, eternal, or ontological Christ is under subjection. Lynn Cohick says both Cyril and Chrysostom, early church fathers, write against the position that Christ is a subordinate being to God the father; Chrysostom indicates that Paul is saying in 1 Cor. 11:3 that Christ is "the same substance as the father." She also writes that if Paul wanted to emphasize the father as ruler in this passage, "he would have chosen the master/slave pair, not the male/female pair." Anthony Thiselton states that "Chrysostom is aware that a parallel between men/women and God/Christ should not give 'the heretics' grounds for a subordinationist Christology." Lucy Peppiatt writes that the persons of the Trinity are coequal and coeternal and points out that Chrysostom warns "against applying the relation of the Godhead directly to the husband-wife relation;" when applied to the Godhead the notions are "too high for us to grasp." The meaning of "head" (in 1 Cor. 11:3) as "authority" was not common

in Paul's day, and many scholars, including Kenneth Bailey, have concluded that Paul is saying that the *origin* (one of the meanings of the word *head* in Greek) of Christ is the godhead, the *origin* of man is Christ, and the *origin* of woman, in the Garden, is man. Kevin Giles tells the story of the modern-day controversy over the Arian heresy. Cohick, *Letter to the Ephesians*, 357. Thiselton, *First Epistle to the Corinthians*, 818. Peppiatt, *Rediscovering Scripture's Vision for Women*, 74–5. Bailey, *Paul Through Mediterranean Eyes*, 298. Giles, *Rise and Fall of the Complementarian Doctrine of the Trinity*, and *What the Bible Actually Teaches on Women*, 21–34.

30. See chapter 4.
31. Mat. 28:10. See chapter 4.
32. Craig Keener writes that he has "never heard a persuasive argument for why Jesus' maleness must be represented by male ministers, but his singleness or Jewishness need not be." William Witt disagrees with the argument that only men can be priests because they represent the body of Christ and says "there is no such teaching in Scripture or the patristic tradition of the church." Keener, *Paul, Women, and Wives*, 110. Witt, *Icons of Christ*, 200–1.

Aida Besancon Spencer states that Jesus "always" describes himself as a human being rather than a male, and in most cases the New Testament writers are also careful to describe Jesus with the generic Greek term "human," *anthropos*, rather than the Greek for a male, *aner*. Spencer says God is the source of everything, including gender, and "transcends gender because God is Spirit and has no form, male or female." Therefore, Jesus' maleness is not what reflects "God's essence." Both male and female, she writes, are created in God's image and so both are needed to reflect his image. She explains that the "masculine biblical language for God ... refers to grammatical, *not* natural gender." Also, both male and female metaphors are used for God; God is not a literal father or mother, and the term "father" is a metaphor like a mother hen and eagle are; God is not defined by any one of these metaphors. "God is in God's own class." Like Spencer, Stanley Grenz points out that in speaking of Jesus Christ as "being made in human likeness" (Phil. 2:7), Paul uses the general Greek word *anthropos* ("human"), rather than the gender specific *aner* ("man"). Grenz also states that "the Nicene Creed declares that our Lord became a human being (*enanthropesanta*), thereby taking to himself the likeness of all who are included within the scope of his saving work." R.K. McGregor Wright says that "gendered imagery for God is metaphorical language." "In no way can we conclude that because Jesus assumed a male humanity that God is sexual (male or female) or that human masculinity is divine." "The divine nature of Jesus, he says, did not become male, nor did the human nature become divine." Also, God is never said in the Hebrew Bible to be "male" (*zakar*). In addition, Wright says, there are no suggestions in Scripture that sexuality is part of the image of God in humanity; rather, it is part of the created order shared with many of God's other creatures, and God is "neither male nor female." Sexuality, Wright points out, is represented in Scripture as a created thing, not an eternal cosmic "principle" of masculine and feminine. "The conclusion must be that sexuality is a created thing and not one of God's attributes." Sarah Sumner points out that John said the Word became "flesh" (*sarx*), not male (*aner*). Spencer, *Beyond the Curse*, 22, and "Does God Have Gender?" 6–11, 12 (also see endnote 41). Grenz, "Biblical Priesthood and Women in Ministry," 281-2. Wright, "God, Metaphor and Gender," 289–91. Sumner, *Men and Women in the Church*, 117, footnote 11.

Chapter 12 – What remains

1. Eph. 1:7-8.
2. See chapter 2 for explanation.
3. Gen. 1:26-28 states that God said, let us make mankind in our image, male and female, and let them rule over the fish . . . and all creatures. Nothing here restricts ruling just to males; rather it specifically includes females. Aida Besancon Spencer writes that "women want to lead along with men because God created them to do so." Spencer, "What are the Biblical Roles of Female and Male Followers of Christ?" 11.
4. Gen. 3:16. See chapter 2 for explanation of the Hebrew grammar in Gen. 3:16 as a prediction rather than a command.
5. Gen. 3:15.
6. Mat. 19:4-6. Gen. 2:24.
7. John 15:13.
8. Mat. 20:25-28.
9. Mark 12:31.
10. See chapter 10 for more explanation.
11. Acts 2:16-18.
12. See chapter 5.
13. See chapter 10.
14. 2 Cor. 5:17.
15. Gal. 3:27-8 states that in Christ there is not male or female, for we are all one in Christ. Craig Keener writes that Paul uses the precise terminology for *male and female* in this verse that appears in the creation narrative; Keener says Paul envisions here a "restoration of the primeval unity of male and female that flourished before the judgment of Gen. 3:16, as part of the new creation (Gal. 6:15)." Keener, *Galatians*, 308.
16. In 1 Pet. 1:1-3, 2:4-5, 9, Peter writes to God's elect, who have a new birth through the resurrection of Jesus Christ and are being built into a spiritual house to be a holy priesthood; he never limits this just to men. Rev. 1:5-6 states that Jesus has freed us from our sins and made us to be a kingdom and priests to serve God; there is no restriction to just men. Rev. 5:10 says the lamb (Jesus) has purchased with his blood those of every tribe and language and people and nation to be a kingdom and priests to serve our God, and they

will reign on earth; some translations say in verse 9 that the lamb purchased "men" from every tribe and language and people and nation, but the original Greek here indicates "mankind," not the Greek word for just men. Rev. 20:4–6 talks about the souls of those who had been beheaded because of their testimony for Jesus, came to life and reigned with Jesus a thousand years; it says they will be priests of God and of Christ and reign with him. Nothing restricts this just to men; rather, women were persecuted and martyred for Christ too. Heb. 5:1 says in some translations that every high priest is selected from "men," but the Greek word here is also reflective of "mankind," and is not the Greek word for just "men." Dorothy Lee addresses the negative female images that are given in Revelation. She explains that the Greek word for city, *polis*, "is in the feminine gender;" she also believes that the 144,000 who have not "polluted themselves with women" refers to "idolatry as sexual adultery." Lee, *Ministry of Women in the New Testament*, 146–9.

17. 2 Tim. 2:11–13 says that if we endure, we will also reign with Christ; nothing implies that this applies only to men. Rev. 20:4–6 states that those who have been beheaded for their witness to Jesus will reign with Christ for a thousand years; women were martyred for their faith too and nothing in this passage restricts those who reign to just men. Rev. 21:27 speaks of those whose names are written in the Lamb's book of life and Rev. 22:3 says the servants of the Lamb will serve him, and his name will be on their foreheads, and they will reign for ever and ever; nothing restricts this just to men. Revelation 5:10 says the Lamb (Jesus) has purchased with his blood those of every tribe and language and people and nation to be a kingdom and priests to serve our God, and they will reign on earth. Nothing in this passage in the original Greek restricts this just to men.

18. See chapter 5.

19. See chapter 6.

20. Hooker, *A Preface to Paul*, 17.

21. See chapter 7.

22. See chapter 9.

23. Eph. 5:25.

24. Eph. 5:21. See chapter 8.

25. Eph. 5:18.

26. For example, see Rom. 12:10, 1 Cor. 12:25, Gal. 5:13, Eph. 4:2–3.

27. Fee, "The Cultural Context of Ephesians 5:18-6:9," 6-7. Also see chapters 7 and 8.

28. James 1:5. Sarah Sumner cites research showing that "more than 90 percent" of married couples made "nearly all decisions" jointly. She quotes one Southern Baptist husband and father of three as stating that decision making should be mutual and if the same Holy Spirit that is leading him is also leading his wife, then they are probably not going to disagree; they will be "led in the same direction." Married seminary professors Aida Besancon

Spencer and William Spencer say that they resolve leadership in specific areas by "gifting, ability, or responsibility." Sumner, *Men and Women in the Church*, 202. Spencer and Spencer, *Marriage at the Crossroads*, 87.

29. **Prayer**: Mat. 6:9–13, Col. 4:2, Eph. 6:18, I Thes. 5:17 (the phrase "brothers" given by some translations relates to the original Greek implying brethren or family and is not deemed here to be gender exclusive). **Bible reading**: Josh. 1:8, Rom. 12:1–2. **Worship**: John 4:24 and many Old Testament verses.

30. Rom. 12:4–8 calls for those in Christ to use their gifts. Some translations describe a "man" or "man's gift" or say "brothers," but the original Greek uses words that are gender inclusive for mankind, not gender exclusive for just men. 1 Pet. 4:10–11 says that each of you should use whatever gift you have received to serve others.

31. Howard Marshall states that within the "context of total submission flowing out of love on both sides [of a marriage], there can develop a freedom for each to be what Christ wants them to be in their high calling as his people." Further, he writes, "the Gospel itself leads us out of patriarchalism into a different kind of relationship that mirrors more adequately the mutual love and respect that is God's purpose for his redeemed people." Marshall says he suspects that "many husbands who are hierarchalists in theory are virtually egalitarians in practice." Alan Johnson says that "in our non-patriarchal culture (one not requiring male honor [above females])," mutual yielding and mutual respect "best fulfill the model of Christ." Marshall, "Mutual Love and Submission in Marriage," 204, 194. Johnson, "A Meta-Study of the Debate over the Meaning of 'Head' (*Kephale*) in Paul's Writings," 28.

32. See chapter 8.

33. Michelle Lee-Barnewall points out that "the only direct instruction Adam is given in regard to his relationship with Eve" is to "cleave," so they may be one flesh. In the coming of Christ, she says, what was broken in the Garden between man and woman is to be restored; the responsibility of the man becomes "giving himself for his wife rather than abandoning or blaming her" and in this way he imitates the "last Adam," Jesus, rather than the first. Lee-Barnewall, *Neither Complementarian nor Egalitarian*, 144.

34. See chapter 4.

35. Mat. 23:37. Also see multiple instances of female imagery for God in the Old Testament, for example, Isa. 42:14.

36. See chapter 4.

37. Brauch, *Abusing Scripture*, 248–9.

38. Bruce, *A Mind for What Matters*, 263, 266. Craig Keener states that while Paul would undoubtedly have been happy to welcome later readers to "listen in" on his message and reapply the principles to other settings, "he no more wrote with such readers in mind than he wrote in a language other than Greek." Bruce asks if Paul addressed a situation in, for example, Thessalonica,

in a particular way, what would he have said to us in our different setting? Keener, *Paul, Wives & Women*, xv.

39. Fee and Stuart, *How to Read the Bible for all its Worth*, 18, 30.
40. Hendricks and Hendricks, *Living by the Book*, 202, 209, 266.
41. Cunningham and Hamilton, *Why Not Women*? Sarah Sumner points out that there is no favoritism with God and [male] chauvinism is "utterly foreign to God's character." Sumner, *Men and Women in the Church*, 125.
42. Marshall, "The Gospel Does Not Change but Our Perception of it May Need Revision," 146.
43. Youth With A Mission (YWAM) states that functioning in teams is one of its 18 core values: "YWAM is called to function in teams in all aspects of ministry and leadership. We believe that a combination of complementary gifts, callings, perspectives, ministries and generations working together in unity at all levels of our mission provides wisdom and safety. Seeking God's will and making decisions in a team context allows accountability and contributes to greater relationship, motivation, responsibility and ownership of the vision (Deut. 32:30–31; 2 Chr. 17:7–9; Prov. 15:22; Eccl. 4:9–12; Mark 6:7–13; Rom. 12:3–10; 2 Cor. 1:24; Eph. 5:21; Phil. 2:1–2; 1 Pet. 4:8)." https://ywam.org/about-us/values/. Accessed 10/21/21.
44. Rob Dixon is a senior fellow for gender partnership with the InterVarsity Institute and has identified ten attributes that are critical for "flourishing" mixed-gender ministry partnerships. Dixon, *Together in Ministry*.
45. Alvin Schmidt references Brittain and Carroll, who say that in the Jerusalem Christians, the sexes mingled in a "pure and noble companionship," but "this perfect society was not destined long to endure." Schmidt, *Veiled and Silenced*, 212.
46. An international team of theologians who are part of the Lausanne Movement have written about the need for this, encouraging churches to "acknowledge godly women who teach and model what is good, as Paul commanded, and to open wider doors of opportunity for women in education, service, and leadership." Further, they state, "We long that women should not be hindered from exercising God's gifts or following God's call on their lives." *The Cape Town Commitment*, 68.
47. Respected historians have recounted that in the Dark Ages it was taught in churches that, based on man as the "head," he should beat his wife to keep her in line. It is unimaginable that this would be taught in churches today. But teaching, for example, that the man is the "head" of the wife, drawing on the more standard English understanding of this word, and not explaining that "head" has multiple meanings in the Greek, or bringing balance that the man is called to lay down his life for his wife, can engender ungodly treatment of women by men who hear or read such messages. Manfred Brauch says the traditional Christian view regarding women has been "nurtured for centuries by misunderstandings and interpretations of words that are, at best, problematic, and may therefore be decidedly unbiblical." He

says this has contributed to the "long and tragic history of women's inferior status, and their restricted roles in the home, church, and society, and their frequent subjugation and abuse in hierarchical marriage relationships." Brauch, *Abusing Scripture*, 152.

48. Wright, *Surprised by Scripture*, 82.
49. William Martin, who had extensive interviews with Billy Graham for a biography of him, writes that this was a "significant departure from the common Evangelical practice of barring women from public roles." Martin, *A Prophet with Honor*, 442. The international cooperation of Christian leaders that Billy Graham began came to be known as the Lausanne Movement and the involvement of women grew. At the third major Congress (in Cape Town in 2010), 35 percent of the nominated delegates from 198 countries were women. I was a committee chair for that Congress, Lausanne Senior Associate for the Partnership of Men and Women, and wrote on that topic. Jane Crane, "History of the Partnership of Men and Women in the Lausanne Movement."
50. Don Williams writes that the power for the Christian life is not in obeying the law of Moses, but in "trusting the Holy Spirit." God is "the God of surprise; we cannot calculate or control him." Williams, *Apostle Paul and Women in the Church*, 26.
51. Holman Christian Standard Bible, 2013.

Works cited

Abegg, Martin Jr., Flint, Peter, Ulrich, Eugene. *The Dead Sea Scrolls Bible, The Oldest Known Bible Translated for the First Time into English*. New York, NY: HarperCollins, 1999.

Aristotle. *Aristotle, Volume XIII: The Generation of Animals*. Translator A.L. Peck. Cambridge: Loeb Classical Library, Harvard University Press. 1963. 4.3 (767b 4-8) and 2.3 (737a 25-30).

_____. *Problemata*, 10.57. As cited in Catherine Clark Kroeger, "Toward an Understanding of Ancient Conceptions of 'Head.'" 5.

Bailey, Kenneth E. *Jesus Through Middle Eastern Eyes, Cultural Studies in the Gospels*. Downers Grove, IL: InterVarsity, 2008.

_____. *Paul Through Mediterranean Eyes, Cultural Studies in 1 Corinthians*. Downers Grove, IL: InterVarsity. 2011.

Barth, Markus. *Ephesians 4-6, A New Translation with Introduction and Commentary*. New York, NY: Doubleday, 1974.

Bauer, W., Arndt, W.F., Gingrich, F.W., Danker, F.W. *A Greek-English Lexicon of the New Testament and Other Early Christian Literature*. Chicago, IL: University of Chicago Press, 1979.

Belleville, Linda. *I Timothy*. Cornerstone Biblical Commentary. (In a volume including *2 Timothy, Titus* and *Hebrews* by other authors.) Carol Stream, IL: Tyndale House, 2009.

_____. "Exegetical Fallacies in Interpreting 1 Timothy 2.11:15," *Priscilla Papers*, 17:3, Summer 2003. 17:3.3-11.

_____. "Teaching and Usurping Authority, I Timothy 2:11-15." In *Discovering Biblical Equality, Complementarity Without Hierarchy*. Ronald W. Pierce and Rebecca Merrill Groothius, Eds. Downers Grove, IL: InterVarsity. 2005. Also published with some updates in *Discovering Biblical Equality, Biblical, Theological, Cultural & Practical Perspectives*. Ronald W. Pierce and Cynthia Long Westfall, Eds. Christa A. McKirland, Associate Ed. Downers Grove, IL: InterVarsity, 2021.

_____. "Women in Ministry: An Egalitarian Perspective." In *Two Views on Women in Ministry*. Stanley Gundry, Series Ed. James R. Beck, General Ed. Grand Rapids, MI: Zondervan, 2001, 2005.

_____. *Women Leaders and the Church, Three Crucial Questions*. Grand Rapids, MI: Baker, 2000.

_____. *Women Leaders in the Bible*." In *Discovering Biblical Equality, Complementarity Without Hierarchy*.Ronald W. Pierce and Rebecca Merrill Groothius, Eds. Downers Grove, IL: InterVarsity, 2005.

Beyer, Elizabeth, General Ed. *Created to Thrive, Cultivating Abuse-Free Faith Communities*. Minneapolis, MN: CBE International, 2021.

Bilezikian, Gilbert. *Beyond Sex Roles, What the Bible Says About a Woman's Place in Church and Family*. Grand Rapids, MI: Baker, 1985.

Bloesch, Donald. *Is the Bible Sexist? Beyond Feminism and Patriarchalism*. Eugene, OR: Wipf and Stock, 1982, 2001.

Brauch, Manfred T. *Abusing Scripture, The Consequences of Misreading the Bible*.

Downers Grove, IL: InterVarsity, 2009.

_____. "I Corinthians." In *Hard Sayings of the Bible*. Walter Kaiser, Jr., Peter H. Davids, F.F. Bruce, Manfred T. Brauch. Downers Grove, IL: InterVarsity, 1996.

_____. "1-2 Timothy." In *Hard Sayings of the Bible*. Walter Kaiser, Jr., Peter H. Davids, F.F. Bruce, Manfred T. Brauch. Downers Grove, IL: InterVarsity, 1996.

_____. "Ephesians." In *Hard Sayings of the Bible*. Walter Kaiser, Jr., Peter H. Davids, F.F. Bruce, Manfred T. Brauch. Downers Grove, IL: InterVarsity, 1996.

Bruce, F.F. *I and II Corinthians*. New Century Bible Commentary. Grand Rapids, MI: Wm. B. Eerdmans, 1971.

_____. *A Mind for What Matters, Collected Essays*. "Women in the Church: A Biblical Survey." 259-266. Grand Rapids, MI: William B. Eerdmans, 1990. Also published in *Christian Brethren Review*, 33 (1982): 7-14.

_____. *An Expanded Paraphrase of the Epistles of Paul*. Palm Springs, CA: Ronald N. Haynes, 1965, 1981.

_____. *The Book of Acts*. Grand Rapids, MI: Wm. B. Eerdmans Publishing Co, 1988.

_____. *The Epistles to the Colossians, to Philemon, and to the Ephesians*. Grand Rapids, MI: Wm. B. Eerdmans, 1984.

_____. *The Epistle to the Galatians*. The New International Greek Testament Commentary. Grand Rapids, MI: Wm. B. Eerdmans, 1982.

_____. *Paul: Apostle of the Heart Set Free*. Grand Rapids, MI: William B. Eerdmans, 1977.

_____. "Women in the Church: A Biblical Survey." *Christian Brethren Review*. 33. 7-14. 1982.

Bruce, F.F., Packer, J.I., Comfort, Philip, and Henry, Carl F.H., *The Origin of the Bible*. Carol Stream, IL: Tyndale House, 1992, 2003, 2012.

Bushnell, Katharine C. *God's Word to Women, One Hundred Bible Studies on Woman's Place in the Church and Home*. Originally published 1921. Republished in Minneapolis, MN: Christians for Biblical Equality, 2003.

Cervin, Richard S. "Does *Kephale* Mean 'Source' or 'Authority Over' in Greek Literature? A Rebuttal." *Trinity Journal* 10 (1989): 85-112.

_____. "On the Significance of Kephale ('Head'): A Study of the Abuse of One Greek Word." *Priscilla Papers*. April 30, 2016.

Clark, Elizabeth A. *Women in the Early Church, Message of the Fathers of the Church*. Collegeville, MN: The Liturgical, 1983.

Cohick, Lynn H. *Ephesians*. A New Covenant Commentary. Eugene, OR: Cascade, 2010.

_____. *The Letter to the Ephesians*. The New International Commentary on the New Testament. Grand Rapids, MI: Wm. B. Eerdmans, 2020.

_____. "Women as Leaders," in *The IVP Women's Bible Commentary*. Catherine Clark Kroeger and Mary J. Evans, Eds. Downers Grove, IL: InterVarsity, 2002.

_____. *Women in the World of the Earliest Christians, Illuminating Ancient Ways of Life*. Grand Rapids, MI: Baker Academic, 2009.

Cohick, Lynn H. and Hughes, Amy Brown. *Christian Women in the Patristic World, Their Influence, Authority, and Legacy in the Second through Fifth Centuries*. Grand Rapids, MI: Baker Academic, 2017.

Comfort, Philip W. "Afterword: Recent Developments," in Bruce, F.F., Packer, J.I., Comfort, Philip, and Henry, Carl F.H., *The Origin of the Bible*. Carol Stream, IL: Tyndale House, 1992, 2003, 2012.

_____. "Texts and Manuscripts of the New Testament," in Bruce, F.F., Packer, J.I., Comfort, Philip, and Henry, Carl F.H., *The Origin of the Bible*. Carol Stream, IL: Tyndale House, 1992, 2003, 2012.

Crane, Jane L. "A Map for Gender Reconciliation." In Lausanne Occasional Paper No. 53, "Empowering Men and Women to Use Their Gifts Together in Advancing the Gospel." In *A New Vision, A New Heart, A Renewed Call*. Volume Two. Lausanne Occasional Papers from the 2004 Forum for World Evangelization hosted by the Lausanne Committee for World Evangelization in Pattaya, Thailand. David Claydon, Ed. Pasadena, CA: William Carey Library, 2005. 659-669.

_____. "History of the Partnership of Men and Women in the Lausanne Movement." In *The Lausanne Movement, A Range of Perspectives*. Edited by Margunn Serigstad Dahle, Lars Dahle and Knud Jorgensen. Oxford, UK: Regnum International, 2014. pdf available at www.FACTorTHEORY.org.

Crowell, Nancy A. and Burgess, Ann W., eds. "Causes and Consequences of Violence Against Women," in *Understanding Violence Against Women*. National Research Council. Washington, D.C.: National Academy, 1996.

Cunningham, Loren and Hamilton, David. *Why Not Women, A Fresh Look at Scripture on Women in Missions, Ministry, and Leadership*. Seattle, WA: YWAM, 2000.

Davids, Peter H. "A Silent Witness in Marriage." In *Discovering Biblical Equality, Complementarity Without Hierarchy*. Ronald W. Pierce and Rebecca Merrill Groothius, Eds. Downers Grove, IL: InterVarsity, 2005.

Deen, Edith. *All of the Women of the Bible*. New York, NY: HarperCollins, 1955.

_____. *Great Women of the Christian Faith*. Uhrichsville, OH: Barbour, 1959

deSilva, David A. *Honor, Patronage, Kinship and Purity, Unlocking New Testament Culture*. Downers Grove, IL: InterVarsity, 2000.

Dixon, Rob. *Together in Ministry, Women and Men in Flourishing Partnerships*. Downers Grove, IL: InterVarsity, 2021.

Ehrman, B. *The Orthodox Corruption of Scripture: The Effect of Early Christological Controversies on the Text of the New Testament*," Oxford: Oxford University Press, 2011, as cited in Philip Payne, "Vaticanus Distigme-Obelos Symbols Marking Added Text."

Elliott, Raymond L. "Bible Translation," in Bruce, F.F., Packer, J.I., Comfort, Philip, and Henry, Carl F.H., *The Origin of the Bible*. Carol Stream, IL: Tyndale House, 1992, 2003, 2012.

Erickson, Millard J. *Christian Theology*. Third Edition. Grand Rapids, MI: Baker Academic, 2013.

Fee, Gordon D. *1 and 2 Timothy, Titus*. New International Biblical Commentary. Peabody: Hendrickson, 1984.

_____. *1 & 2 Timothy, Titus*. Understanding the Bible Commentary Series.

Grand Rapids, MI: Baker, 1984, 1988.

———. "The Cultural Context of Ephesians 5:18-6:9." *Priscilla Papers*. Winter 2002: 16:1. 3-8. Reprinted in 30th Anniversary Edition. Volume 31, Number 4, Autumn 2017.

———. *The First Epistle to the Corinthians*. The New International Commentary on the New Testament. Grand Rapids, MI: Wm. B. Eerdmans, 1987.

———. *God's Empowering Presence, the Holy Spirit in the Letters of Paul*. Peabody, MA: Hendrickson, 1995.

———. "Praying and Prophesying in the Assemblies, I Corinthians 11:2-16." In *Discovering Biblical Equality, Complementarity Without Hierarchy*. Ronald W. Pierce and Rebecca Merrill Groothius, Eds. Downers Grove, IL: InterVarsity, 2005.

———. "The Priority of Spirit Gifting." In *Discovering Biblical Equality, Complementarity Without Hierarchy*. Ronald W. Pierce and Rebecca Merrill Groothius, Ed. Downers Grove, IL: InterVarsity, 2005. Third Edition 2021: *Discovering Biblical Equality, Biblical, Theological, Cultural & Practical Perspectives*.

Fee, Gordon D. and Stuart, Douglas. *How to Read the Bible for All Its Worth*. Grand Rapids, MI: Zondervan, 1981, 2003.

Fitzmyer, Joseph A. *First Corinthians, A New Translation with Introduction and Commentary by Joseph A. Fitzmyer. The Anchor Yale Bible*. New Haven and London: Yale University Press, 2008.

Flint, Peter W. *The Dead Sea Scrolls*. Nashville, TN: Abington, 2013.

Galen. *On the Doctrines of Hippocrates and Plato*, 6.3.21.4. Ed. and trans. Phillip De Lacy, 3 vols. (Berlin: Akademie-Verlag, 1978-84), 2:378. As cited in Catherine Clark Kroeger, "Toward an Understanding of Ancient Conceptions of 'Head.'" 4.

Gasque, Laurel and W. Ward. "Saint Paul, Apostle of Freedom for Women and Men, an Interview with F.F. Bruce." *Priscilla Papers*. Vol. 3, number 2. Spring 1989.

Giles, Kevin. *The Rise and Fall of the Complementarian Doctrine of the Trinity*. Eugene, OR: Cascade, 2017.

———. *What the Bible Actually Teaches About Women*. Eugene, OR: Cascade, 2018.

Gill, Deborah M. and Cavaness, Barbara. *God's Women Then and Now*. Springfield, MO: Grace and Truth, 2007.

Glahn, Sandra. "Artemis of the Ephesians in First-Century Ephesus and Ramifications for How We Read I Timothy." Christians for Biblical Equality International Conference, "Created to Thrive." August 2, 2019. https://www.cbeinternational.org/resource/audio/artemis-ephesians-first-century-ephesus-and-ramifications-how-we-read-1-timothy. Accessed 6/21/21.

———. *Nobody's Mother, Artemis of the Ephesians in Antiquity and the New Testament*. Downers Grove, IL: InterVarsity Press, 2023.

Gordon, A. J. "The Ministry of Women." *The Missionary Review of the World*. New York: Funk & Wagnalls, 1894.

Grenz, Stanley J. "Biblical Priesthood and Women in Ministry." In *Discovering Biblical Equality, Complementarity Without Hierarchy*. Ronald W. Pierce and Rebecca Merrill Groothius, Eds. Downers Grove, IL: InterVarsity. 2005. Adapted from Stanley J. Grenz and Denise Muir Kjesbo, *Women in the Church: A Biblical Theology of Women in Ministry*.

Groothius, Rebecca Merrill. *Good News for Women, A Biblical Picture of Gender Equality*. Grand Rapids, MI: Baker, 1997.

Grudem, Wayne. "Does *Kephale* ('Head') Mean 'Source' or 'Authority Over' in Greek Literature? A Survey of 2,336 Examples." *Trinity Journal* 6 (1985)" 38-59.

_____. *Evangelical Feminism and Biblical Truth, An Analysis of More than 100 Disputed Questions*. Wheaton, IL: Crossway, 2004, 2012.

_____. "The Meaning of *Kephale* ('Head'): An Evaluation of New Evidence, Real and Alleged." *Journal of the Evangelical Theology Study* 44 (2001): 25-65.

Gupta, Nijay K. *Tell Her Story, How Women Led, Taught, and Ministered in the Early Church*. Downers Grove, IL: IVPAcademic, 2023.

Haddad, Mimi. "History Matters: Evangelicals and Women." In *Discovering Biblical Equality, Biblical, Theological, Cultural & Practical Perspectives*. Ronald W. Pierce and Cynthia Long Westfall, Eds. Christa A. McKirland, Associate Ed. Downers Grove, IL: InterVarsity, 2021.

_____. "Priscilla, Author of the Epistle to the Hebrews?" *Priscilla Papers*. Jan. 30, 1993.

Haddad, Mimi and Callaghan, Sean, Contributors. *Is Women's Equality A Biblical Ideal? A Five-Part Series*. Minneapolis, MN: CBE Internationa,. 2021.

Haines-Eitzen, Kim. *The Gendered Palimpset, Women, Writing, and Representation in Early Christianity*. New York, NY: Oxford University Press, 2012.

Harrison, R.K. "Old Testament and New Testament Apocrypha." In Bruce, F.F., Packer, J.I., Comfort, Philip, and Henry, Carl F.H., *The Origin of the Bible*. Carol Stream, IL: Tyndale House, 1992, 2003, 2012.

Hays, Richard B. *First Corinthians*. Louisville, KY: John Knox, 1997.

Hendricks, Howard G. and Hendricks, William D. *Living by the Book, The Art and Science of Reading the Bible*. Chicago, IL: Moody, 1991, 2007.

Hess, Richard S. "Equality With and Without Innocence, Genesis 1-3." In *Discovering Biblical Equality, Complementarity Without Hierarchy*. Ronald W. Pierce and Rebecca Merrill Groothius, Eds. Downers Grove, IL: InterVarsity, 2005.

_____. *The Old Testament, A Historical, Theological, and Critical Introduction*. Grand Rapids, MI: Baker Academic, 2016.

Hoag, Gary C. *Wealth in Ancient Ephesus and the First Letter to Timothy, Fresh Insights from* Ephesiaca *by Xenophon of Ephesus*. Bulletin for Biblical Research Supplement 11. Richard S. Hess and Craig L. Blomberg, Eds. Eisenbrauns (an Imprint of Penn State University Press), 2015.

Holmes, Michael W. *The Apostolic Fathers, Greek Texts and English Translations*. Grand Rapids, MI: Baker Academic, 1992.

Homer. *Odyssey* 9.140, 13.102, 346. As cited in Catherine Clark Kroeger, "Toward an Understanding of Ancient Conceptions of 'Head.'" 4.

Hooker, Morna D. *A Preface to Paul*. New York: NY: Oxford University Press, 1980.

_____. "Authority on Her Head: An Examination of I Cor. XI.10," *New Testament Studies* 10 (1963-64): 410-16. As referenced in Bruce, F.F., I & II Corinthians, 106, and Johnson, Alan, "A Meta-Study of the Debate over the Meaning of 'Head' (*Kephale*) in Paul's Writings," 21-22.

Jobes, Karen H., and Silva, Moises. *Invitation to the Septuagint*. Second Edition. Grand Rapids, MI: Baker Academic, 2000, 2015.

Johnson, Alan F. "A Meta-Study of the Debate over the Meaning of 'Head' (*Kephale*) in Paul's Writings." *Priscilla Papers*. Vol. 20, No. 4. Autumn 2006.

Johnson, Alan F., General Ed. *How I Changed My Mind About Women in Leadership, Compelling Stories from Prominent Evangelicals*. Grand Rapids, MI: Zondervan, 2010.

Kaiser, Walter C. Jr. "Correcting Caricatures: The Biblical Teaching on Women." http://www.walterckaiserjr.com/womenpage2.html, accessed 1.14.19. Published in *Priscilla Papers*, Vol. 19, No. 2, Spring 2005.

_____. *Hard Sayings of the Old Testament*. Downers Grove, IL: InterVarsity, 1988.

_____. *The Promise-Plan of God, A Biblical Theology of the Old and New Testaments*. Grand Rapids, MI: Zondervan, 1978, 2008.

Kaiser, Walter C. Jr., Davids, Peter H., Bruce, F.F., Brauch, Manfred T. *Hard Sayings of the Bible*. Downers Grove, IL: InterVarsity, 1996.

Kateusz, Ally. "Women Leaders at the Table in Early Churches." *Priscilla Papers*. Spring 2020, 14-22.

Kavanagh, Julia. *Women of Christianity, Exemplary for Acts of Piety and Charity. The Pioneer 1852 Narrative of Women's Lives in the Christian Tradition*. Eugene, OR: Wipf & Stock, 2006.

Keener, Craig S. *1 Peter, A Commentary*. Grand Rapids, MI: Baker Academic, 2021.

_____. *Acts*. New Cambridge Bible Commentary. Cambridge, UK: Cambridge University Press, 2020.

_____. *Acts, An Exegetical Commentary. Volume I. Introduction and 1:1-2:47*. Grand Rapids, MI: Baker Academic, 2012.

_____. *Galatians, A Commentary*. Grand Rapids, MI: Baker Academic, 2019.

_____. *The Historical Jesus of the Gospels*. Grand Rapids, MI: William B. Eerdmans, 2009.

_____. *The IVP Bible Background Commentary, New Testament*. Downers Grove, IL: InterVarsity, 1993.

_____. "Learning in the Assemblies: I Corinthians 14:34-35." In *Discovering Biblical Equality, Complementarity without Hierarchy*. Ronald W. Pierce and Rebecca Merrill Groothius, Eds. Downers Grove, IL: InterVarsity, 2005. Third Edition, 2021: *Discovering Biblical Equality, Biblical, Theological, Cultural & Practical Perspectives*.

_____. "Mutual Submission Frames the Household Codes." *Priscilla Papers*. Summer 2021. Vol. 35, No. 3.

_____. *Paul, Women, and Wives, Marriage and Women's Ministry in the Letters of Paul*. Peabody, MA: Hendrickson, 1992.

_____. *Romans*. New Covenant Commentary Series. Eugene, OR: Cascade, 2009.

_____. "Women in Ministry: Another Egalitarian Perspective." In *Two Views on

WORKS CITED

Women in Ministry. Stanley Gundry, Series Ed. James R. Beck, General Ed. Grand Rapids, MI: Zondervan, 2001, 2005.

Kimball, Cynthia Neal. "Nature, Culture and Gender Complementarity." In *Discovering Biblical Equality, Complementarity without Hierarchy.* Ronald W. Pierce and Rebecca Merrill Groothius, Eds. Downers Grove, IL: InterVarsity, 2005.

Kostenberger, Andreas. "A Complex Sentence Structure in I Timothy 2:12." *Women in the Church: A Fresh Analysis of I Timothy 2:9-15.* Andreas Kostenberger, Thomas Schreiner and H. Scott Baldwin, Ed. Grand Rapids, MI: Baker, 1995. (A Third Edition was released in 2016.)

Kostenberger, Andreas J. and Kostenberger, Margaret E. *God's Design for Man and Woman, A Biblical Theological Survey.* Wheaton, IL: Crossway, 2014.

Kroeger, Catherine Clark. "I Timothy 2:12 – A Classicist's View." In *Women, Authority and the Bible.* Downers Grove, IL: InterVarsity, 1986.

_____. "Toward an Understanding of Ancient Conceptions of 'Head.'" *Priscilla Papers.* Vol. 20, No. 3, Summer 2006.

Kroeger, Richard Clark and Kroeger, Catherine Clark. *I Suffer Not a Woman, Rethinking I Timothy 2:11-15 in Light of Ancient Evidence.* Grand Rapids, MI: Baker, 1992.

_____. "Sexual Identity in Corinth." *Reformed Journal.* 28, 1978.

_____. *Women Elders…Called by God?* Louisville, KY: The Office of Women's Advocacy. Women's Ministry Unit. Presbyterian Church (U.S.A.), 1980/2001.

Lampe, G.W. *A Patristic Greek Lexicon* (Oxford: Oxford University Press, 1968, 749). As cited in Brauch, Manfred. "I Corinthians," 601.

The Lausanne Movement. *The Cape Town Commitment, A Confession of Faith and a Call to Action.* Peabody, MA: Hendrickson, 2011.

Lee, Dorothy A. *The Ministry of Women in the New Testament, Reclaiming the Biblical Vision for Church Leadership.* Grand Rapids, MI: Baker Academic, 2021.

Lee-Barnewall, Michelle. *Neither Complementarian nor Egalitarian, A Kingdom Corrective to the Evangelical Gender Debate.* Grand Rapids, MI: Baker Academic, 2016.

Liefeld, Walter L. *1 & 2 Timothy, Titus.* The NIV Application Commentary. Grand Rapids, MI: Zondervan, 1999.

_____. *Ephesians.* Downers Grove, IL: InterVarsity, 1997.

_____. "The Nature of Authority in the New Testament." In *Discovering Biblical Equality, Complementarity Without Hierarchy.* Ronald W. Pierce and Rebecca Merrill Groothius, Eds. Downers Grove, IL: InterVarsity, 2005.

Lightfoot, Neil R. *How We Got the Bible.* Revised and Expanded Third Edition. Grand Rapids, MI: Baker, 2003.

MacHaffie, Barbara J. *Her Story, Women in Christian Tradition.* Minneapolis, MN: Fortress, 2006.

Marshall, I. Howard. "The Gospel Does Not Change but Our Perception of it May Need Revision." In Johnson, Alan F., Gen Ed. *How I Changed My Mind About Women in Leadership.* Grand Rapids, MI: Zondervan, 2010.

_____. "Mutual Love and Submission in Marriage: Colossians 3:18-19 and

Ephesians 5:21-33." In *Discovering Biblical Equality, Complementarity Without Hierarchy.* R.W. Pierce and R.M. Groothius, Eds. Downers Grove, IL: InterVarsity, 2005.

_____. *The Pastoral Epistles.* London: T&T Clark LTD, 2004.

_____. *I Peter.* Downers Grove, IL: InterVarsity. 1991.

Martin, William. *A Prophet with Honor, The Billy Graham Story.* New York, NY: William Morrow, 1991.

Mathews, Alice. *Gender Roles and the People of God, Rethinking What We Were Taught About Men and Women in the Church.* Grand Rapids, MI: Zondervan, 2017.

Metzger, Bruce. *The Bible in Translation, Ancient and English Versions.* Grand Rapids, MI: Baker Academic, 2001.

Mickelsen, Berkeley. "Who are the Women in I Timothy?" Parts I and II. https://www.cbeinternational.org/resource/article/priscilla-papers-academic-journal/who-are-women-1-timothy-21-15-part-1. Who Are the Women in I Timothy 2:1-15 (Part 2) | CBE (cbeinternational.org). Accessed 7.2.21

Mickelsen, Berkeley and Alvera. "What Does *Kephale* Mean in the New Testament?" In *Women, Authority and the Bible*, Alvera Mickelsen, Ed. Downers Grove, IL: InterVarsity, 1986.

Miller, Jeffrey D. "A Defense of Gender-Accurate Bible Translation." In *Discovering Biblical Equality, Biblical, Theological, Cultural & Practical Perspectives.* Ronald W. Pierce and Cynthia Long Westfall, Eds. Christa A. McKirland, Associate Ed. Downers Grove, IL: InterVarsity, 2021.

Nicole, Roger. "Biblical Authority and Feminist Aspirations." In *Women, Authority and the Bible.* Mickelson, Alvera, Ed. Downers Grove, IL: InterVarsity, 1986.

_____. "Biblical Egalitarianism and the Inerrancy of Scripture." *Priscilla Papers.* Vol. 20. No. 2. Spring 2006.

_____. "Biblical Concept of Women." *Evangelical Dictionary of Theology.* Grand Rapids, MI: Baker, 1984.

Norton, Mark. "Texts and Manuscripts of the Old Testament." In Bruce, F.F., Packer, J.I., Comfort, Philip, and Henry, Carl F.H, *The Origin of the Bible.* Carol Stream, IL: Tyndale House, 1992, 2003, 2012.

Olson, David H. and Olson, Amy K. *Empowering Couples: Building on Your Strengths.* Minneapolis: Life Innovations, 2000.

O'Sullivan, James N. *Xenophon of Ephesus: His Compositional Technique and the Birth of the Novel.* UaLG 44: de Gruyter, 1995. The novel is contained in B.P. Reardon, Collected Ancient Greek Novels, 2nd Edition. Berkeley: University of California Press, 2008.

Pack, Roger, Ed. *Artemidori Daldiani Onirocriticon Libri V* (Leipzig: Teubner, 1963) 1.2.7. As cited in Catherine Clark Kroeger, "Toward an Understanding of Ancient Conceptions of 'Head.'" 5.

Payne, Philip B. *The Bible vs. Biblical Womanhood, How God's Word Consistently Affirms Gender Equality.* Grand Rapids, MI: Zondervan, 2023.

_____. "Fuldensis, Sigla for Variants in Vaticanus, and I Cor 14.34-5." *New Testament Studies.* Vol. 41. 1995, 240-262.

_____. "Is I Corinthians 14:34-35 a Marginal Comment or a Quotation?" *Priscilla Papers.* Vol. 33. No. 2. Spring 2019.

WORKS CITED

———. *Man and Woman, One in Christ, An Exegetical and Theological Study of Paul's Letters*. Grand Rapids, MI: Zondervan, 2009.

———. "Oude in 1 Timothy 2:12." Presented at the Evangelical Theological Society Annual Meeting in Atlanta, GA, Nov, 21, 1986. Revised and published as "1 Timothy 2,12 and the Use of Oude to Combine Two Elements to Express a Single Idea." *New Testament Studies* 54 (2008):235-53.

———. "Six Ground-breaking Discoveries, A Summary of 'Vaticanus Distigme-obelos Symbols Marking Added Text, Including I Corinthians 14.34-5." *New Testament Studies* 63 (2017) 604–625.

———. "Vaticanus Distigme-obelos Symbols Marking Added Text, Including 1 Corinthians 14. 34-5." *New Testament Studies*, Vol. 63, Issue 4. October 2017, 604-625.

———. "What About Headship?" In *Mutual by Design*. Elizabeth Beyer, General Ed. Minneapolis, MN: CBE International, 2017.

Payne, Philip B. and Canart, Paul. "The Originality of Text-Critical Symbols in Codex Vaticanus." *Novum Testamentum* LKII, 2. Vol. 42. Fasc. 2. 2000, 105-113.

———. "Distigmai Matching the Original Ink of Codex Vaticanus: Do They Mark the Location of Textual Variants?" *Le manuscrit B de la Bible (Vaticanus graecus 1209): Introduction au fac-simile, Actes du Colloque de Geneve (11 juin 2001), Contributions supplementaires* (ed. Andrist, P.; Lausanne: Editions du Zebre, 2009) 199-226.

Payne, Philip B. and Huffaker, Vince. *Why Can't Women Do That? Breaking Down the Reasons Churches Put Men in Charge*. Boulder, CO: Vinatti, 2021.

Peppiatt, Lucy. *Rediscovering Scripture's Vision for Women, Fresh Perspectives on Disputed Texts*. Downers Grove, IL: InterVarsity, 2019.

Photius. *Commentary on I Corinthians 11:3*, in K. Staab, *Paulus-kommentare aus der griechischen Kirche aus Katenenhandschriften gesammelt und herausgegeben* (Munster: Aschendorff, 1933) 567.1. As cited in Catherine Clark Kroeger, "Toward an Understanding of Ancient Conceptions of 'Head.'" 5.

Pierce, Ronald W. *Partners in Marriage and Ministry*. Minneapolis, MN: Christians for Biblical Equality, 2011.

Pierce, Ronald W. and Groothius, Rebecca Merrill, Eds. *Discovering Biblical Equality, Complementarity Without Hierarchy*. Downers Grove, IL: InterVarsity, 2005.

Pierce, Ronald W. and Westfall, Cynthia Long, Eds. McKirland, Christa L., Co-editor. In *Discovering Biblical Equality, Biblical, Theological, Cultural, and Practical Perspectives*. Downers Grove, IL: InterVarsity, 2021.

Piper, John and Grudem, Wayne, Eds. *Recovering Biblical Manhood and Womanhood, A Response to Evangelical Feminism*. Wheaton, IL: Crossway, 1991.

Pope John Paul II. "Mulieris Dignitatem." Apostolic Letter of the Supreme Pontiff John Paul II on the Dignity and Vocation of Women on the Occasion of the Marian Year. August 15, 1988. http://www.vatican.va/content/john-paul-ii/en/apost_letters/1988/documents/hf_jp-ii_apl_19880815_mulieris-dignitatem.html. Accessed 11.24.20.

Schmidt, Alvin J. *Veiled and Silenced, How Culture Shaped Sexist Theology.* Macon, GA: Mercer University Press, 1989.

Scholer, David M. "I Timothy 2:9-15 and the Place of Women in the Church's Ministry." In *Women, Authority and the Bible.* Alvera Mickelsen, Ed. Downers Grove, IL: InterVarsity, 1986.

_____. "A Biblical Basis for Equal Partnership, Women and Men in the Ministry of the Church." An abbreviated form of a series of articles published as "Women in Ministry," *Covenant Companion* 72:21 (Dec 1, 1983), 8-9; 72:22 (Dec 15, 1983), 14-15; 73:1 (Jan 1, 1984), 12-13; 73:2 (Feb 1984), 12-15;copyright 1983 and 1984 by the *Covenant Press*, Chicago. http://abc-usa.org/wp-content/uploads/2012/07/biblicalbasis.pdf, accessed 5.14.19. Also available at this writing at https://www.fuller.edu/wp-content/uploads/2018/02/Women-in-Ministry-A-Biblical-Basis-for-Equal-Partnership.pdf.

_____. "The Evangelical Debate over Biblical 'Headship.'" In *Women, Abuse, and the Bible, How Scripture Can Be Used to Hurt or Heal.* Catherine Clark Kroeger and James R. Beck, Eds. Grand Rapids, MI: Baker, 1996.

_____. "Women." *Dictionary of Jesus and the Gospels, A Compendium of Contemporary Biblical Scholarship.* Downers Grove, IL: InterVarsity. First Edition, 1992.

Schreiner, Thomas R. "An Interpretation of I Timothy 2:9-15: A Dialogue with Scholarship." In *Women in the Church, An Interpretation & Application of I Timothy 2:9-15."* Wheaton, IL: Crossway. Third Edition, 2016.

Sechrest, Love L. *A Former Jew, Paul and the Dialectics of Race.* London/New York, NY: T&T Clark, 2009.

Spencer, Aida Besancon. *1 Timothy.* New Covenant Commentary Series. Eugene, OR: Cascade, 2013.

_____. *Beyond the Curse, Women Called to Ministry.* Nashville, TN: Thomas Nelson, 1985.

_____. "Does God Have Gender?" *Priscilla Papers.* Vol. 24, No. 2, Spring 2010.

_____. "Jesus' Treatment of Women in the Gospels." In *Discovering Biblical Equality, Complementarity without Hierarchy.* Ronald W. Pierce and Rebecca Merrill Groothius, Eds. Downers Grove, IL: InterVarsity, 2005.

_____. "Leadership of Women in Crete and Macedonia as a Model for the Church," *Priscilla Papers.* Vol. 27, No. 4. Autumn 2013.

_____. "What are the Biblical Roles of Female and Male Followers of Christ?" *Priscilla Papers.* 18:2, Spring 2004.

_____. Spencer, Aida Besancon, and William David. *Christian Egalitarian Leadership, Empowering the Whole Church According to the Scriptures.* Eugene, OR: Cascade, 2020.

Spencer, William and Aida, and Tracy, Steve and Celestia. *Marriage at the Crossroads, Couples in Conversation About Discipleship, Gender Roles, Decision Making and Intimacy.* Downers Grove, IL: InterVarsity, 2009.

Stark, Rodney. *The Rise of Christianity, How the Obscure, Marginal Jesus Movement Became the Dominant Religious Force in the Western World in a Few Centuries.* New York, NY: Harper Collins, 1996.

Stott, John R.W. *The Message of 1 Timothy and Titus.* Downers Grove, IL: Inter-

Varsity, 1996.
_____. *The Message of Ephesians*. Downers Grove, IL: Inter-Varsity, 1979.
_____. *The Message of Galatians*. Downers Grove, IL: Inter-Varsity, 1968
Sumner, Sarah. *Men and Women in the Church*. Downers Grove, IL: Inter-Varsity, 2003.
Taylor, Marion Ann, Ed., and Choi, Agnes, Assoc. Ed. *Handbook of Women Biblical Interpreters, A Historical and Biographical Guide*. Grand Rapids, MI: Baker Academic, 2012.
Thayer, Joseph H. *Thayer's Greek-English Dictionary of the New Testament*. Grand Rapids, MI: Baker, 1977.
Thiselton, Anthony C. *The First Epistle to the Corinthians*. The New International Greek Testament Commentary. Grand Rapids, MI: Wm. B. Eerdmans, 2000.
Tucker, Ruth. *Black and White Bible, Black and Blue Wife, My Story of Finding Hope after Domestic Abuse*. Grand Rapids, MI: Zondervan, 2016.
Tucker, Ruth A. and Liefeld, Walter. *Daughters of the Church, Women and Ministry from New TestamentTimes to the Present*. Grand Rapids, MI: Zondervan, 1987.
Van Leeuwen, Mary Stewart. *Gender and Grace. Love, Work and Parenting in a Changing World*. Downers Grove, IL: InterVarsity, 1990.
_____. "Social Science Studies Cannot Define Gender Differences." *Priscilla Papers*. Vol. 27, No. 2, Spring 2013.
Walker, Larry. "Biblical Languages." In Bruce, F.F., Packer, J.I., Comfort, Philip, and Henry, Carl F.H., *The Origin of the Bible*. Carol Stream, IL: Tyndale House, 1992, 2003, 2012.
Walsh, Julie and Miller, Jeffrey D. "Translating Ephesians 5.33," *The Bible Translator* 74, no. 1, April 2023: 93-109.
https://journals.sagepub.com/doi/epdf/10.1177/20516770231151420
Walter, Victor. "Versions of the Bible."In Bruce, F.F., Packer, J.I., Comfort, Philip, and Henry, Carl F.H., *The Origin of the Bible*. Carol Stream, IL: Tyndale House, 1992, 2003, 2012.
Westfall, Cynthia Long. "Paul and Gender: Highlights and Bombshells." Mutual by Design. CBE International Conference,. July 22, 2017. https://www.cbeinternaional.org/resource/audio/paul-and-gender-highlights-and-bombshells
_____. *Paul and Gender, Reclaiming the Apostle's Vision for Men and Women in Christ*. Grand Rapids, MI: Baker Academic, 2016.
Wijngaards, John. *What They Don't Teach You in Catholic College, Women in the Priesthood and the Mind of Christ*. Lafayette, LA: Acadian House, 2020.
Williams, Don. *The Apostle Paul and Women in the Church*. Woodinville, WA: Sunrise Reprints, An Imprint of Harmon, 1977, 2010.
Winter, Bruce W. *Roman Wives, Roman Widows: The Appearance of New Women and the Pauline Communities*. Grand Rapids, MI: William B. Eerdmans, 2003.
Witherington, Ben III. *Conflict and Community in Corinth, A Socio-Rhetorical Commentary on 1 and 2 Corinthians*. Grand Rapids, MI: William B. Eerdmans, 1995.
_____. *Letters and Homilies for Hellenized Christians, Volume I, A Socio-*

Rhetorical Commentary on Titus, 1-2 Timothy and 1-3 John. Downers Grove, IL: InterVarsity, 2006.

_____. *Letters and Homilies for Hellenized Christians, Volume II, A Socio-Rhetorical Commentary on 1-2 Peter.* Downers Grove, IL: InterVarsity, 2007.

_____. *The Letters to Philemon, the Colossians, and the Ephesians, A Socio-Rhetorical Commentary on the Captivity Epistles.* Grand Rapids, MI: William B. Eerdmans, 2007.

_____. *Reading and Understanding the Bible.* New York, NY: Oxford University Press, 2015.

_____. *Women and the Genesis of Christianity.* Cambridge, UK: Cambridge University Press, 1990.

_____. *Women in the Earliest Churches.* Cambridge, UK: Cambridge University Press, 1988.

_____. *Women in the Ministry of Jesus.* Cambridge, UK: Cambridge University Press, 1984.

Witherington, Ben III with Darlene Hyatt. *Paul's Letter to the Romans, A Socio-Rhetorical Commentary.* Grand Rapids, MI: William B. Eerdmans, 2004.

Witt, William G. *Icons of Christ, A Biblical and Systematic Theology for Women's Ordination.* Waco, TX: Baylor University Press, 2020.

Wright, N.T. *Surprised by Scripture. Engaging Contemporary Issues.* New York, NY: Harper Collins, 2014. Chapter entitled "The Biblical Case for Ordaining Women," also published as "The Biblical Basis for Women's Service in the Church," *Priscilla Papers*, Vol. 20, No. 4, Autumn 2006, 5-10.

Wright, R.K. McGregor. "God, Metaphor and Gender." In *Discovering Biblical Equality, Complementarity without Hierarchy.* Ronald W. Pierce and Rebecca Merrill Groothius, Eds. Downers Grove, IL: InterVarsity, 2005.

Art and photographs

The photograph of a page from the ancient Codex Vaticanus Bible at the Vatican Library (Biblioteca Apostolica Vaticana), and the artwork from Art Resource, are used with permission and credited adjacent to the photograph/art. The cover includes a small portrait of John Chrysostom, a father of the early church, shown in full in chapter 5; Alfredo Dagli Orti/Art Resource, NY.

The artwork from Getty Images is credited here, as titled by Getty Images and in order of appearance in this book: Dead Sea Scrolls Go Digital/Getty Images, Deborah's Song of Triumph/Culture Club via Getty Images, Jesus and the Adulteress/Culture Club via Getty Images, Baptism of Christ/Graphica Arts via Getty Images, Paul and Phoebe/ZU_09 via Getty Images, Bible Manuscripts/ZU_09, Paul Writes to the Ephesians/ZU_09 via Getty Images, Origen of Alexandria/adoc-photos via Getty Images, Among the First Christians a Letter from Paul is Read/ZU_09 via Getty Images, First Council of Nicaea/ZU_09 via Getty Images, Joseph Makes Himself Known to His Brethren/Duncan 1890 via Getty Images.

The photograph of Billy Graham at his San Diego Crusade in 2003 is courtesy of the Billy Graham Evangelistic Association. Used with permission. All rights reserved. www.billygraham.org.

All photos of scholars in this book who are currently living are used with permission of the scholar. Photos of the deceased scholars are used with permission as follows: from a close living relative or in two cases, when such could not be located, a close working colleague gave a written opinion that the scholar would give permission if living; for the photo of F.F. Bruce, per www.ffbruce.com, no one holds the copyright to his photo in this book and there would not be restrictions to its use this book; three photos for scholars from 1920 or earlier are widely used and formal permissions were not obtainable. Photo of Aida Becanson Spencer by Nicole Rim/Gordon-Conwell Seminary.

About the author

Jane L Crane holds a Masters in Peace and Justice from the University of San Diego and conducted two years of doctoral-level research through the Oxford Centre for Mission Studies in Oxford, England. She holds a certificate in non-profit board governance from the Harvard Business School and was the lead person in developing board guidelines for a Youth With A Mission base that are now used internationally.

Crane was an officer on the Board of Directors for one of Billy Graham's last crusades (2003) and opened in prayer for him at San Diego's stadium. She also chaired and co-chaired large Christian events for San Diego that brought together tens of thousands of people from across denominations and cultures, including the March for Jesus and National Day of Prayer.

Crane was a committee chair and Senior Associate for the partnership of men and women for the international Lausanne Movement during its Cape Town Congress in 2010 (considered the largest representative gathering of Christians to that date in history). She has been published on the partnership of men and women in Lausanne and taught about the Scriptures on women on five continents. Videos of her teaching can be viewed at www.FACTorTHEORY.org.

From 2010 to 2014, she developed an Adopt A Widow program in two African countries and authored *Half A Piece of Cloth, the Courage of Africa's Countless Widows*. She includes in that book how traditional African religion and interpretations of Christianity are helping or harming Africa's millions of destitute widows, from young to old.

She has been married to Christopher Crane for more than 40 years, has one adult son, Andrew, and lives in San Diego, California. She considers *Who Leads?* the culmination of her life's work.

With thanks

To my husband, Chris, who has always been supportive of God's calls on my life.

To our son, Andrew, first reader of this book and delight to my heart.

To my dear friend and prayer partner, Evelyn Wills, with whom I share "bowls of laughter."

To my many friends who love God with all of their hearts.

To our gracious God. There is no better life than following you!

www.ingramcontent.com/pod-product-compliance
Lightning Source LLC
Chambersburg PA
CBHW060514090426
42735CB00011B/2220